Called to praise

A collection of calls to worship,
prayers, and anthology material
for use in Christian worship and education,
and for personal reflection

Written and compiled by Donald Hilton

CHRISTIAN
education

Anthologies of resource material compiled by Donald Hilton

Published by Christian Education

> *Liturgy of Life*
> *Flowing Streams*
> *Prayers for Christian Worship*
> > *Volume 1: Seasons and Celebrations*
> > *Volume 2 The Word in the World*
> *No Empty Phrases*

Books published by the United Reformed Church

> *Sounds of Fury*
> *Table Talk*

CALLED TO PRAISE

Published by Christian Education,
1020 Bristol Road,
Selly Oak,
Birmingham
B29 6LB

www.christianeducation.org.uk

First published 2005
ISBN 1-904024-74-2

Collection © Copyright Donald Hilton 2005

Cover illustration by Peggy Chapman
Text illustrations by Phillip Vernon

British Library Cataloguing-in-Publication Data:
A catalogue record for this book is available from the British Library.

Typeset in Palatino Linotype by Creative Pages, www.creativepages.co.uk
Printed and bound in Great Britain by Creative Print and Design (Wales)
Ebbw Vale

Contents

Preface

Preface

Called to praise is a resource book for Christian education and worship. The first part follows the pattern of the Christian Year and is divided into seven sections:

Advent

Christmas & Epiphany

Lent

The Life and Teaching of Jesus.

Holy Week

Easter

Ascension, Pentecost & Trinity

The second part has four sections:

Creation

Mission & Ministry

The Christian Community

Justice & Peace

Each of the eleven sections is subdivided as follows:

- Bible calls to worship for use as opening sentences in Christian services
- Other calls to worship
- Prayers
- An anthology on the theme

A third part offers calls to worship and prayers for use at any season of the year.

Throughout the book neither *Amen*, nor any other formal closing is normally given, but can be added as appropriate. **Bold type** indicates possible congregational participation. Compiled primarily for the use of worship leaders on Sundays and other days, the resources are also offered for use in private devotions and personal reflection.

Copyright restrictions

The spoken word

There are no restrictions when material in this book is used as the spoken word in the worship of a local church or in a church study group.

Copying the material

Where no name is given as the author of an item, the author is Donald Hilton and the copyright is his. These items, whether prayers, calls to worship or anthology items, can be freely used in the life of a local church e.g. in occasional Orders of Service, periodic church magazines, or local study group material. The acknowledgement 'from *Called to praise* published by Christian Education © Donald Hilton' should be indicated against each item so used. For the use of any material in more permanent form, and for all uses beyond the local church, permission should be sought.

To copy any other item which is still within copyright, application must be made in each case to the copyright owner whose details will be found in the *Index of Copyrights* at the end of this book.

Donald Hilton
May 2005

Advent

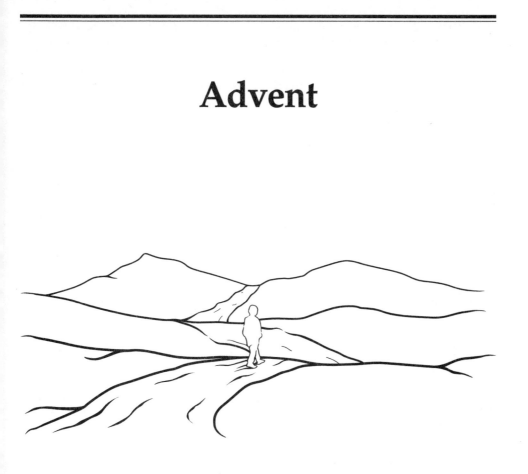

a It will be said on that day, Lo, this is our God; we have waited for him, so that he might save us. This is the Lord for whom we have waited; let us be glad and rejoice in his salvation.
Isaiah 25:9

b Comfort, O comfort my people, says your God. Speak tenderly to Jerusalem, and cry to her that she has served her term, that her penalty is paid, that she has received from the Lord's hand double for all her sins. *Isaiah 40:1–2*

c In the wilderness prepare the way of the Lord, make straight in the desert a highway for our God. Every valley shall be lifted up, and every mountain and hill be made low; the uneven ground shall become level, and the rough places a plain. Then the glory of the Lord shall be revealed, and all people shall see it together, for the mouth of the Lord has spoken.
Isaiah 40:3–5

d Zion said, 'The Lord has forsaken me, my Lord has forgotten me.' Can a woman forget her nursing child, or show no compassion for the child of her womb? Even these may forget, yet I will not forget you. *Isaiah 49:14–15*

e How beautiful upon the mountains are the feet of the messenger who announces peace, who brings good news, who announces salvation, who says to Zion, 'Your God reigns'.
Isaiah 52:7

f In those days John the Baptist appeared in the wilderness of Judea, proclaiming, 'Repent, for the kingdom of heaven has come near.' This is the one of whom the prophet Isaiah spoke when he said, 'The voice of one crying out in the wilderness: "Prepare the way of the Lord, make his paths straight."'
Matthew 3:1–3

g Blessed be the Lord God of Israel, for he has looked favourably on his people and redeemed them. *Luke 1:68*

h See, I am laying in Zion a stone that will make people stumble, a rock that will make them fall, and whoever believes in him will not be put to shame. *Romans 9:33*

i You know what time it is, how it is now the moment for you to wake from sleep. For salvation is nearer to us now than when we became believers; the night is far gone, the day is at hand. Let us then lay aside the works of darkness and put on the armour of light.
Romans 13:11–12

j The Lord is near. Do not worry about anything, but in everything by prayer and supplication with thanksgiving let your requests be made known to God. And the peace of God, which surpasses all understanding, will guard your hearts and your minds in Christ Jesus.
Philippians 4:5–7

k See, I am coming soon; my reward is with me, to repay according to everyone's work. I am the Alpha and the Omega, the first and the last, the beginning and the end.
Revelation 22:12–13

l The one who testifies says, 'Surely I am coming soon.' Amen. Come, Lord Jesus! The grace of the Lord Jesus be with all the saints.
from Revelation 22:20–21

1 Oh hearken, for this is wonder!
Light looked down and beheld Darkness.
'Thither will I go', said Light.
Peace looked down and beheld War,
'Thither will I go', said Peace.
Love looked down and beheld hatred,
'Thither will I go', said Love.
So Light came and shone,
So came Peace and gave Rest,
So came Love and brought Life.
And the Word was made flesh and dwelt among us.

Laurence Housman

2 He is coming as he promised!
He will come into our complacency to stir us to action.
He will pierce our insensitivity to sharpen our discipleship.
He will challenge our false busyness and give us new priorities.
He will deepen our shallow Christmas preparations with new meaning.
Whether we are ready for him or not, he will come.
He has made a promise.

3 Already there is an advent light on the far horizon;
the promise is being formed,
hope is renewed,
the dawn is breaking,
the Word is taking flesh,
and the people of God await their renewal.

4 Come, O come, Emmanuel!
Come to a world that stands in need of love
and to a nation that has forgotten you.
Come to a Church that has lost its nerve
and to congregations that need a renewal of the Spirit.
Come to the weary streets of our cities
and to those who have lost their sense of direction.
Come where the ancient pathways are choked with weeds
and where the signposts of hope have been torn down.
Come to us in our church, our homes, our hearts
and bring your disturbing peace.

5 When Christ comes,
darkness will be light,
despair will be hope,
sadness will be joy,
conflict will be peace,
and we will be called to work,
– when Christ comes.

6 The Advent call is a call to pilgrimage:
to follow a star wherever it leads,
to wait in suspense for a new revelation,
to journey in hope, confident of God's leading,
to believe that the heavens can open,
to watch for an unlikely birth
and see beauty in the dirt of a stable.
The Advent call is a call to pilgrimage.

7 Listen for the gentle knock on the door;
watch for the dawning light that dispels darkness;
wait for the gentle touch of the hand of God;
breathe in the fragrance of the Spirit's promise;
taste and see that the Lord is good,
for the Advent days are upon us
and the journey has begun.

8 We are waiting:
as Elizabeth waited for the birth of a child
until John was born;
as Mary waited, pondering all these things in her heart
until the truth was revealed;
as shepherds waited on the hillside
until the heavens opened;
as wise men journeyed in waiting
until a stable door swung open.
And we are waiting
until…
until God gives what God will give.

9 Advent Lord,
let Christmas come!
Let it come this year
new and fresh
as though for the first time,
so that in its coming
we praise your name
and give you true adoration.

10 Come, Lord, and bless us all!

Bless us with the comfort of your coming
for we need you,
and look for the renewal of every spiritual gift.

Bless us with the challenge of your coming
for we are careless people, casual in our service,
and need a sharp reminder of our duty.

Bless us with the light of your coming
for the world is often a dark place,
and we need new evidence that light will always conquer darkness.

Bless us with the hope of your coming
for we sometimes despair,
and need the re-assurance that evil cannot win the final victory.

Bless us with the humility of your coming
for pride often rules our day,
and we long for the simplicity of your manger birth.

Come, Lord! Your people are waiting.

11 Spirit of the living God,
come and bless us in our Advent worship
so that when the new day dawns,
we may share the joyful sounds of heavenly praise,
see angels dancing in delight,
welcome kings as they kneel in adoration,
greet shepherds as they find a place in the kingdom
and join the circle of universal praise.

12 Prepare the way of the Lord!
Ignore the cul-de-sac of the shopping mall;
    look for the road to a costly birth.
Lower the mountains of greed and self-indulgence;
    seek the valley road to the vulnerability of the newborn.
Clear the path rock-strewn with pride;
    find the road to childlike openness.
Then will the glory of the Lord be revealed
and all flesh shall see it.

13 The sky is deep above the hill,
the silent stars, the frozen tree,
the world so still!

builder of stars beyond our sight,
touch our hearts that are so cold
with fire and light

that fire may leap from heart to heart
across the reaches of the dark!
Shatter the night!

One master and one lasting home!
Awake and kindle, rise to praise!

The Lord will come!

Jane T Clement
From *Behold that Star*

14 Into the loneliness of the human heart;
Come, Jesus; the Christ-child!
Into the barrenness of worship that has become a habit;
Come, Jesus; the Christ-child!
Into a Christmas that has forgotten you;
Come, Jesus; the Christ-child!
Into a Church where symbol has obscured the Presence;
Come, Jesus; the Christ-child!
Into me, and into us, and into this moment;
Come, Jesus; the Christ-child!

15 Spirit of the Lord,
you call us to travel the Advent road.
Forgive us:
our eyes are half-blind,
   though we can see the distant horizon of hope;
our ears are deaf,
   though faintly we hear the first cry of a baby;
our feet are leaden,
   though we have strength enough for the first step of the journey;
our imaginations are limited
   though our spirits are stirred by the thoughts of a birth;
our worship is earthbound,
   though we sense the glory of heaven's gift.
Spirit of the Lord,
still calling us to walk the Advent road,
give us sight and hearing,
grant us swiftness of foot, boundless imagination.
You who are our goal,
be also our path.

16 *Now is the moment to wake from sleep!*   *Romans 13:11*
Stir your people, living God,
open our eyes,
and rouse us from our lethargy.

The Lord is near!   *Philippians 4:5*
Show us your presence, Lord God,
be our companion,
reveal your purpose.

I am the Alpha and the Omega!   *Revelation 1:8*
Encircle us with your power, eternal God,
enclose us in your love,
be our beginning and our ending.

Repent, and believe in the good news!   *Mark 1:15*
Forgive our waywardness, forgiving God,
give us the obedience of Mary,
grant us the peace of the child.

17 This we know, Christmas child;
as we step out to Bethlehem:
    we cannot travel unless we walk in company with others,
    we cannot reach the stable door unless we walk in hope,
    we cannot stay the course unless you give us strength.
But in these Advent days,
the call is strong
and we begin.
Longed-for child, hope of the world,
guide our feet.

18 Jesus Christ,
Son of the Father who calls us to be a pilgrim people,
we pray for those who long to start the journey
    but do not know where to begin;
for those who must begin in loneliness
    and long for companions to travel with them;
for those lost in the valleys of indecision
    who cannot see the beckoning hills;
for those so well-familiar with the yearly Advent journey
    that they have lost the excitement of the pilgrimage;
for those carrying so many burdens
that the way seems never-ending.
For all these, and no less for us,
be a guide, a companion on the way.

19 Father in heaven, as Christmas comes close,
many, passing by, will hear the carols we sing;
    may hearts be touched and memories stirred
    to bring reminders of a former faith.
Many will see the candle lights;
    may the symbol guide them to the Light of the World.
Many will see the pictured scene:
    the child,
    his parents,
    the ox and ass,
    the shepherds amazed, the wise men searching;
may parable and story reveal their inner meaning,
speak of God in humility,
and sow a seed of dawning faith and love.

20 *Great expectations*

When it comes,
do not expect Christmas to be all joy.
Herod lurked in the background the first time round,
and stars are only bright when the night is black.
   Christmas will not be joy for those who live on the streets
   and find the gates closed on their usual shop doorway,
   the library warmth no longer available,
   the benefits office closed,
   and those who shed the occasional coin
   now hurrying by to catch the next party.
      And families' best intention of joyful reunions
      can find the Christmas veneer soon rubbed away;
      old irritations surfacing by Boxing Day
      and ancient arguments refreshed long before the turkey's finished.
         And those who daily eat alone, regretting it,
         find a solitary Christmas lunch
         a double burden;
         crackers need two to pull.
When it comes,
do not expect Christmas to be all joy.

21 *Advent shock*

The great question to us is whether we are still capable of being truly shocked or whether it is to remain so that we see thousands of things and know that they should not be and must not be, and that we get hardened to them. How many things have we become used to in the course of the years, of the weeks and the months, so that we stand unshocked, unstirred, inwardly unmoved.

Advent is a time when we ought to be shaken and brought to a realisation of ourselves. The necessary condition for the fulfilment of Advent is the renunciation of the presumptuous attitudes and alluring dreams in which and by means of which we always build ourselves imaginary worlds. In this way we force reality to take us to itself by force – by force, in much pain and suffering.

This shocked awakening is definitely part of experiencing Advent. But at the same time there is much more that belongs to it. Advent is blessed with God's promises, which constitute the hidden happiness of this time. Being shattered, being awakened – only with these is life made capable of Advent.

Alfred Delp, *a Jesuit priest, hanged in a Nazi prison in 1945 for his opposition to Hitler*
From *Watch for the Light*

22 *Wake-up call*

The first verse reflects the opening Chorale from 'Wachet auf', Bach's Advent Cantata

Wake up, wake up, a voice is crying;
hear the watchman from on high.
Wake up, city of Jerusalem!
The time is short, the bridegroom near.
Take heed – or miss the promised celebration.

Wake up, wake up, the voice still cries,
wake up, all nations of the earth;
the endgame threatens, warfare rife.
Yet peace still beckons at God's bidding.
Strive for reconciliation now.

Wake up, wake up, a child is dying;
wake up those who live in ease.
Hunger reigns, families are starving.
Should the rich feed off the poor?

Choose the way that shares resources.
Wake up, wake up, the earth is weeping,
wake up to heal a grieving globe.
The land is our mother, enjoy it gently;
air, water, soil, protect with care.

Honour all creation gives.
Wake up, wake up, the Church is bleeding,
wake up, those who love its life.
Its wounds are deep, its health decreasing.
Respect tradition, welcome changes.
Fit its life to meet our times.

Wake up, wake up, each Christian pilgrim,
wake up to greet the dawning day.
The night can never bind the faithful;
Christ will come as God has promised,
and Advent point a better way.

23 *Christmas is for the elderly*

Advent and Christmas … are about old people.

Shall I say that again? Advent and Christmas are about old people.

But what about the children? someone asks. And I have to reply that they don't feature in the story.

The Advent stories begin with an elderly couple, Elizabeth and Zechariah; he a priest helping out in his retirement years; she a childless senior citizen.

The Christmas stories end with another elderly couple. One is Simeon, a God-fearing man who regularly visits the temple, the other is Anna, an 84-year-old widow and prophetess. They are the people who witness Jesus being dedicated to God by his parents in accordance with Jewish tradition, and who recognise his uniqueness.

And in between, we have three wise men, of indeterminate age, though if Eastern tradition is to be acknowledged, wisdom should be considered as the gift of years, not of youth.

I claim Advent and Christmas as a time for adults, not out of any dislike for children, but because I fear that viewing these seasons as if they were devoted to and for toddlers, we avoid one of the quirks of God's nature.

God expects old dogs to do new tricks.

God expects people whom the world would deem 'past it', to initiate.

The beginning of Jewish-Christian history involves an old man, Abraham, a nonagenarian, and his equally aged wife Sarah, from whom, God maintains, a nation will spring. He could have chosen a fertile upwardly mobile pair of newly-weds. We would have.

But God is not us. God expects old people –
    to be the sowers of new seed;
    to be midwives of change;
    to be the ones who recognise and name the new directions which
        society has to take;
    to be the ones who applaud and encourage new potential.

Elizabeth and Zechariah became parents in their old age, and Simeon and Anna recognise the uniqueness of Mary's tiny baby, because God will not have people marginalised or written off on account of age.

And when we see the wise men worshipping Jesus, and then going home by another way, we see God's belief and expectation that older folk can change, and will change when they recognise the truth.

John Bell
From *Celebrating the gift of years* (United Reformed Church booklet, 2002)

24 *Prepare the way*

Will the valleys bloom in time
to announce the day of grace
and the travellers arrive
at that strange familiar place?

As the searchers persevere
on a pathway of their prayer
fertile soil among the stones
roots the fragile offerings there

till the lily and the rose
blow on rocky winding slopes
where the deep ravines are filled
by the sum of many hopes.

Then the valleys blaze with light
when the dawn comes up again
for the crooked shall be straight
as our rough ways are made plain.

Margaret Connor

25 *Invitation*

Will you be my guest this Christmas?
I have only an animal's stall,
But if you can bear being crowded,
I'll make sure there's room for all.

The table will not be laden,
But there is bread and wine to share,
And you soon will cease to hunger
If you come and join us there.

If you'll be my guest this Christmas,
I'll promise to be your guide
Through a manger, a cross and an open tomb
To a door the whole world wide.

Joan Brockelsby (altd.)

26 *The lost friend*

I missed him when the sun began to bend;
I found him not when I had lost his rim;
With many tears I went in search of him,
Climbing high mountains which did still ascend,
And gave me echoes when I called my friend;
Through cities vast and charnel houses grim,
And high cathedrals where the light was dim,
Through books and arts and works without an end,
But found him not – the friend whom I had lost.
And yet I found him – as I found the lark,
A sound in fields I heard but could not mark;
I found him nearest when I missed him most;
I found him in my heart, a life in frost,
A light I knew not till my soul was dark.

George MacDonald (1824–1905)

27 *Come home!*

Pilgrim remember
For all your pain
The Master you seek abroad
You will find at home –
Or walk in vain

Anon (7th century)

28 *Long-prepared*

When Luke was opening the heavens to let the angels sing,
Matthew was planning a journey for eastern, travelling kings.

Isaiah had long since done his bit and preached of God's world-wide
reign,
so that visitors three from the far-flung east were simply joining the
train.

And Simeon wasn't a side line; he'd watched and lingered for years,
whilst Anna, long since widowed, had waited with fasting and tears.

So Advent is nothing unusual; it's been in the air for ages,
so that we can now join in the shepherd's song and the pilgrim search
of the sages
in our own time and place.

29   *Living flame*

The Advent candles shine,
to tell the time of Christmas dawning.

The candles, the candles,
how easily the flames could be put out –
a puff of wind would mark their end,
a finger pressed against a thumb would do the trick;
first one, then two, and three, and four – then nothing.

And we from this year's light would journey back to darkness:
no Christmas tree this year,
no cause for decoration, nor for gifts,
no carols, since no child to sing about.

The child, the child,
how easily that child could be put out –
a more determined Herod, parents lacking care,
a traitor lurking with the shepherds,
or simple hunger in an age that saw so much of early death,
or lingering starvation;
then no young man to teach and preach, to heal and save.

The young man, the young man on his cross,
how easily that life could be put out –
a soldier's spear, a hail of stones,
a long slow ebbing of all energy and strength;
all human life hangs merely on a thread.
    And so it was on Calvary hill.
    The light went out;
    the price of being human.

Or so they said,
because they could not wait a mere three days
to find the fullness of the truth.

Advent Promise;
Christmas Lord;
Easter Christ;
your flame will never die,
nor will our faith.

Christmas & Epiphany

Christmas

a The people who walked in darkness have seen a great light; those who lived in a land of deep darkness – on them light has shined.   *Isaiah 9:2*

b A child has been born for us, a son given to us; authority rests upon his shoulders; and he is named Wonderful Counsellor, Mighty God, Everlasting Father, Prince of Peace.   *Isaiah 9:6*

c Do not be afraid; for see – I am bringing you good news of great joy for all the people: to you is born this day in the city of David a Saviour, who is the Messiah, the Lord.   *Luke 2:10–11*

d Let us go now to Bethlehem and see this thing that has taken place, which the Lord has made known to us.
Luke 2:15

e The Word became flesh and lived among us, and we have seen his glory, the glory as of a father's only son, full of grace and truth.   *John 1:14*

f When the fullness of time had come, God sent his Son, born of a woman.
Galatians 4:4

g Though he was in the form of God, he did not regard equality with God as something to be exploited, but emptied himself, taking the form of a slave, being born in human likeness.
Philippians 2:6–7

h Long ago God spoke to our ancestors in many and various ways by the prophets, but in these last days he has spoken to us by a Son, whom he appointed heir of all things, through whom he also created the worlds.
Hebrews 1:1–2

Epiphany

i I am the Lord, I have called you in righteousness, I have taken you by the hand and kept you; I have given you as a covenant to the people, a light to the nations.   *Isaiah 42:6*

j It is too light a thing that you should be my servant to raise up the tribes of Jacob and restore the survivors of Israel; I will give you as a light to the nations, that my salvation may reach to the end of the earth.   *Isaiah 49:6*

k Arise, shine; for your light has come, and the glory of the Lord has risen upon you. For darkness shall cover the earth, and thick darkness the peoples; but the Lord will arise upon you, and his glory will appear over you. Nations shall come to your light, and kings to the brightness of your dawn.
Isaiah 60:1–3

l Jesus spoke, saying, 'I am the light of the world. Whoever follows me will never walk in darkness but will have the light of life.'   *from John 8:12*

m There is no longer Jew or Greek, there is no longer slave or free, there is no longer male and female; for all of you are one in Christ Jesus. *Galatians 3:28*

n Grace was given to bring to the Gentiles the news of the boundless riches of Christ, and to make everyone see what is the plan of the mystery hidden for ages in God who created all things; so that through the church the wisdom of God in its rich variety might now be made known to the rulers and authorities in the heavenly places.
from Ephesians 3:8–10

30 The Advent wait is over,
  Christ is born.
The longing years are fulfilled,
  Christ is born.
The wilderness has blossomed,
  Christ is born.
Creation is complete,
  Christ is born
and you are witnesses to his saving power.
Come and worship.

31 The vulnerable Christ
who trusted himself to human hands
calls us into his gentle presence.
Come, let us adore.

32 This is the expected day;
promised by the prophets,
longed for by the wise ones,
expected throughout our Advent preparation,
already seen by childlike eyes,
and now present for us.
Thanks be to God.

33 Love and joy will now combine,
peace and justice unite;
earth and heaven are one,
for Christ is born on earth,
and the Father's love revealed
in the Christmas birth.
Thanks be to God.

34
Faith lies in the searching;
Hope lives in the longing;
Love springs from God's good grace;
and in the manger lies all three.

35
Behind a stable door,
locked in a mother's love,
lies the child you have waited for.
Poorest of the poor shepherds,
richest of the rich wise men,
worship him,
and bid you join them in thanksgiving.

36
The cry of a child is heard in the night.
Common shepherds raise their sights
as heaven itself speaks justice and peace.
Wise ones fall to their knees
as new insight, fresh discernment, dawns.
Creation quickens into new life,
finding its fulfilment
as the promise of the ages is fulfilled.
For God is with us, the Word is flesh.
We will adore and give thanks.

37
Remember the shepherds' midnight glory
    but do not forget
    weary hours of waiting in wet fields.
Remember those who followed a star
    but do not forget
    the fatigue of anxious search.
Remember Mary, mother of our Lord,
    but do not forget
    the birth pangs of hope.
Remember Christ, the infant child,
    but do not forget
    the long foreshadowed cross.
Remember! Give thanks!
And worship with trembling joy.

38 The pain of birth that Mary bore
is as nothing to the sword that will one day pierce her heart.
The delight of the shepherds at the angel's song
is as nothing to the cry of resurrection joy that will break out of a tomb.
Thanks be to God.

39 Come, you who are pilgrim travellers:
who know the truth
but still search for its fullness;
who have found the goal
but still seek its richness.
Come, join the wise ones of every age,
and worship Christ who is all in all.

40 The risks God takes!
First, to speak the universe into being:
'Let there be!' And there was.
And then to place creation's gifts in human hands;
to nourish or to spoil.
Again, to share with us
the torturous path our feet have taken
through history's long ages.
And now this day:
    to visit us in human form,
    lie cradled in a woman's arms.
What risks!
What trusting love!
Come and worship in humble gratitude!

41 Sing this day,
    sing with the joy of Mary;
rejoice this day,
    rejoice with the welcoming delight of Joseph;
see heaven opened this day,
    see angels dance before shepherds;
step out this day,
    step out towards the goal the wise men saw from far.
The child is born.

42   The promised light of which the prophets spoke
now blazes from a manger;
the light that shines from the stable door
will soon flood the earth with gospel truth,
and we will speak of Christ who is the Light of the World.

43   Good people all:
For you, for you rings out this Christmas call:
  None is too poor:
  the shepherds first heard news and sought his door.
  Too high no state:
  great kings were proud to enter at his gate.
  None dwells too far:
  on the last and loneliest outpost shines his star.
Come one, come all,
kneel, and be one in worship at his stall.

Lilian Cox
adapted from *Sing New Songs*

44   The eternal Word has become human flesh.
Still he comes to his own people
to find that not all will recognise him.
But to those who believe
he will give the power to become children of God.

45   A voice has cried in the wilderness:
    in the wilderness of dreary city streets
      and the loneliness of high-rise flats;
    in the wilderness of poverty
      and the helplessness of unemployment;
    in the wilderness of bereavement
      and the isolation of lost companionship;
    in the inner wilderness of human despair
      and the pain of those who have lost heart.
God answers the cry in the weakness of a child
who, in sharing our loss,
will lead us to an abundant life of hope.

46 Come to church today on tiptoe.
Here is mystery.
Here is promise.
Here is hope.
For God is present
in human form.

47 Before we celebrate your birth, Lord Jesus Christ,
you are already here;
before we give ourselves in service
you have already claimed us.
    Messiah of Israel – you are the Lord of every nation,
    Mary's child – you brought our faith to birth,
    Jesus of Nazareth – you reach out from the village of your birth to
the ends of the earth,
    Son of man – you are the Son of God.
We celebrate your birth in the here and now
but you were in our past,
you are present,
and you are our future.

48 Eternal God,
heaven's gate was raised in Bethlehem
when Jesus came.
Leaving the place of glory
he came to live with us –
    not with mighty power to subdue us,
    nor yet with such glory as would blind our eyes,
    not in such majesty as would set him apart from us,
    nor yet so high that we cannot reach him.
He came as a child in helplessness:
    suckled by a human mother,
    watched over by a human father,
    nurtured in a human family;
    one with them and one with us.
Now raise the gates of our hearts, O God,
break down the doors of our stubborn spirits.
Live with us! Reign amongst us, Emmanuel!

49 Lord Jesus Christ:
  stable-born when even wise men looked in a palace;
  laid in a manger whilst even angels sang 'Glory!';
  vulnerable to the sword of searching soldiers;
  at one with the poor though your first gift was gold,
your birth turns the values of the world upside down.

Eternal king, you lived your life in one nation;
Creator of the universe, the byroads of Galilee were your chosen path,
Perfect Love, you died a villain's death,
Life of life, you lay in a borrowed grave,
From beginning to end you turned life's values on their head.

Come to us, now.
Show us who you are,
and what we should be.
Continue to surprise us,
so that, kept alert,
we are ready again to receive you,
and do your will.

50 Lord, we have tried,
God knows how we've tried
to build a world worthy of its creator
and faithful to the gospel.
But our efforts have crumbled
and our hopes faded.
The new Jerusalem has slipped through our grasp
and even our prayers have not been able to hold it.

But this is a new day,
this is the promised moment,
this is a day of fresh beginning
for with Christ's birth, bright hope is born,
and in his life amongst us
lies new-born resolution.

The cry of a child has given us hope,
an infant has cradled new purpose within us
and we are ready, with him,
to seek the kingdom road
and walk with God.

51
Welcome, child of hope,
Born in this dark and dreary month,
Conceived at a time
When hope was wearing thin.
The hope of your coming
Has sustained a weary nation
Through a long winter.

And now you come,
Bringing joy to a nation
Which has known so much sorrow:
You make our barren, weary hearts
Sing anew with joy.
Tiny, insignificant,
Known to the select few,
You turn lives upside down.
Welcome, child of hope.

The Hengrave Community

52
We longed for your coming amongst us, Lord Jesus Christ,
but await your arrival with anxious hope.
We are ill-prepared:
    the Advent days have been frittered away in ceaseless busyness
    and we have not given ourselves time for thoughtfulness and prayer.
We are unready:
    pressured to meet Christmas before its time
    we have sidestepped its meaning in early celebration.
Forgive us.
But now as the day truly dawns,
in quiet confidence,
we await the promised moment
to receive the undeserved gift.

    Silence

The time has arrived, the day is upon us.
The promise is fulfilled.
God has visited his people in Christ the Son.

Lord, reveal the season of our salvation.
Give us a Christmas that sees the true Gift of your coming,
and grant us celebration that humbles us into worship.

53 God, veiled in history
and shrouded in mystery,
who can stand the day of your coming?

Who can hold their heads high
when you appear?
Who can stand tall and erect
when you visit the earth?

Who can say
they have visited the prisoner,
clothed the naked,
rescued the lost,
housed the refugee,
and forgiven the enemy?

Who is ready
with lamps lit
and faces alert,
eager to open the door
and welcome the bridegroom?

Not us.

Our lives are tired and unfocused;
our ways are selfish and undirected;
our relationships are scarred with bitterness;
our service stumbles with apathy;
our worship is far from the best.

Forgive us, please,
and restore to our spirits
the honesty and eagerness
seen in children of the kingdom.

Open our eyes to greet your arrival
with wonder and joy,
so that new heaven and new earth
are born today
and peace becomes the gift
to every person
and every nation
this Christmas Day
and always.

David Jenkins

54 Forgiving Lord, we confess it.
We could have better used the Advent days now past:
    our prayer could have been deeper,
    and our preparation more careful. Forgive us, we pray.
But this we learn afresh each Christmas time:
    your love is unstinting
    and your mercy constant. Renew our faith, we pray.
Come to us now, through the simplicity of Christmas,
    with a forgiveness that challenges us,
    and a love that is searching.
Touch us through the infant Christ
    so that our discipleship is invigorated
    and our worship enriched. In this hope, we pray.

55 How wonderful to us
that we should find the forgiveness of the Holy One
in the smile of a child.
How marvellous
that we feel afresh the welcoming love of the Eternal One
in a newborn infant.
How far beyond our understanding
that we should find the Everlasting Word
in a manger bed.
As the forgiven ones,
welcomed by the Christ Child
to hear the ancient word that is ever new,
we kneel in adoration.

56 Word made flesh, speak to us
and then through our hands and arms,
our life blood and our sacrifice,
our flesh will learn to speak,
our lives to work
and meet with heaven's gifts,
the needs of those on earth.

57
As once a mother cradled her baby in her arms,
so you, eternal God, ever encircle your creation with love,
and hold each human child in faithfulness.
Faithful God, we worship you.

As once a father kept close watch beside a manger crib,
so you, eternal God, ever keep a guardian care over all that you have made,
and stand as watchman over every human life.
Guardian God, we worship you.

As once wise men brought precious offerings to a newborn child,
so you, eternal God, ever shower the universe with costly gifts,
and give your treasures to the sons and daughters of your love.
Generous God, we worship you.

As once angels broke the bounds of heaven to sing a song of glory,
so still, eternal God, heaven's voice is tuned to earthly need,
and sings its glorious song to every human ear.
Glorious God, we worship you.

58
Not once upon a single time,
not once within a single place,
but now for every time and place
the truth of Christ is born and lives.
And Christmas fills the earth.
Thanks be to God!

59
Thank you, God in Christ, for this unique time.
The Christmas story dawns upon us, fresh and true, yet again.
Thank you for the startling impact of the child in the manger
whose birth stirs our imagination and jolts our complacency.
Thank you that the child, full-grown, will challenge us
and turn our lives upside down.
Thank you for the promise in his birth,
that life has found its purpose, and death has lost its victory.
God in Christ, your people praise you in loving wonder.

60
Light of the world, the bright star of your life is leading us forward.
Shepherd of your people, heaven's truth has opened before us.
Peace of the world, your reconciling love is making a new earth.
Child new-born, you are the promise of our future.
Thanks be to God.

61 Father, in the midst of family Christmas celebration,
we hear the cry of those who live alone.
At the centre of our Christian worship,
we sense the sadness of the persecuted who must pray in secret.
Surrounded by our Christmas plenty,
we remember those whose hunger now will be as yesterday's.
At the heart of our Christmas joy
we remember those for whom Christmas brings sad memories of
former loss and pain.

Father God, encircle your whole family with love;
Saviour Christ, comfort those for whom you lived and died;
Loving Spirit, stand with all who need you.

62 We bring our gold, token of our affluence and ease.
Show us, child of poverty, how best to use our wealth,
to meet the crying need of all the world, and bring relief.

We bring our frankincense, token of our prayers.
Show us, Word made flesh, how spoken prayers may live,
to reach a damaged world with love and aid.

We bring our myrrh, token of healing and true wholeness,
Show us, child of peace, how to take our given skill and love
to ease a warring world, and find a reconciling peace.

63 From the refugee camp and the asylum centre,
from the drab inner cities and the wastelands of the world,
from the villages and towns of poverty,
from homes where fear lurks in the corner
comes a cry,
the cry of a child.
Christ is born though still unrecognised.
Unstop our ears,
open our eyes,
release our compassion
to hear the Christ who ever comes
in the form of those who cry in need.

64 We have made our way to Bethlehem, visited the child,
and knelt at the manger in humility.
Now, eternal Father,
help us to walk into the future
with the same devotion and delight,
to find him in our homes and schools,
in factory, office and in all our working days.

We have offered praise with the shepherds
and felt the joy of heaven on earth.
Now, eternal Son of the Father,
help us to see your glory in our common life,
find heaven's truth afresh on earth
in faithful discipleship and loving service.

We have joined the wise ones as they followed the star,
matching our steps to theirs in the search for truth.
Now, eternal Spirit,
still give us strength of heart and mind
to follow the pilgrim light
and journey in the name of Christ.

65 A child cries in the poverty-stricken countries of the world;
it is the cry of the infant Christ to us.
I was hungry and you gave me food.
A child begs and lives in the streets of neglecting cities;
it is the plea of the forsaken Christ to us.
I was a stranger and you welcomed me.
A child, born with Aids, weeps; lacking medicine and hospital;
it is the anguish of the lonely Christ to us.
I was sick and you took care of me.
Christ is present in the lives of the little ones.
Just as you did it to one of the least of these
who are members of my family
you did it to me.

66 Child of the manger who grew, became strong, and advanced in
wisdom and in favour with God and with God's people, so live in us
that by the power of the strength you give us, the influence of the
wisdom you teach us, and the inspiration of your teaching, we too may
grow fully to know the grace of God.

67   *Rest You Merry*

Whatever the News may be this morning, let me wish you a Merry Christmas. Not the Season's Greetings, not a Festive Yuletide, not even a *Happy* Christmas – but a *Merry* one. For surely, after the still wonder of Christmas Eve, Christmas Day is the year's great occasion for an outburst of sublime merriment: it's astonishing, outrageous, ridiculous and hilarious, that God's amongst us not as a dazzling deity but in the least pompous of human shapes – as a baby, of all things!

And so, first of all, a Merry Christmas to all babies; and to their mothers; and to their fathers; and to their brothers and sisters; for you've got the best of *all* Christmas presents. And a Merry Christmas to much maligned innkeepers, too. It's hardly your fault if the rooms are full up and someone arrives at the last minute without a booking; but it's much to your credit if you manage to squeeze a deserving case into what nowadays would be called 'The Annexe'.

A Merry Christmas to shepherds; to all farming folk who have to keep an eye on the beasts when other folk are off duty – and to all who have to do night duties. A Merry Christmas to Wise Men – especially those who can see God's hand at work in the stars, and are prepared to put themselves out to pay tribute to him. A Merry Christmas to soldiers, even, who show mercy. Isn't there, somewhere, a legend about the soldier who, overhearing the message of Peace and Goodwill, rejected the order to slay the innocents and became himself a martyr? Oh, and a Merry Christmas to donkeys – even if there's no scriptural evidence of their being involved in the affair at all. And a Merry Christmas to friendly Egyptians. And to Jews, without whom we wouldn't have had a Christ. Happy Chanukkah!

A Merry Christmas to the Church – High, Low and In-Between – One and Many – Young and Old – misunderstood, nagged and teased by the media, yet surviving, against all the odds, to keep the Mass in Christmas. To say the very least – without you there wouldn't be any Christmas carols or bells or the Gospel story preserved. Merry Christmas, then, to all organists, choristers, sextons, vergers and bell-ringers. And of *course* a Merry Christmas to all curates, vicars and rectors, all priests, ministers and evangelists, all officers and superintendents, monks and nuns, elders, overseers and clerks, all deacons and deaconesses, deans and rural deans, *arch*deacons, provosts, and canons.

Merry Christmas, then, to all critics, prophets, mavericks and cranks; not to mention (though not in the same breath) all humanists, rationalists, atheists, agnostics *and* heretics … Christmas is here for you, too, whether you take it or leave it. And if I may presume to offer it, a Merry Christmas to our Moslem, Hindu, Sikh and Buddhist brothers and sisters. And with as much deference – a prayer, perhaps, rather than a greeting – a Merry

continued...

Christmas to the poor, the ill, those lonely, depressed, in prison or lately bereaved.

Who shall I end with? I choose those who are seeking now to incarnate the Gospel in their lives – house-churches, prayer groups, and unofficial, experimental 'para-churches'. To everyone, then: forget the News. Today there is only one News: Merry Christmas!

Gerald Priestland
Abridged from *Yours faithfully* based on a BBC broadcast in December 1978

68 *A little baby thing*

They all were looking for a king
   To slay their foes and lift them high:
Thou cam'st a little baby thing
   That made a woman cry.

O Son of Man, to right my lot
   Naught but thy presence can avail;
Yet on the road thy wheels are not,
   Nor on the sea thy sail!

My how or when thou wilt not heed,
   But come down thine own secret stair,
That thou mayst answer all my need –
   Yea, every bygone prayer.

George MacDonald (1824–1905)

69 *My Bethlehem*

This is my little town,
My Bethlehem,
And here, if anywhere,
My Christ Child
Will be born.

I must begin
To go about my day –
Sweep out the inn,
Get fresh hay for the manger
And be sure
To leave my heart ajar
In case there may be travellers
From afar.

Elizabeth Rooney

70   *Born at Christmas*

Why pick on Christmas to be born?
I mean, 's a funny old time;
Cold and dark, snow and ice,
And then, to crown it all,
Not comfortable at home
But on a journey, in a cave,
Fleeing by night across the border.
It makes you quail to think of it.
But then, it wasn't his idea,
Not that it ever is, of course,
But this child, no one really knows
When he was born, or where.
These tales of Christmas are our tales,
Not his. We are the ones that need them,
At every time, to keep our hope alive.
This child was born tomorrow.

W S Beattie

71   *Rend the clouds*

Light of lights! All gloom dispelling
Thou didst come to make thy dwelling,
Here within our world of sight.
Lord, in pity and in power,
Thou didst in our darkest hour
Rend the clouds and show thy light.

Praise to thee in earth and heaven
Now and evermore be given,
Christ who art our sun and shield.
Lord, for us thy life thou gavest,
Those who trust in thee thou savest,
All thy mercy stands revealed.

Thomas Aquinas (1225–74)

72 *Christmas facts*

It isn't true, of course,
All that about
Shepherds and kings,
The circumstantial details of that birth.
It seemed appropriate
So they put it in,
Just like a parable.
But ever since
We've called it history.

There must have been a birth,
A life, a departing.
The name was Jesus.
All beyond those basic facts
Is taken over as a battlefield
By scholarship.

Within those narratives
We used to take as gospel
Is there now any single thing
We can say for sure
This happened
As it is set down?
These were his actual words,
These deeds
Were his?

W S Beattie

73 *Priorities*

It's strange that Paul
did not recall,
or failed to mention
stable or stall;
ignored angels' wings
and journeying kings
yet wrote at such length
about many more things.
Surely,
if in only one letter,
he could have done better.

Had no story portrayed
a virginal maid?
Was the Magnificat song
much later relayed?
Or was it Paul's choice
to focus his voice
not on parable tale
but on argument's force?
Remember,
Paul's letters were early dated;
when Gospels four were still awaited.

74   *Cosmic celebration*

Christmas is a cosmic celebration of the beginning of something that we cannot adequately describe. It is a liturgy that sings of a new covenant between the God of eternity and man in history.

Pope Paul VI

75   *Overture*

The birth stories are a powerful overture to the great gospels of Matthew and Luke that, like so many good overtures, convey in a nutshell the message which is later to be developed.

Hans Küng

76   *So fair a fancy?*

Christmas Eve, and twelve of the clock,
   'Now they are all on their knees,'
An elder said as we sat in a flock
   By the embers in hearthside ease.

We pictured the meek mild creatures where
   They dwelt in their strawy pen,
Nor did it occur to one of us there
   To doubt they were kneeling then.

So fair a fancy few would weave
   In these years! Yet, I feel,
If someone said on Christmas Eve,
   'Come, see the oxen kneel

In the lonely barton by yonder coomb
   Our childhood used to know,'
I should go with him in the gloom,
   Hoping it might be so.

Thomas Hardy

77 *This Holy Night*

The Eve of Christmas, cold and crisp, is here,
And night's dark curtain splashed with stars sublime;
The silence speaks, the Infinite seems near,
And That Which is Eternal, enters time.

Was it like this at Beth'lem long ago?
Did Mary, in the pain of giving birth,
Sense the Transcendent, immanent, – and know
Almighty God, as Babe, had come to earth?

The pregnant silence speaks of those who pine
Under the pain of hatred, fear or strife,
But steadfast faith and shining hope combine
To birth afresh His Love, the Source of Life.

God comes to heal us on this holy night:
But only poor and humble find their sight.

Beryl Chatfield

78 *Tenacious mystery*

...Bethlehem was charming and moving and strange, and one does not
mind either there or in Jerusalem whether the shrines are rightly
identified or not, because the faith of millions of pilgrims down the
centuries has given them a mystical kind of reality, and one does not
mind much their having been vulgarised, for this had to happen, people
being vulgar and liking gaudy uneducated things round them when
they pray; and one does not mind the original sites and buildings
having been destroyed long ago and others built on their ruins and
destroyed in their turn, again and again and again, for this shows the
tenacious hold they have had on men's imaginations.

Rose Macaulay
From *Towers of Trebizond*

79 *Basilica of the Nativity, Bethlehem*

We lit slim tapers
where a silver star
marked the spot
under bulbous hanging lamps –
tarnished chains swaying.

The cattle never knew
a scene like that.

Surveying
the accumulated myth,
tourist hype,
shekels for everything,
we questioned our emotions' rise:
'Why here?
It could have happened anywhere.'

But above the cave
we saw the unchanging nature
of those rocks;
gazed on a pavement
laid by Constantine
and in the tesseras' golden gleam
glimpsed countless streams
of those who'd found
their spiritual El Dorado there.

Then we said:
'Here
is as good as anywhere.
Why **not** here?'

Margaret Connor

80 *Love hurts at Christmas*

Christmas-time is happy-time.
Lay in the food and booze
(To make quite sure that you can manage it),
Presents and cards, and those infernal jingles;
Dreaming of a Christmas like no one's ever known.
Pretend, dress up, and play your part,
(But inside, clowns are sad, they say).
   Well-fed, well-housed, in work,
   Look at the people of the streets,
   The dispossessed, the victims,
   Spare a dime, then turn away
   A shiver down your spine
   Because you know that really you're like them:
      Alone and destitute
      of the true riches
      that at Christmas-time
      we try to celebrate
      so cheerfully.
      Yet never quite anaesthetise the pain
      of being who we are
      when the bright sword
      of your reality
      compels our worship
      in our own despite.
And wondering always
If that pain
Is not the thing most real
In our shamed human life.

W S Beattie

81 *Albania 1990*

It was the winter of 1990. The event was a Carol Service. The venue was a cemetery; the country in which it took place, Albania. A thousand and more people turned up. The minister who led the service had just been released from prison after twenty-eight years. For forty years a rigid, atheistic government had banned the Bible, and destroyed or closed the churches. The worship of God was forbidden; 'Jesus' an alien name. Few in the cemetery, therefore, knew any carols but the memory of Christmas and carol services lingered. They turned for help to a group of elderly women, young when the regime began who, public worship forbidden, had quietly sung their hymns at home, whispered prayers only heard by God, and so maintained a slender tradition of worship. They were the faithful remnant waiting for re-birth. Adeste fideles! O come all ye faithful!

82 *Gifts to bring*

'Gold,' said one, 'is what I bring,
Gold to honour heaven's King.'
    Wise men came;
    Men of fame:
    Gifts to bring,
    Praise to sing.
We will honour heaven's King.

'Myrrh I bring, to show my care;
Myrrh to heal the wounds he'll bear.'
    Wise men came;
    Men of fame:
    Gifts to bring,
    Praise to sing.
Men will make the cross he'll bear.

'Frankincense is mine to share;
Frankincense, the sign of prayer.'
    Wise men came;
    Men of fame:
    Gifts to bring,
    Praise to sing.
God in Christ has met our prayer.

'Joy we'll bring, from all on earth;
Joy to welcome Jesus' birth.'
    We must sing!
    Let bells ring!
    Every voice
    Now rejoice!
Season of our own new birth.

From *Sing New Songs*

83 *Wisdom*

What would have happened
if there had been Three Wise Women
instead of Three Wise Men?

They would have asked directions,
arrived in Bethlehem on time,
cleaned the stable from floor to rafters,
helped deliver the baby,
brought practical gifts,
and there would have been peace on earth.

Anon

84 *Journey*

We don't know
how long they were on the way
yet the journey was crucial
with awareness slowly growing.
And what had made them start?
A rumour blazoned on a night sky?
A rumour precisely timed?

It was risky
leaving their countries,
dangerous to spurn
security of timeworn paths –
safe, familiar modes of thought.
There must have been moments
when they questioned their purpose,
asked if it was all worthwhile
chasing the way of a star.

As to their gifts –
gold seemed simple –
a percentage on income
but the rising incense of prayer
was a daily grinding effort;
the twisting agony of separation
from wives who told them
they were mad to go
and sons who refused to follow –
that was the myrrh of their offering.

In the end
they must have realised
they'd staked their lives
on a rumour – but arriving
knew they'd proved it.

Margaret Connor

85

Searching faith

The star did not continually shine.
We lost it
often
when mists put out the light,
obscuring the distant pass between the mountain peaks.
Fog we feared.
We walked like blind men,
or stood, indecisive in our waiting,
scanning the nearby ground
for the blurred footprints of previous travellers
in the search for truth.

Strangely, the daytime was the worst
when all seemed clearer to the casual eye,
and others,
cynical of our queries and consulting,
strode firmly by,
following some predetermined goal
along a well-worn path that asked no questions.
Undeterred by changing scenes,
new vista possibilities could be ignored
and obstacles soon brushed aside.
They reached some place of comfort ease,
without the pain of search.

Little consolation to know
that it was ever thus:
   that faith is patient
   waiting, godly
   indecision, search
   'not knowing', more honest than blind certainty,
   and the true goal little known until it's found.

But always, as we journeyed,
we heard and felt, as from a distant land,
the cry of glory
beneath a stable roof.

86 *Magi's Pilgrimage: Found*

Footsore, yes. But now at the end of this endless trail
       with autumn come
and change the order of the day, the holy grail
       draws us home.

It is unexpected, the finding of it (I'd rather say
       the being found):
we'd looked in tip-toe places, traced the star's white way –
       but missed the ground

from which we grow, in whom we live, and where the leaves
       turn to gold ...
Perhaps we, too, may cast sham loves for one who weaves
       new from old ...

And we are reached for, energised. This autumn Son
       heralds our spring.
We thought we'd finished, find we've only now begun
       our journeying ...

Kate Compston

87 *No certainties*

For us there are no certainties, no star
blazing our journey, no decisive dream
to reassure hurt hearts or warn us when
it's time to move. The shepherds, harassed men,
are given answers to the questions they
have never thought to ask. Told where to go
and what to look for. We try out our way
unlit with angels, wondering 'How far?'
Yet in the story we find who we are:
the baby is told nothing, left to grow
slowly to vision through the coloured scheme
of touch, taste, sound; by needing learns to pray,
and makes the way of flesh, dark stratagem
by which God is and offers all we know.

Jennifer Dines

88   *First Light*

Where first did it shine at the moment of birth,
That new glint of dawn in the darkness of earth?
Did the light at the end of the tunnel begin
In a shed round the back of the Bethlehem inn?

Did it shine on rough shepherds from angel-clad hills
Divinely directed round ridges and rills?
Or glow on the gifts of the men who were wise
And came to the stable with stars in their eyes?

Or was there a gleam from a Nazareth bed
Of a Nazarene born and a Nazarene bred?
Were those at the cradle his own kith and kin
With no proclamation, no heavenly din?

The fact or the fiction, the what-might-have-been.
A natural event or a Christmas card scene,
It matters but little whatever is said,
That luminous spirit is still being bred:
Confined in the womb of each soul on the earth
The love-light of healing lies ready for birth.

Chris Avis

89 *Jesus is our light*

Lord God, you sent your Son into the world
to be its one true light.

Brighter than the lamp
which warns the ship of danger,
    Jesus is our Light.
Greater than Orion's glory
blazing on a winter's night,
    Jesus is our Light.
More faithful than a candle
reflecting our face,
    Jesus is our Light.

      As the torch's flame
      banishes the fear of the night – So Christ you are our light.
      As the orange light in our cobbled street
      guides us safe to home – So Christ you are our light.

Brighter than the temple lamps
whereby the dancer danced,
    Jesus is our Light.
Greater than the Christmas lights
blazing down Oxford Street.
    Jesus is our Light.
More faithful than the firefly
illuminating nature's night,
    Jesus is our Light.

Philip Wren

Lent

Lent – General

a As a parent disciplines a child so the Lord your God disciplines you. Therefore keep the commandments of the Lord your God, by walking in his ways and by fearing him.

Deuteronomy 8:5–6

b I sought the Lord, and he answered me, and delivered me from all my fears. Look to him, and be radiant; so your faces shall never be ashamed. O taste and see that the Lord is good; happy are those who take refuge in him.

Psalm 34:4–5, 8

c Create in us a clean heart, O God,
put a new and right spirit within us.
Do not cast us away from your
    presence,
never take your holy spirit from us.
Restore to us the joy of your salvation,
and sustain in us a willing spirit.

adapted from Psalm 51:10–12

d I love the Lord, for he has heard my voice and my supplications.
He has inclined his ear to me, therefore I will call on him as long as I live.
What shall I return to the Lord for all his bounty to me?
We will lift up the cup of salvation and call on the Lord by name.
I will pay my vows to the Lord in the presence of all his people.
I will bring a thank-offering and call on the name of the Lord.

adapted from Psalm 116:1–2, 12–13, 17

e O Lord, you have searched me and known me. You know when I sit down and when I rise up; you discern my thoughts from far away. *Psalm 139:1–2*

f Come now, let us argue it out, says the Lord: though your sins are like scarlet, they shall be like snow; though they are red like crimson, they shall become like wool. *Isaiah 1:18*

g This is the covenant that I will make with the house of Israel says the Lord: I will put my law within them, and I will write it on their hearts; and I will be their God, and they shall be my people. No longer shall they teach one another, or say to each other, 'Know the Lord', for they shall all know me, from the least of them to the greatest.

from Jeremiah 31:33–34

h With what shall I come before the Lord, and bow myself before God on high? He has told you, O mortal, what is good; and what does the Lord require of you but to do justice, and to love kindness and to walk humbly with your God? *Micah 6:6, 8*

i Beware of practising your piety before others in order to be seen by them; for then you have no reward from your Father in heaven.

Whenever you give alms, do not sound a trumpet before you.

When you are praying, do not heap up empty phrases … for your Father knows what you need before you ask him. *from Matthew 6:1–8*

j Work out your own salvation with fear and trembling; for it is God who is at work in you, enabling you both to will and to work for his good pleasure.

from Philippians 2:12–13

Lent – Pilgrimage & Reflection

a The Lord said to Abram, 'Go from your country and your kindred and your father's house to the land that I will show you. I will make of you a great nation, and I will bless you, and make your name great, so that you will be a blessing. *Genesis 12:1–2*

b Your statutes have been my songs wherever I make my home. I remember your name in the night, O Lord, and keep your law. This blessing has fallen to me, for I have kept your precepts.
Psalm 119:54–56

c Now see all this; and will you not declare it? From this time forward I make you hear new things, hidden things that you have not known. They are created now, not long ago; before today you have never heard of them.
Isaiah 48:6–7

d Jesus went on with his disciples to the villages of Caesarea Philippi; and on the way he asked his disciples, 'Who do people say that I am?' And they answered him, 'John the Baptist; and others, Elijah; and still others, one of the prophets.' He asked them, 'But who do you say that I am?' Peter answered him, 'You are the Messiah.' *Mark 8:27–29*

e I appeal to you therefore, brothers and sisters, by the mercies of God, to present your bodies as a living sacrifice, holy and acceptable to God, which is your spiritual worship. Do not be conformed to this world, but be transformed by the renewing of your minds, so that you may discern what is the will of God.
from Romans 12:1–2

f By faith Abraham obeyed when he was called to set out for a place that he was to receive as an inheritance; and he set out, not knowing where he was going. *Hebrews 11:8*

g Since we are surrounded by so great a cloud of witnesses, let us also lay aside every weight and the sin that clings so closely, and let us run with perseverance the race that is set before us, looking to Jesus the pioneer and perfecter of our faith. *Hebrews 12:1–2*

Lent – Call & Temptation

h Hear, O Israel: the Lord is our God, the Lord alone. You shall love the Lord your God with all your heart, and with all your soul, and with all your might. Keep these words that I am commanding you today in your heart.
Deuteronomy 6:4–6

i If you are unwilling to serve the Lord, choose this day whom you will serve; … but as for me and my household, we will serve the Lord.
from Joshua 24:15

j Thus says the Lord, he who created you … he who formed you … : Do not fear, for I have redeemed you; I have called you by name, you are mine.
from Isaiah 43:1

k As he walked by the Sea of Galilee, Jesus saw two brothers, Simon, who is called Peter, and Andrew his brother, casting a net into the lake – for they were fishermen. And he said to them, 'Follow me, and I will make you fish for people.' Immediately they left their nets and followed him.
Matthew 4:18–20

a Jesus said, 'The time is fulfilled, and the kingdom of God has come near; repent, and believe in the good news.
Mark 1:15

b Jesus said, 'If any want to become my followers, let them deny themselves and take up their cross and follow me. For those who want to save their life will lose it, and those who lose their life for my sake, and for the sake of the gospel, will save it. *Mark 8:34–35*

c Jesus said, 'Why are you sleeping? Get up and pray that you may not come into the time of trial.' *Luke 22:46*

d Blessed be the God and Father of our Lord Jesus Christ, who has blessed us in Christ with every spiritual blessing.
Ephesians 1:3

e John, writing to the church at Sardis, said: 'I know your works; you have a name of being alive, but you are dead. Wake up, and strengthen what remains and is on the point of death, for I have not found your works perfect in the sight of my God.' *from Revelation 3:1–2*

f John, writing to the church at Laodicea, said: 'I know your works; you are neither cold nor hot. I wish that you were either cold or hot. I reprove and discipline those whom I love. Be earnest, therefore, and repent.'
Revelation 3:15, 19

g 'Listen! I am standing at the door, knocking; if you hear my voice and open the door, I will come in to you and eat with you, and you with me.'
Revelation 3:20

Lent – Mothering Sunday & Family Life

h The fear of the Lord is the beginning of knowledge; fools despise wisdom and instruction. Hear, my child, your father's instruction, and do not reject your mother's teaching. *Proverbs 1:7–8*

i They said to Jesus, 'Your mother and your brothers and sisters are outside, asking for you.' Jesus replied, 'Who are my mother and my brothers?' And looking at those who sat around him, he said, 'Here are my mother and my brothers! Whoever does the will of God is my brother and sister and mother.'
from Mark 3:32–35

j Jesus took a little child and put it among them; and taking it in his arms, he said to them, 'Whoever welcomes one such child in my name welcomes me, and whoever welcomes me welcomes not me but the one who sent me.' *Mark 9:36–37*

k 'My soul magnifies the Lord, and my spirit rejoices in God my Saviour, for he has looked with favour on the lowliness of his servant. Surely, from now on all generations will call me blessed.' *Luke 1:46–48*

l Whenever we have an opportunity, let us work for the good of all, and especially for those of the family of faith. *Galatians 6:10*

m You are no longer strangers and aliens, but you are citizens with the saints and also members of the household of God. *Ephesians 2:19*

90
Walk gently through these coming weeks
with quiet eagerness;
many have gone before you,
and by humility, quietness, and persistent prayer
have found signposts to an inner harmony
and pathways to a deep-felt peace.

91
The Lenten journey is no easy ride:
the paths are rough and sometimes desert-dry,
the roads uncertain and the resting places few;
but you will find friends to travel with you,
ancient clues to guide you on your way.
And always there will be the hopeful expectation
that you are walking in the steps of Christ.

92
No one will tempt us in the weeks of Lent
to find a stone and turn it into bread,
or leap from temple rooftop with majestic ease.
No crowds will kneel before our feet,
promising to call us king if we will do their will.
Our tempting will be different:
    to hear again his 'Follow me' – and turn aside,
    or hear a cry of human pain – and close our ears;
    to waste the moment that we set aside for prayer,
    or spurn the opportunity for study's growth;
    to reject a trivial luxury and call it discipline,
    or see a call to serve as one more burden.
These may be the desert stumblings on our Lenten road.

93
To stop and think;
    that is the gift God offers in our Lent.
To pause and reflect;
    that is what God lays within our reach.
To look life in the face and ask its meaning;
    that is the opportunity God gives.
To see within ourselves and ask just who we are;
    that is an awesome task God offers.
And then step out to meet the Easter call.

94 Seed sown in the field, coins lost in the home,
lilies fading, children growing, bread breaking,
rich men dining, beggars sighing, shepherds guiding;
everyday sights for everyday people –
this is where Jesus saw signs of the kingdom.
And now, for us?
This is the Lenten call:
    to look around at all the world,
    to think of all our daily life,
    and see what cries aloud
    of kingdom come!

95 **Jesus asked, 'Who do you say that I am?'**
And will his Church today search him out
and use this Lent to know his mind?

Jesus said, 'It is written, my house shall be a house of prayer.'
And will his Church today give dedicated time
and use this Lent for fresh devotion?

Jesus said: 'Why are you sleeping?'
And will his Church today wake from its slumber
and use this Lent to do his work?

96 *Use two voices. When the ten lines of the first two columns have been spoken,*
line by line, both voices read the six sentences of the third column in unison.

First voice:	*Second voice:*	*Both voices:*
Son of a carpenter,	Calling God, Father;	We trust ourselves
One with his people,	Creating new family;	through this Jesus
Draining the old wine,	Fermenting the new wine;	To the Kingdom
Open to everyone,	Narrowing the gate;	he points to,
Deliverer of captives,	Binding the free;	To the Father behind it,
Bringer of peace,	Stirring up strife;	With the disciples
Creator of unity.	Dividing asunder;	everywhere
Hope for the hopeless,	Destroying our hopes;	who live for it.
Crucified for all,	Compelling cross-bearers;	
Emptying the tomb.	Going ahead of us.	

Sheffield Urban Theology Unit
From *The Eucharist of the Radical Christ*

97 Lent calls us
to journey along a Way
that stretches into unseen distances,
to hold to a Truth
that is great beyond our fullest understanding,
and embrace a Life
that calls us to maturity.
Lent calls us to follow Jesus
who is the Way, the Truth, and the Life.

98 In these coming weeks,
if our ears are open,
Jesus will come with a message of hope and challenge.
If we are clear-sighted,
Jesus will come with a vision of renewal and confidence.
If we are alert to his teaching,
Jesus will turn our lives upside down.
If we will live with him,
Jesus will teach us the meaning of suffering.
If we will let 'self' die with him,
Jesus will show us the road to life.

99 Jesus did not travel alone –
he chose twelve friends and more
to walk the road to Jerusalem.
Come now,
in worship, study, thoughtfulness and love,
let us walk the road together
and follow him.

100 God has created us to do him some definite service. He has committed
some work to each one of us which he has not committed to another. We
have our mission. We may never know it in this world, but we shall be
told it in the next. Therefore, trust him. Wherever, whatever you are,
you can never be thrown away. If you are in sickness, your sickness may
serve him; in perplexity, your perplexity may serve him; if you are in
sorrow, your sorrow may serve him. He knows what he is about.

John Henry Newman (1801–1890) adapted

101
While we deliberate, God reigns;
When we decide wisely, he reigns;
When we decide foolishly, he reigns;
When we serve him in humble loyalty, he reigns;
When we serve him self-assertively, he reigns;
When we rebel and seek to withhold our service, he reigns;
He reigns: the Alpha and Omega,
Which was, and which is, and which is to come.

William Temple

102
This call to worship could be spoken by several voices

If God be for us, who can be against us?
  – and we see Jesus, wrestling alone in desert temptation.

If God be for us, who can be against us?
  – and we see Jesus facing the rigidity of Law and the hypocrisy of
    religion.

If God be for us, who can be against us?
  – and we see Jesus locked in solitude in Gethsemane garden.

If God be for us, who can be against us?
  – and we see Jesus facing the power of Rome.

If God be for us, who can be against us?
  – and we see Jesus betrayed by his friends.

If God be for us, who can be against us?
  – and we see Jesus hanging, limp, upon a cross.

Since God is for us, none can be against us!
  – and we see Jesus in resurrection light.

103
For use the Sunday before Palm Sunday, perhaps at the end of worship

Prepare the branching palms to strew along his way,
approach Jerusalem's gates.
The lengthening days of Lent will close
and a new drama begin.
The Passover prepared, the crowds will gather,
and soldiers, facing troubled times,
will look for trees to make a cross,
whilst God will look for one who proves obedient to the end,
and for those who will walk with him.
So be it.

Pilgrimage & Reflection

104 Loving Father, in the name of Jesus
who increased in wisdom and in years,
and in divine and human favour,
help us in these weeks of preparation
to be who we are,
and grow towards what we might become
in his name.

105 Lord Jesus Christ,
we have heard your call to walk the Christian way,
and have received your ministry of healing and reconciliation.
Now, send us on our pilgrim way.
Give us strength to keep the faith,
insight to know where you are leading,
and love for all our companion travellers.

106 Saviour Christ, we remember that the journey you took to the cross
was not a neatly planned seven week journey
with the end always clearly in sight,
and the assurance of a glorious resurrection a guaranteed certainty,
but was a treacherous, uncharted walk
with few signposts
and a dwindling number of friends.
If we are to walk with you even a few steps in this season
first grant us honesty,
then courage to face the uncertainty of faith,
and at the last a simple trust
that God is in control.

107 As Simon and Andrew mended broken nets,
you came, Christ the fisherman, and called them to follow you;
as Matthew sat at his desk, counting his dues,
you came, Christ the carpenter, and invited him to work with you;
as Paul travelled towards Damascus,
you came, journeying Christ, and showed him a new road to travel;
as Simon the Zealot sought freedom's path by violence,
you came, liberating Christ, and pointed him towards the power of peace.
Come again, Christ of all peoples,
come where we are, come to who we are,
and make us your disciples.

108
Lord Jesus Christ, let me seek you by desiring you,
and let me desire you by seeking you.
Let me find you by loving you,
and love you by finding you.
I acknowledge, Lord, with thanksgiving
that you have made me in your own image,
so that I can remember you, think of you, and love you,
but confess that the likeness is so worn,
and darkened by the smoke of sin,
that it cannot do that for which it was made.
Let it be that in these coming weeks,
my seeking will lead to finding,
my finding to a renewal of your spirit within me,
so that your image shines bright and clear.

based on a prayer by **Anselm** (1033–1109)

109
As winter darkness edges into light,
and timid shoots begin to show their green,
so, with the brightness of the noonday sun,
bring us closer to your Easter presence,
and kindle our wavering faith into new life.

In a God-forsaking world that idolises self,
and measures possibility in human terms alone,
then, with the sharpness of a sword,
reveal again your active power that daily touches earth,
and raise our Lenten sights to see your guiding hand.

In a Church that rarely matches vision with its hope,
and ever finds a gap between its prayers and life,
now, with the word of a prophet,
set our spirits free to sound the depths of faith,
and turn our feet to walk the pilgrim way.

In personal lives that lag behind our best intention,
and often miss the times of grace we seek,
please, with demanding encouragement,
give us now a widening perspective ,
and spur us on towards your promised goal.

Call & Temptation

110 Thou, our source,
Who rises and shines forth in all things,
May your whole being be honoured in our hearts;
May the unity of all things be made clear.
Your one desire shall then act with ours,
as in all light and sound, so in all forms around us;
Grant what we need each day in bread and insight;
Loose the cords of the mistakes that bind us
as we release the strands we hold of others' guilt;
Do not let outward appearances delude us,
but free us from what holds us back;
From you is all unity,
all the potential of life,
the song that resonates in all things;
From age to age renewing.
We affirm this with our whole beings. Amen

The Aramaic prayer of Jesus created from ancient manuscripts. Translator
unknown

111 Lord, there is more than a touch of laziness
in what we have called 'commitment' in ourselves;
and more than a touch of commitment
in what we have labelled 'casual' in others.
There is an inner silence in the most talkative
and a powerful word of insight hiding in the most silent.
There is a deep need for stillness in the most active among us
and a powerful urge to work in the seemingly passive.
There is a shyness in those whose talents stand out a mile
and a wealth of possibilities in those slow to come forward.
Help us to use this time of Lenten reflection
to see ourselves and others with greater clarity,
to nurture the gifts you have given each one
and then to offer the wholeness of our church life
into the purposes of your kingdom.

112 The kingdom of God is at hand: be ready to welcome it;
The kingdom of God is within you: declare its presence;
for the kingdoms of this world
will become the Kingdom of our God,
and he will reign for ever and ever.

113

Hidden beneath the apple's skin and flesh,
tucked away within the core,
forgotten and ignored,
lies your promise, O God,
the seeds
   from which new life may spring,
   through which the tree may be renewed,
   that speak of hope for tomorrow.

Enter the heart of me,
germinate my life,
and reveal to me the prospect and the possibility
that you have placed in every tomorrow.

May your will and way be nevermore
forgotten or ignored.

Adrian Bulley

114

Lord,
be hearing to my deafness;
be sight to my blindness;
be a gentle touch to my insensitivity.
Be care in my neglect;
be wisdom for my ignorance;
be depth to my superficiality.
And call, and call again,
until I hear and see and know.

115

Patient Companion,
you listened gently to your disciples when they misunderstood you,
and when they looked for power rather than service
you still held them in your care;
you did not reject them when they followed their own way,
and even when they deserted and denied you
you were still faithful to them.
   We who follow them still misunderstand,
   still seek power, and forget to serve,
   still desert, reject, and fail.
Have mercy on us, patient Companion.

**Mothering Sunday
& Family Life**

116 Eternal God, we offer you adoration and praise;
by your own power and love
you watch over us as would a father
and nurture us as would a mother.
You did not display yourself alone in kingly majesty
nor treat us as a lord would treat a servant;
against all we expected you came in humility and loss
in Jesus the Christ.
We ask this prayer, eternal God:
  In our family life
  and all our human contacts,
  create in us
  what we have seen in him.

117 Loving Father, we thank you for the gift of home and family life.
Thank you for the family into which we were born or were nurtured;
  for its security and trust,
    for given freedom to grow, discover and learn,
    for the pain and delight of sharing.
Thank you for the home-life we have helped to create;
    as husband and wife dependent on each other,
    as parents in shared responsibility,
    as children learning to give,
    as those who welcome visitors and friends.
Thank you for the homes we have visited;
    for the welcome given and friendship received,
    for the awareness of different patterns of family life,
    for memories that will last for ever.
Thank you for the homes we have created alone;
    in enforced or chosen solitude,
    in the sadness of bereavement,
    in advancing older age.
Thank you for the homes that shelter us;
    when we choose no longer to live alone,
    when our affairs fall into the hands of others.
Thank you for the home you have promised us;
    in which there are many mansions,
    in which we rest in your love,
    and where you rule supreme.

118   *He will feed his flock like a shepherd*
          ...and gently lead those that are with young. Isaiah 40:11

God of love,
We pray for parents, mothers and fathers, as they care for their children.

In the joy and hesitancy of the months of pregnancy
we pray for the growing child, the waiting mother, the anxious father:
    Saviour Christ, be a shepherd to them
    and gently lead those that are with young.

In the delight and anxieties of a child's early days and months
we pray for those recently become parents:
    Saviour Christ, be a shepherd to them
    and gently lead those that are with young.

In the welcome and adjustment when a growing family receives a new baby
we pray for parents and siblings as patterns and relationships change:
    Saviour Christ, be a shepherd to them
    and gently lead those that are with young.

In teenage years when freedom is both welcomed yet feared
we pray that young and old alike may find strong resources of love:
    Saviour Christ, be a shepherd to them
    and gently lead those that are with young.

In family conversations when young people search for a job or further education
we pray that guidance may found for the right way forward:
    Saviour Christ, be a shepherd to them
    and gently lead those that are with young.

When bags are packed for a future home outside the parents' care
and pride, joy and sadness are mixed
we pray that love will keep its strong bond, and trust renew its life:
    Saviour Christ, be a shepherd to them
    and gently lead those that are with young.

As customs vary and family patterns change
we pray for tolerant understanding and generous acceptance.
    Saviour Christ, be a shepherd to us all
    and gently lead us in the ways of love.

119   Be to us, O God, as each most needs.
          Be father, mother, brother, sister, friend,
          Be lover, neighbour, confidante, companion,
          Be strength and hope to us,
          And make one family of trust and care.

Pilgrimage & Reflection

120   *True Lent*

Now quit your care,
  And anxious fear and worry;
    For schemes are vain
    And fretting brings no gain.
To prayer, to prayer! –
  Bells call and clash and hurry
    In Lent the bells do cry,
      'Come buy, come buy,
    Come buy with love the love most high!'

To bow the head
  In sackcloth and in ashes,
    Or rend the soul,
    Such grief is not Lent's goal;
But to be led
  To where God's glory flashes,
    His beauty to come nigh,
      To fly, to fly,
    To fly where truth and light do lie.

For is not this
  The fast that I have chosen? –
    The prophet spoke –
    To shatter every yoke,
Of wickedness
  The grievous bands to loosen,
    Oppression put to flight,
      To fight, to fight,
To fight till every wrong's set right.

For righteousness
  And peace will show their faces
    To those who feed
    The hungry in their need,
And wrongs redress,
  Who build the old waste places,
    And in the darkness shine.
      Divine, divine,
Divine it is when all combine!

Then shall your light
  Break forth as doth the morning;
    Your health shall spring,
    The friends you make shall bring
God's glory bright,
  Your way through life adorning;
    And love shall be the prize.
      Arise, arise,
Arise and make a paradise!

Percy Dearmer (1867–1936)
From *The Oxford Book of Carols*

121 *Unadorned*

Lent is a tree without blossom, without leaf,
Barer than blackthorn in its winter sleep,
All unadorned. Unlike Christmas which decrees
The setting-up, the dressing-up of trees,
Lent is a taking down, a stripping bare,
A starkness after all has been withdrawn
Of surplus and superfluous,
Leaving no hiding place, only an emptiness
Between black branches, a most precious space
Before the leaf, before the time of flowers;
Lest we should see only the leaf, the flower,
Lest we should miss the stars.

Jean M Watt

122 *Contentment*

He that is down need fear no fall,
    He that is low no pride;
He that is humble ever shall
    Have God to be his guide.

I am content with what I have,
    Little it be or much:
And, Lord, contentment still I crave,
    Because thou savest such.

Fullness to such a burden is
    That go on pilgrimage:
Here little, and hereafter bliss,
    Is best from age to age.

John Bunyan (1622–88)

123 *Creation and action*

He rang Julia a few days later to arrange a meeting. She was as cheerful as ever and asked him how his work was going.
'Better not to ask.'
'Do you know what the secret is?'
'Tell me.'
'The secret is that there is no secret. You just get on with it. You just do the work.' She could hear him snort at the other end of the phone. 'You think I'm joking? This is as serious as I get!'

Deirdre Madden
From *Authenticity*

124 *Depth in silence*

The only initiation into silence is silence. And when the silence is continuous it ceases to be merely negative – not talking – and it begins to have the quality of depth.

Michael Ramsey
Source unknown

125 *The anonymous Christ*

He comes to us as one unknown, without a name, as of old by the lake-side he came to those men who knew him not. He speaks to us the same word: 'Follow thou me!', and sets us to the tasks which he has to fulfil in our time. And to those who obey him, whether they be wise or simple, he will reveal himself in the toils, the conflicts, the sufferings which they shall pass through in his fellowship, and as an ineffable mystery, they shall learn in their own experience who he is.

Albert Schweitzer (1875–1965)
From *The Quest for the Historical Jesus*

126 Sour-sweet days

Ah my dear angry Lord,
Since thou dost love, yet strike;
Cast down, yet help afford;
Sure I will do the like.

I will complain, yet praise;
I will bewail, approve;
And all my sour-sweet days
I will lament, and love.

George Herbert (1593–1633)

127 The misunderstood past

'Seeing how you're so interested in history,' Roderic said as they ate, 'perhaps when you retire you might think to study history, to do a degree.'

'Me!' Dan said. 'At a university? Sure I have no education worth talking about. They'd never let me in.'

'They don't always require formal qualifications for mature students,' Julia argued 'and in any case, you know far more about history already than any student coming in with a Leaving Certificate.'

Still he wasn't convinced. 'I just don't know. I'm not sure that the way they go about things there would suit me. I have my own way of seeing things.' Abruptly he put down his knife and fork. 'We know nothing', he said. 'We like to think we know it all, but the half of it we're making up. Just imagine if in a thousand years' time, people were trying to know about us: what life was like in Dublin now. Who we were and what we were. What we believed and what we wanted. And all they had to help them to work it out was Glasnevin Cemetery, a few bits of jewellery, bracelets, and earrings, and what they could dig up from the Naas dual carriageway. Can you imagine what you'd come up with? Can you *imagine*?'

Julia said it was the same with painting, that the artists of the past would be amazed if they could see what had happened to their work: altarpieces taken out of churches and broken up, the central image displayed in Washington, the right panel in Berlin, the predella in London. What would they have thought to see those religious images displayed in blank white rooms beside court portraits, beside images that to them would have been wholly profane?

Deirdre Madden
From *Authenticity*

128   *God of love*

Blest be the God of love.
Who gave me eyes, and light, and power this day,
Both to be busy, and to play.
But much more blest be God above,
Who gave me sight alone,
Which to himself he did deny;
For when he sees my ways, I die:
But I have got his sun, and he hath none.

What have I brought thee home
For this thy love? Have I discharged the debt,
Which this day's favours did beget?
I ran; but all I brought was foam.
Thy diet, care and cost
Do end in bubbles, balls of wind;
Of wind to thee whom I have crossed,
But balls of wildfire to my troubled mind.

Yet still thou goest on,
And now with darkness closest weary eyes,
Saying to man, 'It doth suffice:
Henceforth repose; your work is done.'
Thus in thy ebony box
Thou dost enclose us, till the day
Put our amendment in our way,
And give new wheels to our disordered clocks.

I muse, which shows more love,
The day or night, that is the gale, this the harbour;
That is the walk, and this the arbour;
Or that the grass, this the grove.
My God, thou art all love.
Not one poor minute 'scapes thy breast,
But brings a favour from above;
And in this love, more than in bed, I rest.

George Herbert (1593–1633)

129 *Truth keeps exploding*

Religious systems are always churning, changing, interacting and growing. There is a human tendency to try to stop that process and to feel secure in the conviction that the worshipper now possesses the total truth and no more change will be necessary. That is when religious people begin to make exclusive claims like: This is the only true church. Our Bible is the inerrant Word of God. Our pope is infallible. It never works. The 'unchanging truth of God' is always changing. Truth keeps exploding.

I want us to take the various ingredients of Christianity and ask, 'What was the God experience that caused our religious forebears to interact with the culture and knowledge of their day and in the process to write Scriptures, create creeds, develop doctrines and promulgate dogma?' Once we can uncover that driving experience then we can try to discern how we might explain that experience in the language of our day. This is why all religious systems are constantly in flux. They either change or they die. An unchanging religion always becomes idolatrous.

I want to honour my religious past without being controlled by it. I want the freedom to explore my faith tradition without the institutional put-offs that come with such authoritarian pronouncements as, 'the Bible says' or 'the Church teaches'. So my goal in ministry is to walk inside my faith tradition without being bound by it, to carry on a constant dialogue between my faith and the 21st century which I inhabit, to accept no formulation of God as final, and to walk into the mystery of God every day.

John Shelby Spong
Reprinted by permission of WaterfrontMedia. (See index of copyrights)

130 *Uncertainty is inclusive*

...I would argue that my certainty differs from the certainties of my critics in that being so clear that uncertainty is inevitable, I am free to collaborate with any Christian believer who is willing to collaborate with me. In contrast, those Christians who demand certainties as essential to belief must be exclusive. In the end, demanding certainty about faith is essentially schismatic (as is illustrated by the wretched history of Christian quarrelling). The central question for the future of Christian faith is whether it is possible to sustain realistic hope while at the same time deepening humility and opening us up to deeper truth.

David E Jenkins, former Bishop of Durham
From *The Calling of a Cuckoo*

131 *Theology at 120°*

A short, uncomplicated article on the Christian idea of God had to be done for a Hindu magazine. Nothing modern, something quite ordinary. The subject had been discussed in all the theological textbooks, of course. ... However, what was written there and what one had studied with adequate zeal only a few years ago now seemed so inadequate, so irrelevant, so untrue. Theology at 120°F in the shade seems, after all, different from theology at 70°F. Theology accompanied by tough chapattis and smoky tea seems different from theology with roast chicken and a glass of good wine. Now, who is really different, theos or the theologian? The theologian at 70°F in a good position presumes God to be happy and contented, well-fed and rested, without needs of any kind. The theologian at 120°F tries to imagine a God who is hungry and thirsty, who suffers and is sad, who sheds perspiration and knows despair.

The theologian at 70°F and with a well-ordered life sees the whole world as a beautiful harmony with a grand purpose, the church as God's kingdom on earth and himself as promoter of the real culture of humanity. The theologian at 120°F sees the cracks in the soil and the world as a desert; he considers whether it wouldn't be wiser to keep the last jug of water till the evening; he wishes the heat was a few degrees less and he has to exert all his Christian faith to find a little bit of sense in this life wherein he plays such a very insignificant role, because he depends on so many people.

Klaus Klostermaier
From *Hindu and Christian in Vrindaban*

132 *Half-truths*

Our highest truths are but half-truths,
Think not to settle down forever in any truth.
Make use of it as a tent in which to pass a summer's night,
But build no house of it, or it will be your tomb.
When you first have an inkling of its insufficiency
And begin to descry a dim counter-truth looming up beyond,
Then weep not, but give thanks
It is the Lord's voice whispering,
 'Take up thy bed and walk.'

J J Balfour
Source unknown

133 *Called to pilgrimage*

In politics and theology our generation has a pathetic craving for certainty, and a failure to recognise that we always live in the interim. Tomorrow's experience may prove today's so-called 'truth' to be partial. Christians are people of faith called to pilgrimage, not people of the law clutching our creeds. Confidence we may have; certainty never. Confidence undergirds faith whereas certainty, ending enquiry, destroys it.

From an address to the General Assembly of the United Reformed Church 1993

134 *Community*

This we have learned in the community of faith;
for this we give thanks:
    until we hear with each other's ears,
    the Word is indistinct, unclear;
    until we see with each other's eyes,
    we live in shadowed half-light;
    until we walk as pilgrim friends,
    we stumble and are quick to fall;
Until we love,
and let love conquer all mistrust and fear
we are pale shadows of the Christ we serve.

135 *Luxurious fast*

What luxury it is to fast!
Unless you normally eat enough,
or to excess,
fasting makes no sense.
The starving can't fast;
they've no base line
from which to begin.
Did you ever see a really poor person at a Lent Lunch?

Those rejected chocolates
are only a deprivation
because life is normally soft-centred
and cream-filled.

'No thanks! It's Lent.'
And the wine glass stays empty.
But where's the spirit in it
if the cellar is ready to pour out excess blessing
to the tune of Easter bells?

continued...

Remember!
Those forty days and nights
lasted a lifetime.
Even if it was short.

136　*Beyond belief*

I've a fellow feeling
for Thomas –
he asked questions –
and so do I.

I've struggled
under stranglehold
of doctrine
and tangled long
with creeds
which seldom meet
my needs.

Yet as I try
to understand,
floundering at times
on sinking sand
or even giving up
my search,

I've sometimes found
on such a day
I'm lifted up
and turned around,
then gently led
another way.

Margaret Connor

137　*Glory to God!*

Every enlargement of the human mind, every example that God has created us as enquiring, searching, rational creatures who, faced with the so-called obvious, ask, 'But why?' is evidence of God's greatness. Every question mark laid alongside rigid tradition, every door pushed open against the odds, is an example, not only of human greatness but of the ever-widening activity of the God who made us.

Beethoven breaks new ground by adding the human voice to a symphony, Shostakovich produces a sound of music quite different from all that has gone before it. Picasso pioneers new art forms, architects conquer problems of space, poets learn to express the profound in simple ways, a mathematician proclaims 'Eureka!', scientists wrestle with ideas, materials, and formulae until new truth dawns, space craft probe the universe, and archaeologists bring the past into the future, and those with eyes to see, praise the glory of God.

From an address to the General Assembly of the United Reformed Church 1993

Calling and Temptation

138 *Selection process*

There on the skyline –
Something about that bush.
A trick of the light?
The angle of the setting sun?
It almost looks as though it were alight!
Flames rising from a bush.
How strange! How beautiful!
The flames pass through it and it remains itself
Unharmed by the touch of the fire.
   I'm going closer.
   This is a riddle set for me.
   It summons me. I must respond.
   This pointer, which is in my world
   Yet goes utterly beyond it,
   Contradicts it.
Whose fire is this?
Let each one do as he may please,
But it is mine to search,
That I may know what truth I see.
Afterwards, to do such things
As I may be selected for,
But now, in trepidation,
To approach.

W S Beattie

139 *Prepared in the desert*

In the Bible, the desert is a place both of testing and encounter with
God. Every mission of proclaiming and witnessing the kingdom must
be prepared in the desert, where the proximity of death stirs up our will
to live and makes us experience the isolation which leads us to hunger
for communion.

Gustavo Gutierrez
Source unknown

140 *I need the wilderness*

When You, Lord, say, 'Turn stones to bread!'
　　You enable me to do it;
To take each hard event of life
　　And grow in stature through it.

And when I hear your order, 'Jump
　　Into some place of danger!'
I know you'll always tag along,
　　As I face foe or stranger.

You send me out to win the world
　　And pray for its conversion
And teach me all the politic
　　Of love without coercion.

But Satan loves to parody
　　And set me in confusion:
I ask, 'Is this the voice of God,
　　Or only an illusion?'

So, Lord, I need the wilderness,
　　With you and Satan calling, –
That I may there discern for sure
　　If I'm upright or falling.

Beryl Chatfield

141 *Managing without God*

Our coming of age leads us to a true recognition of our situation before God. God would have us know that we must live as people who manage our lives without him. The God who is with us is the God who forsakes us (Mark 15:34). The God who lets us live in the world without the working hypothesis of God is the God before whom we stand continually. Before God and with God we live without God. God lets himself be pushed out of the world on to the cross. He is weak and powerless in the world, and that is precisely the way, the only way, in which he is with us and helps us.

Dietrich Bonhoeffer
From *Letters and Papers from Prison*

142 *Reckoning*

How long shall I consider
this shabby state
to be the sum of my endeavour?
How shall I render
that missed opportunity
which I cloak as prudence,
that lost cause
too easily surrendered
under a tag of common sense,
and the pretence
at understanding others
when their needs
so often irritate?
Will those moments by the bush
with my shoes off
still sustain
through days and nights
of weak self-condemnation?
I don't ask to be a saint
but – oh, let grace
now tilt a wing towards me
and in its cover
may I blot out one mistake.

Margaret Connor

143 *The secret of discipleship*

I will tell you the secret. God had had all there was of me. There have
been men with greater brains than I, men with greater opportunities;
but from the day I got the poor of London on my heart, and a vision of
what Christ could do with the poor of London, I made up my mind that
God would have all of William Booth there was. And if there is anything
of power in the Salvation Army today, it is because God has all the
adoration of my heart and all the power of my will, and all the influence
of my life.

William Booth, founder of the Salvation Army

144 *Disciples*

They threw down their nets
and they followed Him.
There was no time to
calculate profit or loss.
There was no time to
call home for a second opinion.
It seemed absolute madness.
It seemed like death.
But it was a wise madness,
a necessary death.
The old faith dropped
and sank beneath waves.
The new faith walked on water,
beckoning on to Jerusalem
and the dry hills around.

Steve Turner

145 *Something hidden*

Blest are the ears that hear, the eyes that see,
When God reveals himself in human guise;
Unlearned, little gifted, lightly prized –
Yet they beside the Lake of Galilee,
Saw something that was hidden from the wise,
And seeing, humbly followed after Christ.

Anon

146 *Who wouldn't?*

The Master said,
    'Come, follow.'
    That was all.
Earth-joy grew dim,
My soul went after him.
I rose and followed,
    That was all.
Who wouldn't follow if
    They heard him call?

Anon

147 *The unknown best*

He called the unknown best from Peter, James,
And all the rest, who met him face to face,
And lent their lives to his amazing grace
Of humour, irony and insight; flames
Of lambent love in him seared out the shames
Of life-long littleness in them, till base
Was base no more, and even commonplace
Became uncommon, till their names
Grew strong to move a world that would have thought
Them simple, stupid, ordinary men,
As once they had been, helpless for the task –
Till Christ upcaught in them the gold he sought,
Drew forth their deepest selves …
Can he again
Do it, if you or I have faith to ask?

Anon

148 *Christ's alone*

Who answers Christ's insistent call
Must give himself, his life, his all,
Without one backward look.
Who sets his hand upon the plough,
And glances back with anxious brow,
his calling has mistook.
Christ claims him, wholly for his own;
He must be Christ's, and Christ's alone.

John Oxenham

149 *People of a person*

Christians are not people of a book. We are people of a person. Jesus Christ is the Word of God. He and none other. He and no book of words. We are people of faith, who use a particular and precious book as a major and crucial resource. And thus we stand with Jesus struggling with his Scriptures in the wilderness, and with Peter and Paul in rejecting the tradition which would have denied Christ to the Gentiles because in their own experience, reinforced by that of others, they knew the old tradition to have been superseded.

From an address to the General Assembly of the United Reformed Church 1993

150   *Mixed messages*

He called me once,
well, more than once,
and that's the trouble
        – he alters his voice and calling place.

Once he spoke whilst I was working,
(like James and John at fishing, and Matthew at his desk).
My working place was a laboratory
and science my self-chosen mode of thought.
    But was it him –
    or just the impulse of a Christian friend
    who said I'd make a minister?

And then again in Durham:
an overwhelming force, heavy as cathedral stones.
I almost saw him face to face
and felt his breath upon my cheek.
    But was it him –
    or just tradition's heavy weight;
    two thousand years insisting they were right?

Once, he took me by surprise, almost tricked me, so it seemed.
The gospel-preacher's voice was coarse, strident in its affirmations;
no room for doubt, no time for questioning.
But something gentler slipped between the unbending words,
and touched the deeper strata of my soul.
    But was it him –
    or a tempting hope of certainty,
    I knew to be unfaithful to my pilgrim search?

Autumnal sun shone on one visitation.
The air was clear, the fields still green with flowering life.
Reaching a summit, the valley stretched beyond my sight
and life seemed one with all creation.
This time the voice was silence.
    But was it him –
    or nature's soft seducing;
    romantic notions winter's storm would soon dispel?

All this could be ignored,
except for its insistence
and the pressure from within and from without
to see and listen, hear and pay attention,
and then to be.

Family Life & Mothering Sunday

151   *Mother/father God*

As truly as God is our father, so just as truly is he our mother.
In our father, God Almighty, we have our being; in our merciful
mother we are remade and restored. Our fragmented lives are knit
together and made perfect. And by giving and yielding ourselves,
through grace, to the Holy Spirit we are made whole.

I saw that God rejoices that he is our father, and that God rejoices that
he is our mother, and God rejoices that he is our very husband, and
our soul his beloved wife. And Christ rejoices that he is our brother,
and Jesus rejoices that he is our saviour. These are five great joys, as I
see it, which he wills us to delight in – praising him, thanking him,
loving him, and blessing him for ever.

I am he,
the power and goodness of fatherhood;
the wisdom and lovingness of motherhood;
I am he,
the light and race of all blessed love.
I am he,
the great supreme goodness of every kind of thing;
I am he
who makes you love.

Julian of Norwich

152   *The birth of God the Father*

(God) makes a new promise to the new king David, foretelling the role
of David's son Solomon: 'And when thy days be fulfilled, and thou
shalt sleep with thy fathers, I will set up thy seed after thee, which shall
proceed out of thy bowels, and I will establish his kingdom. He shall
build an house for my name, and I will stablish the throne of his
kingdom for ever.' And then, out of the blue, the promise of a quite new
relationship: *'I will be his father and he shall be my son.'* (2 Samuel 7:12–14a)

This is the first time that God has been perceived as a father: God the
Father. The father-son relationship is quite different from a king-subject
or a lord-vassal relationship.

David Boulton
From *The Trouble with God*

153 *Celebrating Mothering Sunday?*

A day to celebrate a mother's love;
Thank you, God.
A day for gratitude too often unexpressed;
A day for care returned for care long given;
Thank you, God.
A day to focus on our source, our given life, our safe belonging.

But are there tears and cries of pain this day?
Does 'mother' mean to all what now it means to us?
How does the child-grown-old
    whose mother's love was never born,
    whose mother's tongue was ever sharp,
    whose mother's manner fast destroyed young hopes and growth,
live through this day?

And what of those whose memory is less of mother's vibrant health
    and more of lengthy sickness, early death, or painful separation?
And those who once in pain and fear
    heard angry words their parents spoke,
    knew love used as weapon,
    saw marriage crumbling at their feet,
    were forced to choose between the two they loved?
How do they live this Mother's Day?

    Loving God, who sowed the seeds that fathered us,
    who mothered us with living food
    who joins both joy and pain in one deep sacrament of life,
    and holds all children in one loving group,
    speak to us this day
    and draw the circle of your care around us all.

154 *The gift*

A bunch of daffodils clutched tight within an infant grasp,
a smiling face above, infused with pride.
'For Mummy', he said. 'Just for her',
and meant it.
And all the hype of market stall and florist shop,
extortion with its easy advertising,
false pressure, and the flowers forced to bloom,
suddenly,
seemed worth it.

155   *The child becomes the model*

The contemporaries of Jesus defined childhood in terms of the future. Children were the 'Israel to be'. Only when a male child reached adolescence did he become 'Israel'. Many other ancient communities acted similarly and the attitude still persists. In contrast, the gospels record a startling incident for which there were no Jewish precedents.

They even brought babies for him to touch; but when the disciples saw them they scolded them for it. But Jesus called for the children and said, 'Let the little ones come to me, do not try to stop them for the kingdom of God belongs to such as these. I tell you that whoever does not accept the kingdom of God like a child will never enter it.' Luke 18:15-17

We sentimentalise the event if we give it an aura of holiness. These were ordinary children playing in the area; certainly with dirty feet and probably with runny noses. Similarly, we take the edge off the story if we write it up for children in terms of: 'The disciples tried to turn the children away because Jesus had had a busy day and was very tired. But, even though he was weary, Jesus still...' etc. The significance of the stories is much more pointed. Jesus was not expected to reject them because he was tired **but because they were children**. The disciples were accepting the current view of childhood; Jesus was offering a new view. Our assumption is that children must change and become like us. This incident asserts that it is adults who must change and become like children. The child becomes the 'kingdom model'. Maturity is measured in terms of childlikeness.

Adapted from the chapter 'Children in the Church' in *For Saints and Sinners*

156   *Gifts for the Table*

Children do not come to church empty-handed; they bring gifts. Their gifts not only allow the children to understand and interpret the events of the (Communion) Table, but may also provide neglected resources for our adult understanding which we shall only find available to us if we are willing to take them from the hands of our children. There is much about the service that children immediately recognise. 'Table' is familiar to them. The willingness to drink from the same cup – or more likely a can of coke – used by their friends is more natural to them than to most adults. 'Sharing', often with a generosity to shame adults, will long since have been part of their lives. They are not strangers to the idea that a tiny portion of food can be a symbol of a full meal. Imaginative play at nursery or primary school will have allowed picnics and feasts of a miniscule but highly significant amount; and for older children midnight feasts at school or church camps will have taught them that the importance of eating together is measured much more by the experience itself than by the quantity of food involved. Children's experience of eating and drinking can assist our adult appreciation of the table event.

Abbreviated from *Table Talk*

157 *The lovesick father*

Not long ago I heard from a pastor friend who was battling with his fifteen-year-old daughter. He knew she was using birth control, and several nights she had not bothered to come home at all. The parents had tried various forms of punishment, to no avail. The daughter lied to them, deceived them, and found a way to turn the tables on them: 'It's your fault for being so strict.'

My friend told me, 'I remember standing before the plate-glass window in my living room, staring out into the darkness, waiting for her to come home. I felt such rage. I wanted to be like the father of the Prodigal Son, yet I was furious with my daughter for the way she would manipulate us and twist the knife to hurt us. And of course, she was hurting herself more than anyone. I understood then the passages in the prophets expressing God's anger. The people knew how to wound him, and God cried out in pain.

'And yet I must tell you, when my daughter came home that night, or rather the next morning, I wanted nothing in the world so much as to take her in my arms, to love her, to tell her I wanted the best for her. I was a helpless, lovesick father.'

Now, when I think about God, I hold up that image of the lovesick father, which is miles away from the stern monarch I used to envision. I think of my friend standing in front of the plate-glass window gazing achingly into the darkness. I think of Jesus' depiction of the Waiting Father, heartsick, abused, yet wanting above all else to forgive and begin anew, to announce with joy, 'This my son was dead, and is alive again; he was lost, and is found.'

Mozart's *Requiem* contains a wonderful line that has become my prayer, one I pray with increasing confidence: 'Remember, merciful Jesu, That I am the cause of your journey.' I think he remembers.

Philip Yancey
From *What's So Amazing About Grace?*

158 *Infant baptism*

We baptise children because they are already God's. They are not outside his kingdom until it occurs to them to enter it or until it occurs to us to push them into it. Christ redeemed us on the first Good Friday without any thought or action on our part. It is right therefore that, as he acted in the first instance, without waiting for any sign of faith from us, so baptism, the sign of the benefits of his kingdom, should come to us without waiting for any sign of faith or desire on our part.

Bernard Lord Manning
Source unknown

159   *Step-parents*

It's so difficult for the step-parent to strike a balance between caring too much and caring too little.

The horror step-parents – the ones who end up in court, or in newspapers, or in jail – don't think about it. They don't care. The child of their partner is a pain, a chore, and a living reminder of a dead relationship. But what about the rest of us? the ones who are desperate to do the right thing?

There's nothing special about us. We are not better human beings because we have taken on the parenting of a kid who is not our biological child. You get into these things without thinking about them, or if you think about it at all, you imagine that it will work itself out somehow. Love and the blended family will find a way. That's what you think.

But the blended family has all the problems of the old family, and the problems that are all its own. You can't give your stepchild nothing but kindness and approval, because no parents can ever do that. And yet you do not have the right to reproach a stepchild the way a real parent does....

Step-parents – the ones who are trying their best – want to be liked. Parents – real parents – don't need to be liked.

Because they know they are loved.

It is a love that is given unconditionally and without reservation. A parent has to do very bad things to squander the love of their child. A step-parent just doesn't get that kind of love.

And, increasingly, I believed that there was nothing you could do to earn it.

Tony Parsons
From *man and wife*

160   *Grandparents*

That's who gets forgotten in a divorce. The grandparents. These old people who worship the little boys and girls who are produced by their own grown-up, messed-up children, the fallible somehow begetting the perfect. Divorce makes grandparents feel as though all that unconditional love they have to give is somehow surplus to requirements.

Tony Parsons
From *man and wife*

The Life and Teaching of Jesus

a Jesus said: 'You have heard that it was said, "You shall love your neighbour and hate your enemy." But I say to you, Love your enemies and pray for those who persecute you, so that you may be children of your Father in heaven.' *Matthew 5:43–45a*

b When the sabbath came, Jesus entered the synagogue and taught. They were astounded at his teaching, for he taught them as one having authority. *Mark 1:21*

c In the morning, while it was still very dark, Jesus got up and went out to a deserted place, and there he prayed. *Mark 1:35*

d Jesus said: 'Very truly, I tell you, we speak of what we know and testify to what we have seen, yet you do not receive our testimony. If I have told you about earthly things and you do not believe, how can you believe if I tell you about heavenly things?' *John 3:11–12*

e Jesus Christ was declared to be Son of God with power according to the spirit of holiness by resurrection from the dead. *Romans 1:4*

f God is faithful; by him you were called into the fellowship of his Son, Jesus Christ our Lord. *1 Corinthians 1:9*

g As you ... have received Christ Jesus the Lord, continue to live your lives in him, rooted and built up in him and established in the faith, just as you were taught, abounding in thanksgiving. *Colossians 2:6–7*

h Long ago God spoke to our ancestors in many and various ways by the prophets, but in these last days he has spoken to us by a Son, whom he appointed heir of all things. *Hebrews 1:1–2*

i We have a great high priest who has passed through the heavens, Jesus, the Son of God. Let us therefore approach the throne of grace with boldness, so that we may receive mercy and find grace to help in time of need. *from Hebrews 4:14–16*

j We declare to you what was from the beginning, what we have heard, what we have seen with our eyes, what we have looked at and touched with our hands, concerning the word of life – this life was revealed, and we have seen it and testify to it. *1 John 1:1–2*

k The Father has sent his Son as the Saviour of the world. God abides in those who confess that Jesus is the Son of God, and they abide in God. *from 1 John 4:14–15*

l We know that the Son of God has come and has given us understanding so that we may know him who is true; and we are in him who is true, in his Son Jesus Christ. He is the true God and eternal life. *1 John 5:20*

m Do not be afraid; I am the first and last, and the living one. I was dead, and see, I am alive for ever and ever; and I have the keys of Death and of Hades. *from Revelation 1:17–18*

161
Jesus said, 'Follow me',
and we will.
Seek and find him first in this act of worship:
    discover him in each other's faith;
    let silence become his voice;
    discern him in the Scriptures;
then, nurtured and loved, follow him into your every day.

162
There is a Way for us to follow,
a Truth for us to seek,
a Life for us to live.
His name is Jesus the Christ,
and we have met to worship him.

163
God in Christ is searching for us,
    as a shepherd would search for a lost sheep,
    as each of us would search for a missing silver coin,
    as a parent would longingly reach out towards a wayward child.
There is joy in heaven as, being found,
we learn to love and worship him.

164
This is the miracle of God's accepting grace –
that we bring to worship the little we have:
    five small loaves and two fish, or a widow's mite,
    a glimpse of faith or an awakening love,
    a moment of truth or a brief sense of gratitude,
    a slender hope or a thirsting spirit.
And God takes what we bring,
multiplies, enriches, and increases it,
so that it becomes his gift to us.
Thanks be to God.

165
Jesus said, 'My house shall be a house of prayer for all nations.'
As we meet in this city (*town, village*)
so we join our praise with people of every continent,
link prayers that rise from every nation,
join hands with women, men, and children across the world,
and find in faith,
one family, one community of loving trust.

166 We meet in the name of Jesus Christ;
prophet, priest and king,
saviour, lord and counsellor,
no name enough,
no thought too high.
Love alone can hold him close
to meet within our worship.

167 Beyond our reach
    yet closer than our breath.
Higher than highest thought
    yet lodged within our hearts.
In worship, simple and profound,
we meet the Lord of Life.

168 Jesus Christ is a candle of hope in the darkness,
a beckoning on the horizon,
a promise of flowering in the desert,
gentle rain in summer's drought,
and a glimpse of the sun on a dark winter's day.
    He it is, who touches us into life,
    calls us to renewal,
    and promises us his presence.
Come now, to worship and praise.

169 Through the hymns we will sing,
by the words we will read,
within the silence we will share,
Jesus Christ is waiting to speak.

Through the fellowship we share,
by the memories we bring,
within laughter and tears,
Jesus Christ is present.

Through the tradition to which we belong,
by our preparing for our future,
within our arriving and departing,
Jesus Christ stands with us.
Thanks be to God.

170 Jesus, the Christ, you stand above all time:
    past and present are an eternal now,
    all that was and is to be is fulfilled in you;
        you are the eternal Lord.

Jesus, the Christ, you are beyond all space:
    you fill all things, you are all in all,
    you outpass sea and star, outreach the heavens;
        you are the universal Lord.

Jesus, the Christ, you are closer than breath:
    as fresh as the air, as intimate as a smile,
    as life-giving as blood, as tender as love;
        you are Lord who stands with his people.

171 Child of the manger,
we watch you with love for the humility of your birth,
and your vulnerable presence among us.

Son of the carpenter,
we rejoice in the ordinariness of your early life
held in the love of parents and the security of a family.

Teacher of faith,
we treasure your words that both challenge and comfort;
timeless in their truth, powerful in persuasion.

Prophet of courage,
we stand in awe at your daring as you faced those who would destroy you,
and turned angry questions into an opportunity to speak of God's kingdom.

Man of loneliness,
in wondering devotion we see your inner strength as you faced the
    darkness,
and wrestled alone in the desert and in Gethsemane.

Suffering Christ,
our hearts bow down to see you accepting pain and loss, carrying your own
    cross,
and bearing insult and humiliation on Calvary hill.

And if that was the end we would ourselves be lost, bereft and forsaken.
But no,
Risen and glorious Christ,
in joy and gladness, we welcome you in resurrection might,
for death has died; you are the eternal Lord.
In birth and life, in death and resurrection
you rightly claim our loyalty and love, our endless adoration.

172   Saviour Christ, we confess our folly:
 though you are quick to teach,
  we have been slow to learn;
 though you love to share your knowledge of the Father,
  we neglect the simple truth you offer;
 though with persuasive words you open up the way to life,
  we prefer to choose our own road;
 though with love you explain both life and death,
  we take one for granted, and fear the other.
Give us a teachable spirit so that,
hearing your stories,
and relishing your words,
we may understand,
and in our understanding
find new life.

173   Forgiving Lord of life,
we confess to narrow minds and closed ears.

When life has beckoned with disturbing new truth
we have sat back in complacent ease.
When others have been excited by fresh ideas
we have tamed their enthusiasm by our dull response.
We have dismissed advancing science as 'beyond us'
without trying to understand.
We have called new patterns of art 'ridiculous'
without giving them a second thought.
We have closed our ears to new music
without spending time to listen.
We have retreated before questions that probed our faith
without wondering whether your voice is within the question.

But please do not give up on us.
Enlarge our minds and open our ears and eyes,
disturb our complacency and point us to new truths,
so that our understanding may be constrained by nothing,
other than your kingdom's truth.

174   Christ of compassion, grant that even in the midst of our unfaithfulness
and folly we may still hear your forgiving word and, resting in your
love, find new strength to recover our discipleship and find our way
back to you. May our renewed service find greater strength in greater
gratitude, and deepening faith through deeper love.

175 It is the baby we remember;
the baby who was just like any other baby,
and yet was God indeed.

It is the boy we remember;
growing up like any other boy,
asking questions of his teachers,
obedient to his parents, yet rising beyond them,
knowing the joy and pain of human growth,
and ever learning more of himself and of his God.

It is the young man we remember;
sometimes angry, always loving,
sometimes knowing, always searching,
holding the presence of God within his own life,
and giving it as a gift to others.

It is Jesus we remember;
God in man, Word made flesh,
Lord and servant, saviour and victim.
May the memory refresh us,
and bring us closer to you, O God,
with thankful adoration and praise.

176 God and Father,
we praise and thank you for our Lord Jesus Christ.
He is our Law,
yet comes to us with such compassion
that we obey, not by obedience alone,
but by our own free will.
He is Prophet to our lives,
yet speaks his piercing truth in such a way
that binds us to his truth with love.
His transfigured life
brings us to our knees
as though before a searing flame
yet illuminates and guides,
and gives us new resources for our living.
    God and Father,
    may we stand with Christ upon the mountain-top
    of glorious light and hope,
    and then descend to meet him once again
    in life's routine and agony.

177 For your lively words that still strike home,
for your stories that come alive for our own time,
for your insight into our inner thoughts and outward behaviour,
for your homely words about heavenly truth,
we give you thanks,
Jesus, our teacher and Lord.

For your ideas that leap two thousand years,
for your truths that make us stop in our tracks,
for your deep understanding of human nature,
for your instinctive grasp of how we think,
we give you thanks,
Jesus, our teacher and Lord.

178 Thank you, God,
for those who first responded to the call of Christ:
for Peter, rough and ready, up and down – but never losing his first vision,
for Simon the Zealot, easy prey to violence – but finding new purpose in
love,
for Mary Magdalene, Joanna and the women who witnessed the
resurrection,
for Thomas, whose insight lifted the gospel above the sight of human
eyes,
for Paul, startled in his travels and finding a new direction for his life,
for the unnamed ones, who walked with the disciples in loving
community.

Thank you, God,
for those who have heard Christ's voice through the generations:
for the desert fathers who heard his voice in loneliness and chosen
poverty,
for the persecuted who listened in prison cell and exiled lands,
for those who saw their Lord in the faces of the poor,
for those who confronted injustice in the name of Christ and paid a price,
for those with unrecorded names known only by remembered love and
care.

Thank you, God,
for those who, by the call of Christ, have been our servants and supporters:
for those within our families from whom we heard the name of Christ,
for those within our churches who ministered his love,
for those who visited in us in times of need,
for those who shared our joys and celebrations.

Father,
out of such blessings may we hear Christ's voice afresh,
and turn our thankfulness into loving service in his name.

179

Jesus, teacher and friend,
like a pearl of great price or a treasure in a field,
   help us to value your word above all else.
Like a seed growing secretly,
   help us to nurture the truth you have given.
Like those drawn to the feast from highway and byway
   help us to be ready to receive your invitation.
Like a coin mislaid, a lost sheep or a rejecting son,
   help us to return to your loving care.
Like yeast in the dough, a light in the darkness,
   help us share your gospel word.

180

Jesus, Lord,
you are a sign of all we might become.   *based on the seven signs*
In the Father's name, be for us   *of John's Gospel*
   the vintage wine that invigorates our bland lives;
   the life-force in whom we can trust;
   the strength that lifts us from our helplessness;
   the bread on which we feed;
   the guide who leads us across troubled waters;
   the healer who lifts the scales from our blind eyes;
   the resurrection power that calls us from the tomb,
that we may grow to the maturity
which is God's purpose for us.

181

Living Christ of all times and all peoples,
break out of the stereotypes
in which our narrow blindness imprisons you!

When we speak of you only as a personal saviour,
   show us again your care for all peoples,
   and how you are working in the structures of human society.
When we imprison you in the Church,
   remind us that you came because God so loved the world,
   and how you are working in places we fail to see or cannot visit.
When we lock you into the first century,
   tell us again that you have no boundary of time or place,
   and reveal yourself to us where we live and work.
Widen our vision, Lord,
deepen our insight,
and bring us to renewed obedience.

182
Universal Christ, ascended Saviour;
unlimited by time,
all constraints broken,
and with compassion made supreme,
speak your word of love for all to hear,
  guide us to justice in every land,
  grant us power to proclaim your reign,
  bridge the gaps that divide us,
  heal the wounds that hurt our peace,
  and let your kingdom come.

183
Make us wise, O Lord, to reverence that which is worthy,
and having seen the pearl of great price,
to desire it above all things,
and with glad heart to surrender all else,
that we may thereby attain it.
For your name's sake.

Anon
Source unknown

184
Jesus,
if human frailty becomes a burden to us,
if sickness seizes us in mind or flesh,
if the pain of loved ones becomes more than we can bear;
  Jesus, healer,
  be our health.

Jesus,
if life's deep questions overpower us,
if ignorance leads to prejudice or hate,
if human folly spoils the life that you have given;
  Jesus, teacher,
  be our wisdom.

Jesus,
if ever human friendship spoils or withers,
if loneliness becomes the path we tread,
if it should seem that violence is winning;
  Jesus, friend,
  be our companion.

First published in *Seasons & Celebrations* National Christian Education Council

185
Christ of peace,
show us that your compassion can still change people's hearts.
Bring your promised peace to the warring nations,
inspire those who lead,
and influence all our relationships with others.

Christ of wisdom,
give good judgment to those who make world-changing decisions.
Grant understanding to those who shape family life,
enthuse those who teach children and young people,
and lead us all into the knowledge of your purpose.

Christ of hope,
lift your people from the blight of disillusionment.
Give the promised assurance of your presence in human life,
renew our conviction that your loving intention will be fulfilled,
and restore our belief in our God-given purpose.

186
Jesus, Lord,
bring your wholeness to our broken world,
renew the gift of faith to those whose trust has wavered,
raise new signposts for a Church that has lost its way,
revive compassion in those absorbed in themselves,
deepen the gifts of the spirit for those locked into materialism,
   and since we ourselves are touched by all these faults,
   lay these gifts also in our unworthy hands.

187
Jesus of Nazareth,
no one has lived or spoken as did you,
your words were seamless with the life you lived.

You spoke of love – then lived compassion day by day.
You disturbed the superficial – and lived yourself a life of integrity.
You warned of suffering – then accepted thorns, and nails and spear.
You challenged untruth – and lived a transparent life.
You pleaded for community – then drew together a diverse group of
   friends.
You pointed others towards faith – and lived a life of utter trust in
   God.
You said that we should love God – then proved your own love in life
   and death.
You heralded the kingdom – and lived in its here and now.
Christ of God,
what else can we do, except to follow you?
You have the words of eternal life.

188 This is our deepest hope, God of earth and heaven:
that by our faith we may walk the way of Christ,
that by our lives we may proclaim his truth,
that by our worship we may honour his name,
and in our dying, live with him for ever.

189 Way of my life, I will walk in your path.
Truth of my life, I will live by your words.
Life of my life, I will trust in your power.
Way, truth, and life,
     walk with me,
     speak to me,
     live in me.

190 Lord Jesus,
be the word on my tongue,
     and the sight of my eyes;
be the way of my feet,
     and the gift in my hands;
be the outreach of my heart,
     and the love of my life;
be my beginning and my end,
and my all in all.

191 This we affirm in the name of Jesus Christ:
when evil stands proud, the humility of Christ is stronger;
when war rages, the peace of Christ can conquer hatred;
when disillusionment saps our strength, the hope of Christ can renew us;
when our trust in God falters, the love of Christ still holds us;
when all seems lost, Christ will find us.

192 Christ of enduring love,
give us the power to love,
and thus, whether to our gain or loss,
whether recognised or ignored,
to be your people
seeking your will in your world.

Jesus Christ

193   *Here is a man…*

Here is a man who was born in an obscure village, the child of a peasant woman. He worked in a carpenter's shop until he was thirty, and then for three years was an itinerant preacher. He had no credentials but himself. While he was still a young man, the tide of popular opinion turned against him. His friends – the twelve men who had learned so much from him and had promised him their enduring loyalty, ran away and left him. He went through a mockery of trial; he was nailed upon a cross between two thieves and when he was dead he was taken down and laid in a borrowed grave through the pity of a friend.

Yet I am well within the mark when I say that all the armies that ever marched and all the parliaments that ever sat, and all the kings that ever reigned, put together, have not affected life upon this earth as has this one solitary life.

Anon

194   *Images of action*

Jesus is the Way, the Truth, and the Life. Those are startling religious images. Each one speaks of openness, movement, growth, and development. Each one precludes stagnation, or a tight definition. With what honesty the gospel-writers show us Jesus, the Lord they worship, wrestling with his own doubt and questions in desert temptations, struggling with doubting fear in Gethsemane, and even on the cross, feeling himself to be a God-forsaken man, not sure that he's 'got it right'. In all those examples, we see Jesus driven, not by credal certainty, but by an agonised reaching out for ultimates that still evade him. How can we expect to avoid question marks when even our Lord knew their pain and their excitement.

It would take only a very little god to give neat precise answers to life's questions; uniform apples plucked from a low-branched doctrinal tree and ready-packed for easy consumption.

But our God is very big.

From an address to the United Reformed Church General Assembly 1993

195 *Jesus the pilgrim*

We will understand Jesus better if we stop seeing him as the man who has all the answers and learn to see him as a man who offers us the essential clues about life and then tells us to go and live it. It means more work for us but that is the privilege of being human. It involves the risk that our journey to truth may be slow or spasmodic but that is the price of maturity.

Jesus' own uncertainty found focus in his agonised cry, 'My God, my God, why have you forsaken me?' That is the ultimate question. And Jesus died not knowing the answer. There is no convincing vindication of the life he chose. He died, as he had lived, in the confidence of faith rather than absolute certainty.

It is the inevitable conclusion to his life. In his incarnation Jesus totally identified himself with our human nature and experience. It means far more than that he looked like a man, ate, drank and slept like a man. It implies a complete sharing of our human experience in loving self-identification with us. Therefore, he must share our uncertainty and search. He must be a pilgrim with us, living the life of faith. The incarnation is the key to under-standing the atonement of Jesus. As he was born like us, so he must die like us with no concessions and no privileges. Silence is the only answer to his ultimate question because it is our only answer as well.

From *Questions Jesus wouldn't answer*

196 *Child of process*

Thou art the Way
Hadst thou been nothing but the goal
    I cannot say
If thou hadst ever met my soul.

I cannot see –
I, child of process – if there lies
    An end for me
Full of repose, full of replies.

I'll not reproach
The road that winds, my feet that err.
    Access, Approach
Art thou, Time, Way, and Wayfarer.

Alice Meynell (1847–1922)

Life of Jesus

197   *It's hard to be a carpenter*

I wonder what he charged for chairs
At Nazareth.
And did men try to beat him down,
And boast about it in the town –
'I bought it cheap for half a crown
From that mad carpenter.'
And did they promise and not pay,
Put it off to another day,
O did they break his heart that way,
My Lord, the Carpenter?
I wonder did he have bad debts,
And did he know my fears and frets?
The Gospel writer here forgets
To tell about the Carpenter.
But that's just what I want to know.
Ah! Christ in glory, here below,
Men lie and cheat each other so,
It's hard to be a carpenter.

G A Studdert-Kennedy (1883–1929)

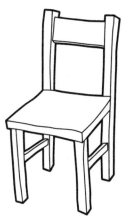

198   *Toll gate to the kingdom*

Suddenly the beggar children whom we had met at the toll gate
emerged. They held out their hands and barred our way.
'What are you doing?' I asked.
'We're playing at toll collectors.'
'What frontier is this?'
'This is the beginning of the kingdom of God.'
I wanted to explode with anger, but I restrained myself. Why shouldn't
I play their game? So I did.
'What must I do to enter into your kingdom?'
The children laughed. The oldest one said:
'Unless you become like children again, you will not enter the kingdom of God.'
'Who rules in your kingdom?'
'We rule in this kingdom. The children. The kingdom is ours.'
'And what duty must I pay?'
'Give us something to eat.'
'Is that all?'
'There is no kingdom you can enter so easily. All you must do is give

continued...

away what you possess. Then you belong to it.'
I didn't know whether it was a game or in real earnest. I said:
'All right. Here is the duty for your kingdom.'
And I gave them a couple of loaves of bread and some fruit. Their faces
shone. They gave way. We were allowed to pass. We had crossed this
frontier as well.

Gerd Theissen
From *The Shadow of the Galilean*

199 Foxes have holes...
No home
   no wife
      no family –
no wonder
he looked with longing
at cosy habitations
of birds
    and foxes.

Itinerant
yet with homely skills,
a dab hand
at campfire meals,
his speciality
was grilled fish
on the beach
at dawn ...
     ... but that
was another matter.

Before that
soldiers slit the robe
his mother wove with love;
a winding sheet of pain
became the stuff
of his rebirth
and maybe then
he dreamed again
    of homing birds
and foxes
   gone
     to earth.

Margaret Connor

200   *Beyond factual reporting*

.... the Gospels are not neutral reporting. They are not written primarily to provide objective information (whatever that would mean) about the historical figure Jesus of Nazareth, but rather to persuade their audiences of the truth of a religious message. Although arguments continue over the precise genre of the Gospels, there is little to suggest that they were ever intended as straightforward factual accounts and even less to suggest that they were written in accordance with the ideals and methods of modern historiography. Scholarly views differ over whether they are to be read as mainly myth and religious propaganda with the occasional historical datum accidentally thrown in, or mainly as historical reminiscence overlain with material expressing post-Easter faith, but all responsible modern interpretations of the Gospels recognize that whatever they may tell us about the historical Jesus, they also construct their meanings in ways that go beyond literal factual reporting.

Eric Eve
From Farmington Paper PR14

201   *Eyes that do not see*

The story of the healing of the blind man of Bethsaida forms a pair, not only with the later story of blind Bartimaeus, but also with the earlier story of the deaf mute. Between these stories Jesus for the second time feeds a crowd from meagre resources and then has a discussion with his disciples in the boat on the way to Bethsaida in which the disciples yet again fail to understand what Jesus is trying to tell them so that Jesus is moved to complain, 'Do you not yet perceive or understand? Are you hearts hardened? Having eyes do you not see, and having ears do you not hear? The position of this incident between the healing of a deaf man and the healing of a blind man is surely no accident; Mark wants us to see that Jesus is struggling to open the ears and eyes of his disciples, a task that ironically proves more difficult than restoring perception to the literally deaf and literally blind.

Mark 7:31–37

Mark 8:1–10
Mark 8:13–21

Eric Eve
From Farmington Paper PR14

202 *Upside down truth*

Christ turned the world's accepted standards upside down. It was the poor, not the rich who were to be blessed; the weak, not the strong, who were to be esteemed; the pure in heart, not the sophisticated and the worldly, who understood what life was about. We should love our enemies, bless them that curse us, do good to them that hate us, and pray for them that despitefully use us, in order that we may be worthy members of a human family whose Father is in heaven.

So Christ spoke. No-one has fully carried out his sublime behests, but it is due to his words that some, at least, have tried.

Malcolm Muggeridge

203 *Locked away*

When Jesus spoke his words of Life to those who gathered round,
His canny tongue cut like a knife tradition's ties that bound.

> *Locked away, locked away in scripture's binding hold,*
> *'I light the way to dawning day', the prisoners were told.*

When Jesus spoke his words of Light to those who ruled in power,
They drove in nails of fear and fright and made earth's darkest hour.

> *Locked away, locked away in death behind a stone:*
> *'The pest is gone, let life go on', said Herod from his throne.*

When Jesus speaks his words of Love within the church concealed,
Tradition needs a mighty shove to see his truth revealed.

> *Locks away! Unlock the way and set the Spirit free:*
> *The Easter light within our plight, the Power in you and me!*

Chris Avis

204 *Passive resistance*

It was the New Testament which really awakened me to the rightness and value of passive resistance, and love towards one's enemies. When I read in the Sermon on the Mount such passages: 'Resist not him that is evil, but whosoever smites thee on thy right cheek, turn to him the other also'; or 'love your enemies, bless them that persecute you, that you may be sons of your Father which is in heaven', I was simply overjoyed.

Mahatma Gandhi
Source unknown

205 *Drawn from the everyday*

When Jesus talked about this wonderful place (the Kingdom of God), he always talked about it in terms drawn from the everyday, the mundane world around him. The language of Jesus, consequently, was concrete and specific. The scenery of his parables and aphorisms consisted entirely of everyday events and topics, of ordinary times, places and persons. He spoke of dinner parties, of travellers being mugged, of truant sons, of corrupt officials, of a cache of coins found in a field, of poor peasants, of precious pearls, of the hungry and tearful, of lawsuits and conscription, of beggars and lending, of birds and flowers, of purity and defilement, of the Sabbath, of wealth, and occasionally of scholars. He also referred to common concerns for food, clothing and shelter, of parents' gifts to children, of a speck in the eye, of true relatives, of sowing and planting, of jars with broken handles, of evil demons, of doctors and the sick, of crushing debt, of vineyard workers, of weeds and gardening, and of wedding celebrations. He talked about camels and needles, about friends and enemies, about priests and Levites, about shrewd managers and persistent widows. His images were drawn from the scene he and his neighbours experienced on ordinary days …

While he spoke unceasingly in mundane terms, his listeners must have perceived that he always had some other subject in mind, to judge by their reported reactions. His basic metaphor … was God's reign or God's estate, but he never (in the parables) spoke about it directly. He regularly compared it to something else, without telling his followers how the two things were alike or related. … His language is highly figurative. It is non-literal or metaphorical.

Robert Funk
From *Honest to Jesus*

206 *Jesus never wrote anything*

Jesus never wrote anything – except on one occasion, in the sand! He spoke, he lived; and that's all. It's important. Look at the Greek philosopher Socrates and his disciple, Plato. Socrates didn't write anything, either, and it was Plato who put the teachings of his master into writing. So we study Plato's works, although Socrates is the person in whom we're interested.

This is even more true in the case of Jesus. At the source of the good news, the gospel, we find the person of Jesus. Had he produced writings, we might have been tempted to regard him only as a master of wisdom. But because he lived, simply, to the full, as he did, we have to go back to his person.

It is this person, with all his mystery, who made an impression on the disciples.

Etienne Charpentier
From *How to Read the New Testament*

207 *Deaf ears*

The Beatitudes contain a message that could save the world. What a pity that Christians have been listening to this message for two thousand years, but they're like stones lying in the water for centuries, never soaking up a single drop.

Mahatma Gandhi

208 *Teaching by parable*

The simplest sights he met,
The sower flinging seed on loam and rock;
The darnel in the wheat; the mustard tree
That has its seed so little, and its boughs
Wide-spreading; and the wandering sheep, the nets
Shot in the wimpled water – drawing forth
Great fish and small – and a hundred such
Seen by us daily, yet never seen aright,
Were pictures for him from the book of Life,
Teaching by parable.

Edwin Arnold
Source unknown

209 *So natural, yet so wise*

He spoke of grass and wind and rain,
And fig trees and fine weather;
And made it his delight to bring
Heaven and earth together.

He spoke of lilies, corn and vines,
The sparrow and the raven;
And words so natural, yet so wise
Were on men's hearts engraven.

T T Lynch
Source unknown

Holy Week

Palm Sunday

a Lift up your heads, O gates!
and be lifted up, O ancient doors!
that the King of glory may come in.
Who is the King of glory?
The Lord, strong and mighty,
the Lord, mighty in battle.
Lift up your heads, O gates!
and be lifted up, O ancient doors!
that the King of glory may come in.
Who is this King of glory?
The Lord of hosts, he is the King of
glory. *Psalm 24:7–10*

b See, a king will reign in righteousness. He will be like a hiding place from
the wind, a covert from the tempest,
like streams of water in a dry place, like
the shade of a great rock in a weary
land. *from Isaiah 32:1–2*

c Rejoice greatly, O daughter Zion!
Shout aloud, O daughter Jerusalem! Lo,
your king comes to you; triumphant
and victorious is he, humble and riding
on a donkey. *from Zechariah 9:9*

d Hosanna to the Son of David!
Blessed is the one who comes in the
name of the Lord! Hosanna in the
highest heaven! *from Matthew 21:9*

e Great and amazing are your deeds,
Lord God the Almighty! Just and true
are your ways, King of the nations!
Lord, who will not fear and glorify
your name? For you alone are holy. All
nations will come and worship before
you. *from Revelation 15:3–4*

Monday to Wednesday

Calls to Worship for these days are taken
from Mark 11 – 14 where the gospel writer
sets out the events of Holy Week day by
day.

Monday

f Then they came to Jerusalem. And
Jesus entered the temple and began to
drive out those who were selling and
those who were buying in the temple,
and he overturned the tables of the
money changers and the seats of those
who sold doves; and he would not
allow anyone to carry anything
through the temple. He was teaching
and saying, 'Is it not written, "My
house shall be called a house of prayer
for all the nations?" But you have made
it a den of robbers.' *Mark 11:15–17*

Tuesday

g Jesus said: 'Whenever you stand
praying, forgive, if you have anything
against anyone; so that your Father in
heaven may also forgive you your
trespasses.' *Mark 11:25*

h 'Have you not read this scripture:
"The stone that the builders rejected
has become the cornerstone; this was
the Lord's doing, and it is amazing in
our eyes?"' *Mark 12:10–11*

i One of the scribes ... asked Jesus,
'Which commandment is the first of
all?' Jesus answered, 'The first is,
"Hear, O Israel: the Lord our God, the
Lord is one; you shall love the Lord
your God with all your heart, and with
all your soul, and with all your mind,
and with all your strength." The
second is this, "You shall love your
neighbour as yourself."'
from Mark 12:28–31

a If anyone says to you at that time, 'Look! Here is the Messiah!' or 'Look! There he is!' – do not believe it. False messiahs and false prophets will appear and produce signs and omens, to lead astray, if possible, the elect. But be alert; I have already told you everything.
Mark 13:21–23

b Jesus said: 'About that day or hour no one knows, neither the angels in heaven, nor the Son, but only the Father. Beware, keep alert; for you do not know when the time will come.' *Mark 13:32–33*

c Jesus said: 'Keep awake – for you do not know when the master of the house will come, in the evening, or at midnight, or at cockcrow, or at dawn, or else he may find you asleep when he comes suddenly. And what I say to you I say to all: Keep awake.' *Mark 13:35–37*

Wednesday

d While Jesus was at Bethany in the house of Simon the leper, as he sat at the table, a woman came with an alabaster jar of very costly ointment of nard, and she broke open the jar and poured the ointment on his head. Some ... said in anger, 'Why was the ointment wasted in this way?' ... But Jesus said, 'She has done what she could; she has anointed my body beforehand for its burial.
from Mark 14:3–9

e Judas Iscariot, who was one of the twelve, went to the chief priests in order to betray Jesus to them. When they heard it, they were greatly pleased, and promised to give him money. So he began to look for an opportunity to betray him. *Mark 14:10–11*

Maundy Thursday

f The fear of the Lord is instruction in wisdom, and humility goes before honour. *Proverbs 15:33*

g 'Truly I tell you, unless you change and become like children, you will never enter the kingdom of heaven. Whoever becomes humble like a child is the greatest in the kingdom of heaven.' *from Matthew 18:3–4*

h Jesus got up from the table, took off his outer robe, and tied a towel around himself. Then he poured water into a basin and began to wash the disciples' feet and to wipe them with the towel that was tied around him. *John 13:4–5*

i After he had washed their feet, had put on his robe, and had returned to the table, he said to them, 'If I, your Lord and Teacher, have washed your feet, you also ought to wash one another's feet. For I have set you an example, that you should
do as I have done to you.'
from John 13:12–15

j Clothe yourselves with humility in your dealings with one another, for 'God opposes the proud, but gives grace to the humble.' *from 1 Peter 5:5*

Good Friday

k My God, my God, why have you forsaken me? Why are you so far from helping me, from the words of my groaning? *Psalm 22:1*

l The stone that the builders rejected has become the chief cornerstone. This is the Lord's doing; it is marvellous in our eyes. *Psalm 118:22–23*

a He was despised and rejected by others; a man of suffering and acquainted with infirmity; and as one from whom others hide their faces he was despised, and we held him of no account.   *Isaiah 53:3*

b All we like sheep have gone astray; we have all turned to our own way, and the Lord has laid on him the iniquity of us all.   *Isaiah 53:6*

c Is it nothing to you, all you who pass by? Look and see if there is any sorrow like my sorrow, which was brought upon me.   *Lamentations 1:12*

d While Jesus was going up to Jerusalem, he took the twelve disciples aside by themselves, and said to them on the way, 'See, we are going up to Jerusalem, and the Son of Man will be handed over to the chief priests and scribes, and they will condemn him to death; then they will hand him over to the Gentiles to be mocked and flogged and crucified; and on the third day he will be raised.'   *Matthew 20:17–19*

e From noon on, darkness came over the whole land until three in the afternoon. And about three o'clock Jesus cried with a loud voice, 'Eli, Eli, lema sabachthani?' that is, 'My God, my God, why have you forsaken me?   *Matthew 27:45–46*

f Jesus said, 'Now my soul is troubled. And what should I say – 'Father, save me from this hour'? No, it is for this reason that I have come to this hour. Father, glorify your name.'   *John 12:27–28*

g Jesus said, 'Now the Son of Man has been glorified, and God has been glorified in him. If God has been glorified in him, God will also glorify him in himself and will glorify him at once.   *John 13:31–32*

h So they took Jesus; and carrying the cross by himself, he went out to what is called The Place of the Skull, which in Hebrew is called Golgotha. There they crucified him, and with him two others, one on either side, with Jesus between them.   *from John 19:16–18*

i Irrespective of the law, the righteousness of God has been disclosed, and is attested by the law and the prophets, the righteousness of God through faith in Jesus Christ for all who believe.   *Romans 3:21–22*

j If God is for us, who is against us? He who did not withhold his own Son, but gave him up for all of us, will he not with him also give us everything else?   *from Romans 8:31–32*

k Taking the form of a slave, being born in human likeness, and being found in human form, he humbled himself and became obedient to the point of death – even death on a cross.   *from Philippians 2:7–8*

l Worthy is the Lamb that was slaughtered to receive power and wealth and wisdom and might and honour and glory and blessing!   *Revelation 5:12*

Palm Sunday

210 Blessed is he who comes in the name of the Lord!
Blessed is the faithful worshipper with joyful hosanna;
blessed are those who lead the people in their praise.

Blessed is the child whose innocence reveals the kingdom;
blessed are those who live by honesty and justice.

Blessed are the homes where God is named and honoured;
blessed are the disciples ready to follow and serve.

God's blessing be on you, and God's blessing be on me,
as we worship the Lord with joyful Hosanna!

211 Hosanna!
Let the palms wave,
let the children sing,
let all disciples follow the king
who goes before us into Jerusalem.
Hosanna!

212 Join with those who cry, 'Hosanna!'
Stretch out the cloaks that mark the royal path.
Follow those whose love leads them to follow him.
Come, let us worship the king who walks in humility.

213 *Jesus said, 'My house shall be called a house of prayer for all nations.'*

This is the invitation today:
bring thoughts of those you know in other lands,
    and those that picture books have let you see,
bring memories of holidays abroad, in lands of sun, or snow and ice,
    and new-found friends you met;
bring the sadness that you feel for lands where hunger rules,
    and joy for those whose life is full and fair.
Welcome them into this house of prayer, every one,
as they would welcome you to where they meet this day,
for Jesus said,
'My house shall be called a house of prayer for all nations.'
This is the week of danger.

214 As Jesus stands above Jerusalem,
the fickle crowds are waiting in the streets below;
politics have chosen religion as a weapon;
Rome's might is holding its breath and soldiers are sharpening their swords;
Pharisees and Sadducees are on the lookout for young upstarts;
the disciples will daily switch between longing hope and fearful apprehension.
This is the week of danger.
Will we journey with him?
Will we watch with him?

Maundy Thursday

215 Come not only to worship, serve, and give,
come first to receive;
draw close to be honoured and valued,
kneel if you will but also be lifted up;
the king is here who wants to serve us,
the lord who washes feet.

216 The teacher and Lord has knelt before us,
the Word is flesh and acts God's love in human life.
In broken bread and poured out wine
we find symbols of true humanity
and signs of God's good purpose.
Come, and find resources for discipleship.

217 Remember the days now long since gone
when, with haste and fear, Israel took unleavened bread
and fled the land in search of freedom.
Remember the times when Jesus, eating with his friends,
made table fellowship a time of spiritual growth.
Remember the five thousand, the Zacchaeus meal, the home at Bethany,
where food and drink became a sign of loving welcome.
Remember the upper room where broken bread and outpoured wine
became a promise that would be fulfilled in death.
Remember, and giving thanks, prepare to receive.

The following two calls to worship can be used separately or together

218
Let's have a meal!
The table is prepared, the seats arranged,
hymns are chosen and the Bible opened.
Our tradition is well known
from the stories in the Scriptures.
Industry and commerce have played their part
to bring us bread and wine.
So, let's have a meal.
Let's have a meal!
The promise is secure;
the Lord is with his people
and invites us to eat and drink with him.
So, let's have a meal.

219
Do not come to this time of worship alone.
Bring, in your imagination and your love,
    the weary who plead for consolation,
    the hungry who cry daily for enough to eat,
    the thirsty who long to find their lives refreshed.
Then come, and only with them,
find your life renewed.

Good Friday

220
The vulnerable babe who lay within his manger,
now, long-prepared
    by wrestling in the desert,
    by knowing rejection and loss,
    by growing confidence in God's intention,
has found the strength
to lie in weakness on a cross.
Let wise men still adore,
and humble workers find heaven's glory still as close.

221
The man who carried his own cross
will bear the burden of this day alone
but we can walk with him
and learn afresh the influence of his life
and the purpose in his dying.

222 The shouts of 'Hosanna!' have faded away,
palm-waving children have gone back to their games,
the crowds have had their field-day, the soldiers have done their job,
the politicians have slipped back into their old ways,
and even the close disciples have merged into the background.
Now, he is alone,
only we are left to hear the cry:
'Could you not watch with me for one hour?'
We meet to bear the mystery of undeserved suffering,
and to pray to receive the gift of undeserved love.

223 He was born for us!
Holy, holy is the Lord.
He lived for us!
Holy, holy is the Lord.
He will die for us!
Holy, holy is the Lord.
He will rise for us!
Holy, holy is the Lord.

224 We were not there when Jesus died
but by the mystery of love
and the gift of faith,
we stand with him this day
to marvel at the way he lived,
wonder at the spirit of his dying,
and thus, to worship him.

225 On this solemn day
we sense again the mystery and the depth
of God's redeeming love.
We bow our heads in sorrow as Christ dies
and offer thanks for all he was, and is.

226 Out of a fractured world we come, saving Christ.
Re-member us, and make us whole.

Palm Sunday

227 Lord Jesus, as you walked your steadfast way to Jerusalem, facing the risk of humiliation and even death, but always confident that you were in the hands of your Father in heaven, so help us to trace this holy week with growing faith and confidence. As we meet in worship, help us to be faithful companions and so, at the end, to stand with each other before your cross in penitence, and rejoice with each other as we know your risen presence.

228 Hosanna to the King of kings!
He is coming to his city to take his rightful place.
Hosanna to the Lord of lords!
He is coming to his people to claim the obedience due to him.
Hosanna to the only Ruler of the Church!
He is coming to be with us and receive our humble worship.

229 Lord Jesus Christ,
enter this day not only into Jerusalem
but into our hearts.
May the 'hosannas' we sing never turn to 'crucify';
instead, may we walk with you into the city,
and into our homes,
our workplaces and our schools.
The waving palms, once held aloft within Jerusalem
have long since died,
and now we greet you with acts of loving service,
with ready obedience,
and with lives made rich by worship and praise.

230 Blessed is the Christ who comes in the name of the Lord;
blessed this and every day.
　The conqueror Lord still rides a donkey,
　the victor's sword remains a palm leaf,
　and his army is drawn from the ranks of the humble.
　The king is a servant, the servant a king,
　and children always sing his praise.
　　Human pride is shown as vanity,
　　priorities upturned,
　　and the world made new.
Blessed is the Christ who comes in the name of the Lord;
blessed this and every day.

231 Welcome, timely visitor!
The doors are open wide;
the red carpet is ready for your gentle steps.
Praise is on our lips, love is in our hearts,
and our lives wide open to your presence.
You are the one we have been waiting for;
a weary world longs for your smile.

If only we deserved you!
If only we could be sure we will be faithful to you!
If only the palms would remain fresh and green!
If only our 'Hosanna' could dispel for ever the demon 'crucify'!
If only we were not who we are…

But still you come,
and always with forgiving love.
Renew us yet again.
Help us to walk with you wherever this week will take us;
    through joy and sadness,
    through acceptance and rejection,
    through life and death.

232 Christ of the humble road,
you chose to enter the city with strength born of gentleness;
a conqueror who knew he would be a victim;
rich in majesty but destined to die with thieves;
surrounded by a cheering crowd but ready for a cross.

And thus have you inspired your people through the ages:
    to wear the cloak of true humility,
    to walk the extra miles of service,
    to care and serve, not looking for reward,
    to use themselves in poured out love.

Your love is still strong to bless;
still you walk with humble tread,
still are you ready to lose for our gain,
and still you come to bless us with your presence.
Grant us holy grace,
that by the power of the Holy Spirit
we may walk the selfsame road with you.

233

Lord Jesus Christ,
...over the broken glass of our world,
the rumours meant to hurt,
the prejudice meant to wound,
the weapons meant to kill,
ride on...
trampling our attempts at disaster into the dust.

> **Ride on,**
> **ride on in majesty.**

...over the distance
which separates us from you,
and it is such a distance,
measurable in half-truths,
in unkept promises,
in second-best obedience,
ride on...
until you touch and heal us,
who feel for no one but ourselves.

> **Ride on,**
> **ride on in majesty.**

...through the back streets
and the sin bins
and the sniggered-at corners of the city
where human life festers
and love runs cold,
ride on
bringing hope and dignity
where most send scorn and silence.

> **Ride on,**
> **ride on in majesty.**

For you, O Christ, do care
and must show us how.
On our own,
our ambitions rival your summons
and thus threaten good faith
and neglect God's people.
In your company and at your side,
we might yet help to bandage and heal
the wounds of the world.

> **Ride on,**
> **ride on in majesty,**
> **and take us with you.**

John L Bell

234 *As he came near and saw the city, he wept over it.*

Jesus Christ, creator of peace and spring of hope,
this day we share your anguish for the cities of the world
– still we have not loved the things that make for peace.

We weep for the divided cities:
where brother fights with brother,
where anger feeds on hatred,
where prejudice blinds the eyes of compassion
and even religion divides,
where children are early taught to hate
and old men relish ancient wrongs.

We weep for the cities of oppression:
where iron law imprisons freedom,
where thought is curbed and conscience stifled,
where the questing spirit is called a traitor,
where art and civilising truth grow barren
and each must think as does his neighbour.

We weep for the cities of poverty:
where children live but die too soon,
where eager hands can find no work,
where hunger rules and aid is short,
where mothers clutch uncomprehending young
and where the little we could do, we fail to do.

We weep for our cities, and for ourselves;
we have not learned the things that make for peace.

Silence

Lord,
turn tears to love,
and love to work.
Turn work to justice,
and all that makes for peace.

235 Christ of all peoples and races,
we share your tears.
Nations are divided,
families have lost their peace,
and the Church speaks with a divided voice.

Christ of the neglected ones,
we share your tears.
Hunger is rampant,
the starving are weak,
and the Church's aid is thinly spread.

Christ of the Nazareth home,
we share your tears.
Mothers weep and fathers grieve
while children live a blighted life,
and the compassion of the Church falls short.

Christ of justice,
we share your tears.
Trade is unfair,
debts increase
and the voice of the Church is louder than its action.

Do not staunch our tears,
do not ease our pain
till justice reigns, compassion abounds
and your Church holds kingdom values.

236 Lord of truth,
you turned the tables on them;
    not in a flash of uncontrolled anger
    but to make room for the forgotten ones who wanted to pray.
You set free the sacrificial doves
    not in a pique of temper
    but to give wings to worship in a world-wide faith.
You raised your voice in the holy place
    not for dramatic effect
    but so that all might hear the whisper of God.
Lord of truth and life,
if we in our complacency should need your disturbing word,
then come to the temple of our heart and mind
and trouble us.

Maundy Thursday & the Lord's Supper

237   The sleep of Peter falls on our unwilling eyes;
we wake but sleep again; the flesh is weak.
> The hungry suffer, and we sleep,
> the lonely cry in their despair, yet still we sleep,
> the homeless grieve, the work-less are discounted, and we sleep on.
> cities are ravaged, communities destroyed,
> young children die before they live
> and still we sleep.

'Could you not stay awake with me one hour?'

The Judas kiss is offered from our lips;
mere token love, not settled in our hearts.
> Our words adore you but our lives deny,
> our worship has no growing root in truth,
> the gesture of affection lives only to impress.

'Would you betray me with a kiss?'

Good Lord, if sleep must come to us,
let it give rest that leads to work.
If here we give a token of our love
let it become true – to heart, and mind, and power.

238   Lord Jesus,
at your hour of greatest need your friends left you, lonely.
We confess: **we would probably have done the same**.
Lord Jesus,
whilst you struggled in the anguish of prayer your friends slept.
We confess: **we would probably have done the same**.
Lord Jesus,
When soldiers took you by force your friends denied they ever knew
   you.
We confess: **we would probably have done the same**.
Lord Jesus,
whilst the crowds chose between you and Barabbas your friends were
   silent.
We confess: **we would probably have done the same**.

If such a time should come again,
for us or for your Church,
we do not know what we would do.
**But through your mercy and your constant love,
we pray for strength to remain faithful.**

239 We give this money; it reminds us of what we daily spend,
but also of people who daily struggle to earn enough.
We give it so that our church can go on serving God and others.

We bring this bread; it reminds us of the food we daily receive,
but also of people who live in constant hunger.
We bring it in the name of Jesus who is the bread of life.

We offer this wine; it reminds us that our thirst is daily quenched,
but also of those whose wells run dry.
We offer it in the name of Jesus, who is the true vine.

240 We take this bread;
It represents human work and effort.
It is the staff of life that sustains our daily living.
It is a sign alike of human richness and human poverty.
It is a symbol of the body of Christ that was broken to make us whole.

We take this wine;
It represents the work of the farm, the vineyard, and the factory.
It is the vine, the grape and the fruit of the harvest.
It is a sign alike of human fellowship and human folly.
It is a symbol of the blood of Christ poured out in love for us.

241 *People will come from east and west, from north and south,*
and will eat in the kingdom of God.

Father, in the name of Jesus,
we pray that this table may be a place of unity
where each accepts all others,
where none are turned away,
where bread and wine are taken in community,
and justice and peace combine.

We pray that what here we see, and hear, and know
may become resources for our daily life,
signs of a kingdom,
and promise of the future you are preparing for us.
So let it be.

Good Friday

242

Lose not your crown of thorns, Christ our King,
hold fast the mocking robe of purple,
for these are symbols of true kingship.
> Humility has won this day –
>> met evil with goodness and given life new hope.
> Defeat is now victory –
>> and nakedness bears the richest robe.
> Weakness has become strength –
>> and the world is conquered by gentleness.

Christ, for God's sake,
and for ours,
do not forfeit the piercing thorn;
embrace the insult of the purple rags,
for we behold our king!

243

The sufferings of the world are yours, eternal Christ,
> you bear the sin and shame of humankind
> as though they were your own.

The agony of rejection too is yours, suffering Lord,
> you faced rebuff and loss in earthly flesh,
> your friends slept in your hour of need,
> and on the cross it was as though your God had died.

Come now, that we who walk this holy day
may sense the purpose of your pain,
find hope in every sorrowing memory of your loss,
and in your frail mortality,
find life.

244

Lord Jesus Christ, brought through temptation to obedience,
and through suffering to perfection,
lift our eyes to the cross which is both death and life
that we, sensing by our love the hurt you bore,
may also know, by the love you show,
the richness you have won for us.

245   Cross-carrying Jesus,
as you stagger on your lonely journey
time slips
worlds reel.

Forgive us that we turn away
embarrassed
uncaring
despairing.

Help us to stay with you
through the dark night
to watch and wait
to know the depths of your anguish
and to realise that you carry us,
forgive (even) us,
love us.

Forgive us
that we get on with our work unthinking
that we gamble unknowing with precious things.

Cross-carrying Jesus,
nailed to the tree of life,
forgive us
and grant us your salvation.

Kate McIlhagga
From *First Light*

246   Stigmatised God,
in Christ you tasted the bitterness of rejection
and bore the fear and prejudice of others.
Give strength to those who carry
that same weight today,
living hope to those in despair,
and the fullness of your love to the exhausted.
And give your people grace
that we may see in others the marks of your Son,
Jesus Christ our Lord.

Richard Watson
Source unknown

247
Suffering Lord, you know it all:
    the pain that grips the body in untimely death,
    the agony of bloody wounds,
    the tortured limbs,
    and that deep sense of frail humanity.

Forsaken Lord, you know it all:
    rejection at the hands of scornful men,
    the fleeing footsteps of those once close,
    the callous glance of soldiers' eyes,
    neglect within the hour of need,
    and a devastating loss of God.

Lord in loneliness, you know it all:
    the scapegoat's banishment,
    the visionary's isolation,
    the curt dismissal of an alien world,
    and the slow erosion of long-held vital dreams.

Suffering, forsaken Lord in loneliness,
bear well the hurt, the pain, the loss.
The world must have just one
who stands obedient to the end.
Thanks be to God.

248
Father, on this strange and awesome day,
when evil rears its ugly head,
when light is dark,
the sun hides its face,
and we must walk by faith
because we have no sight,
we speak our sadness.
    The Light of the world has been put out.
    Joy has become sorrow.
    Goodness has fallen by the wayside.
    Life has died,
and we are left to mourn until the end of time.

What should we do?
If patience is what we need, and hope;
if faith is now required, and trust;
then, Father, hasten these precious gifts to us,
that we may learn to live –
even in the darkness and in loss.

Palm Sunday

249 *Great Day*

It was a great day, Lord,
that day you rode into Jerusalem.
I never saw my cloak again, of course,
and if I had,
with that lot trampling on it,
it wouldn't have been much good.
But it seemed worth it, then.

What went wrong?
We wanted to protect you, Son of David.
We would have fought and died for you
and for your Kingdom,
but then you went off on your own
and let them take you.
Some leader! Some Messiah!
You cheated us,
and who likes being cheated?
You're no use now.
Let's have Barabbas,
he won't give in so easy.

Now, afterwards, I wonder.
Why did you let us do it?
You must have known,
for we have tried to make the kingdom in this world
so many times,
and every time we fail.

I understand, a little: was this the day you became one with us,
with all our hopes and fears,
as is necessary for a scapegoat.
We laid our shouts of praise upon your back
like the lash of a Roman whip
or the weight of a Roman cross.

But now a new word is being spoken,
the word of resurrection;
one I never heard before.
What has been happening, Lord?

W S Beattie

250

The Donkey

When fishes flew and forests walked
    And figs grew upon thorn,
Some moment when the moon was blood
    Then surely I was born.

With monstrous head and sickening cry
    And ears like errant wings,
The devil's walking parody
    On all four-footed things.

The tattered outlaw of the earth,
    Of ancient crooked will;
Starve, scourge, deride me: I am dumb,
    I keep my secret still.

Fools! For I also had my hour;
    One far fierce hour and sweet:
There was a shout about my ears,
    And palms about my feet.

G K Chesterton (1874–1936)

251

Alone

No one could have prepared him for this week;
for the swinging changes of a fickle crowd,
the growing enmity of leaders holding on to power,
the easy-worded hopes of closest friends,
the quick advancing threat of brutal death.
No one could have prepared him.
When did the awful possibility dawn:
    the fearful insights of Isaiah –
        'a man of suffering and acquainted with grief',
    the torment that had long disturbed his mother's dreams –
        'a sword shall pierce your heart'?
When did the politics of James and John
    seem not a foolish error but become a threat –
        'can we sit at your right hand in glory?'
When did he know beyond all doubt
that he was in this
alone?
And no one could save him.

252 *Thy road is ready*

Lord, come away!
Why dost thou stay?
Thy road is ready; and thy paths, made straight
With longing expectations wait
The consecration of thy beauteous feet.
Ride on triumphantly; behold we lay
Our lusts and proud will in thy way!

Hosanna! Welcome to our hearts! Lord, here
Thou hast a temple too; and full as dear
As that of Sion, and as full of sin:
Nothing but thieves and robbers dwell therein:
Enter, and chase them forth, and cleanse the floor:
Crucify them, that they may never more
Profane that holy place
Where thou hast chose to set thy face!
And then if our stiff tongues shall be
Mute in the praises of thy deity,
The stones out of the temple wall
Shall cry aloud and call
Hosanna! And thy glorious footsteps greet!

Jeremy Taylor (1613–1667)

253 *Perplexed*

I didn't understand it,
but when you're nine
and your dad joins the crowd
and shouts 'Hosanna!'
you go along and think it fine.

Even Miriam at seven
tugged mother's skirt,
picked up a palm leaf
and waved it;
bright eyes alert.

'Remember this day', Dad said,
'It's big! It's new! It's deep!
It will change our lives!'
But Friday night,
I saw him weep.

254 *Not the end...*

To the city
On a donkey
Jesus came one sunny day:
People shouting,
No one doubting
Jesus Christ had come to stay.
But the cheering
Turned to jeering
And the gladness
Turned to sadness
When they took our Lord away.

In the temple
An example
Of the evil men he made:
Made them angry,
Filled with envy,
And their hatred on him stayed.
So they took him,
Friends forsook him,
Then they tried him,
Crucified him,
In a tomb his body laid.

But our story
Ends in glory,
For his death was not the end:
New life springing,
New hope bringing,
Now he's everybody's friend.
Every Sunday
Christ is risen,
Every new day
Life is given,
On his love we can depend.

Michael Taylor
From *Sing New Songs*

Maundy Thursday
and the Lord's Supper

255 *And sup in glory*

St. Peter once: 'Lord dost thou wash my feet?' –
　　Much more I say: Lord dost thou stand and knock
　　At my closed heart more rugged than a rock,
Bolted and barred, for thy soft touch unmeet,
Nor garnished nor in any wise made sweet?
　　　　Owls roost within and dancing satyrs mock.
　　　　Lord, I have heard the crowing of the cock
And have not wept: ah, Lord, thou knowest it.
Yet still I hear thee knocking, still I hear:
　　'Open to me, look on me eye to eye,
That I may wring thy heart and make it whole;
And teach thee love because I hold thee dear
　　　　And sup with thee in gladness soul with soul,
　　　　And sup with thee in glory by and by.'

Christina Rossetti (1830–94)

256 *Well-practised*

Could he have washed the disciples' feet
unless he had first
talked with a five-times adulterous woman,
welcomed lepers,
identified children as kingdom people,
seen the real issue around the woman who bled,
told a story about a good Samaritan,
praised an enemy soldier,
ignored Sabbath restrictions,
and so learned
to break the rules?

257   *The servant*

In the servant is comprehended the second person of the Trinity,
and in the servant is comprehended Adam,
that is to say all men.
And therefore when I say 'the Son'
that means the divinity which is equal to the Father,
and when I say 'the servant'
that means Christ's humanity
which is the true Adam.
The lord is God the Father,
the servant is the Son Jesus Christ,
the Holy Spirit is the equal love
which is in them both.

Julian of Norwich (c.1342–1420)

258   *I did sit and eat*

Love bade me welcome; yet my soul drew back,
     Guilty of dust and sin.
But quick-eyed Love, observing me grow slack
     From my first entry in,
Drew nearer to me, sweetly questioning,
     If I lacked any thing.

'A guest', I answered, 'worthy to be here'.
     Love said, 'You shall be he.'
'I the unkind, ungrateful? Ah, my dear,
     I cannot look on thee.'
Love took my hand, and smiling did reply,
     'Who made the eyes, but I?'

'Truth Lord, but I have marred them; let my shame
     Go where it doth deserve.'
'And know you not', says Love, 'who bore the blame?'
     'My dear, then I will serve.'
'You must sit down', says Love, 'and taste my meat.'
     So I did sit and eat.

George Herbert (1593–1633)

259

You wash our feet

We confess it, Lord;
King of the castle we would love to be:
with servants at our beck and call;
our word the law,
our wishes granted,
every whim and fancy met.

We confess it, Lord;
First in the contest, we would love to be:
chosen before others,
winning the game,
applauded, cheered, acclaimed.

We confess it, Lord;
Front of the queue, we would love to be:
first pick of the food,
vintage of the wine,
best seats at the table.

> And then you come.
> You kneel before our pride;
> you wash our feet,
> you offer bread and wine,
> equally to all,
> and call us friends,
> with no distinction made.

The castle walls are breached by love;
the team renewed in glad co-operation;
the table's round, the seats are free,
and welcomed by forgiving love,
we eat and drink
with grateful hearts.

From *Table Talk*

260 *Forget the complications*

Bread and wine –
who knows what they signify?
echoes of sacrifice
an immolated king
a ritual feast
breaking the ultimate taboo
with holy flesh and blood
all decked and dressed about
with every image that the mind can fashion
or devotion dream.

images of straw
words spun by scholars
dry bread, bitter wine
I do not want to eat this meal

but nor did he
my Brother
nor drink the wine of suffering and death
yet it was necessary.

Give me the bread and wine
forget the complications
the only thing that matters
is the human love.

W S Beattie

261 *Telling the story*

With broken bread and outpoured wine,
by table friendship in the Lord,
by spoken word and imitated act,
the story of Christ's love is here re-told;
the old, old story, ever new.

Let what we here rehearse in words
become the way we live in truth;
stories become life; – a chronicle of faith;
the narrative of self-giving love
become the book of life we write.

262 *The logic of Eucharistic hospitality*

....on Christmas Eve in St. Paul's (Richmond, Virginia, USA.), a well-known leader of Temple Beth Ahabah and his wife came to the midnight Eucharist. That was in itself not unusual – the two congregations had worshipped together on eight different occasions that fall. But when the time for communion came, these two came forward with their hands outstretched to receive the bread and wine that for us Christians symbolized the body and blood of Christ. I reject no-one at the altar rail whose hands are open, and so this Jewish couple did receive the sacrament. I saw this temple leader about a week later on the streets of downtown Richmond. After exchanging the pleasantries of the new year, I said, 'Joe, we were so pleased to have you and your wife at church on Christmas Eve. Thank you for coming.'

He then said, 'I'll bet you were a little surprised when we decided to receive communion.'

'I was', I admitted. 'Tell me what it meant to you.'

'We thought about it a lot before we did it, Jack,' he continued, 'but let me ask you some questions to show you how we came to that decision.'

'Okay,' I responded, eager to hear.

'Was not the communion service of the Christian Church said to have originated in the Last Supper, which was supposed to be a Jewish Passover?' he asked.

'Yes,' I responded, 'that is a major strand of our tradition.'

'Were not all those fellows who attended the Last Supper Jews?' he pressed on.

'Yes, they were,' I affirmed.

'Were any of those disciples at that meal baptized or confirmed?' he continued.

'Not to my knowledge,' I responded, interested in the direction he was going.

'Well, we figured that if unbaptised Jews could receive communion from Jesus at the start of the Christian faith, then we could receive it from you in thanksgiving for the dialogue that had brought us close together again!'

It was, to my mind, irrefutable logic and made me begin to realise that all the barriers we institutional people had placed into the life of the church as a way of keeping pure and exclusive our claims to be the sole agents of God on this earth were now inoperable.

John Shelby Spong
From *Here I Stand*
Reprinted by permission of WaterfrontMedia (see index of copyrights)

263 *Zacchaeus relived*

Across the road from the seminary where I worked in Madurai (India) was
a jail with more than a thousand prisoners. Week by week, students and
staff from the seminary went over in the heat of a Sunday afternoon, sang
hymns, preached, and celebrated the eucharist. About seventy prisoners
attended, the vast majority Hindus. No bar was put on who could or who
could not receive communion. Receiving communion, being accepted, was
a sign of the gospel of forgiveness which had been preached. This activity
was not part of any effort to 'convert' Hindus but nevertheless from it came
a steady trickle of baptisms. What had happened was that Jesus' encounter
with Zacchaeus had been relived: first table fellowship, then repentance
and membership of the new community. This seemed to me a far more
beautiful and gracious practice than setting preconditions on coming to 'the
Lord's table – something the Lord never did.

Timothy Gorringe
From *The Sign of Love*

264 *Table justice*

This table would be bare except Christ died
and turned a barren hill into a festival of love,
but now the bread and wine are placed within our hands
and we, by grace and generous invitation,
are one with him in loving solidarity.

This table would be bare except for those
who ploughed the field and sowed the seed,
used tractor, hoe, and mill, and skill,
to bake and slice, and so prepare this food;
and those who tended vine and grape
to gladden hearts and make a celebration;
and now are one in solidarity of service.

Is there greed within these table gifts?
Have others suffered as they worked?
Was work less honoured than is right?
So is our celebration marred by sin?
If so, then offer not alone these gifts
but also prayers of heart and will,
that honest work may find its right reward,
justice prevail,
and all of life be soon renewed
by God's redemptive power.

From *Table Talk*

265 *Who shall we exclude?*

So who shall we exclude from this our table feast?
Let's keep out men;
their reputation for aggression ill-fits this gentle meal.
But Jesus was a man.
He turned the other cheek,
washed feet and served,
showed the nature of true manhood,
and taught and lived that strength in weakness is combined.
So men must be invited.

Then women; they surely will not mind,
grown used to living in the margins of the church; they need not come.
Keep Mary out? And Martha, too, both full of Bethany welcome?
Exclude Priscilla, so generous in her hospitality?
and Magdala, freely forgiven? and Phoebe, herself a minister?
and more than half, two thirds or more, of every church we know?
No! Women must be invited.

What then of those who stumble to the feast? They never would be
missed:
the lame or blind, or those who walk with sticks,
the elderly who take too long, or soon forget they ever came?
Or foreigners who speak in alien tongues, and wear peculiar clothes.
Or strangers who have not learnt our ways, and fail to sit, or rise, or sing?
But pause before you raise the warning hand.
Would he invite the woman by the well?
Were lepers so readily dismissed,
or the beggar who could not see Jericho but saw the Lord?

Children then; that's where we draw the line; the table's not for them:
too young to understand the truth,
inclined to noise and scuffing feet,
half-people, not yet ready to believe,
with no experience yet worthwhile,
and lacking words to speak the pain they feel when doors are shut.
But down the ages sounds an ageless plea,
and is there anger in the echoing cry?
'Let the children come to me, do not try to stop them
the kingdom of God belongs to such as these.'

So throw the table open wide!
No barriers raised, no fence, no moat!
The table is the Lord's. It is not ours.

From *Table Talk*

Good Friday

266 *They never hurt a hair of him*

When Jesus came to Golgotha they hanged him on a tree,
They drove great nails through hands and feet, and made a Calvary;
They crowned him with a crown of thorns, red were his wounds and deep,
For those were crude and cruel days, and human flesh was cheap.

When Jesus came to Birmingham, they simply passed him by,
They never hurt a hair of him, they only let him die;
For men had grown more tender, and they would not give him pain,
They only just passed down the street, and left him in the rain.

Still Jesus cried, 'Forgive them, for they know not what they do,'
And still it rained the winter rain that drenched him through and through;
The crowds went home and left the streets without a soul to see,
And Jesus crouched against a wall and cried for Calvary.

G A Studdert-Kennedy (1883–1929)

267 *The Lamb*

Little lamb, who made thee?
Dost thou know who made thee?
   Gave thee life, and bid thee feed
   By the stream and o'er the mead;
   Gave thee clothing of delight,
   Softest clothing, woolly, bright;
   Gave thee such a tender voice,
   Making all the vale rejoice?
Little lamb, who made thee?
Dost thou know who made thee?

Little lamb, I'll tell thee,
   Little lamb, I'll tell thee:
   He is callèd by thy name,
   For he calls himself a lamb.
   He is meek and he is mild;
   He became a little child.
   I a child, and thou a lamb,
   We are callèd by his name.
Little lamb, God bless thee!
Little lamb, God bless thee!

William Blake (1757–1827)

268 *Stage Craft*

Upon the darkest stage the world has known
the Lord of life bowed down to death,
the sun eclipsed in shame and,
lights dimmed low,
the day became as darkest night.
Three hours the drama played its course:
    a pantomime of justice,
    a tragedy beyond our understanding,
    a mystery to stretch imagination, love, and hope.

      The stage, no longer one bleak hill
      but reaching from the chosen place,
      now touches every corner of the earth,
      enters every hour of time,
      and tolls the bells of heaven
      with sorrow borne on hope.

And three days more, the changing scene
reveals bright morning joy,
the sunshine glory pierces darkest night,
and ushers in a resurrection life; an age new-born.

Now all the world's his stage;
a star turn in a garden,
a strolling player on Emmaus Road,
touring Jerusalem, Judea, Samaria
and the ends of the earth.

      Released from bonds of time and place,
      his actions and his words are one.
      There is no interval,
      he needs no prompter's cue,
      for he is always with us now,
      his presence real in living fellowship,
      of which the symbols are the bread and wine
      we gladly share.

From *Table Talk*

269 *A question of wood*

He who grew up
with wood around
ran with infant feet on sawdust ground
who in childhood played
with wooden toys made by a caring father
yet with youthful hand
learnt to whittle wood
shaping pieces to his own command.

What dreadful irony
decreed that wood should be
his instrument of death
and could it be
that Joseph once embraced
that traitor tree?

At the very end
did wood become his enemy or friend?
Did splinters stab his arms
when outstretched
for the nailing of his palms?
Or did dear familiarity
carve comfort even then
evoking honest kindly men
ladles or the mother's chair
and a working carpenter?

Peggy Poole

270 *Master carpenter*

O Christ, the master carpenter,
who at the last through wood and nails
purchased our whole salvation;
wield well your tools in the workshop of your world,
so that we, who come rough hewn to your bench,
may here be fashioned to a truer beauty by your hand.

Source unknown

271 *Forgive – it is me*

There in a garden, when God called my name,
I could not face him because of my shame,
trust I had broken, I ate from his tree,
God forgive Adam, – for Adam is me.

There in a garden Christ knelt down in prayer,
I helped them find him and I led them there,
they took him and killed him on Calvary tree,
God forgive Judas, – for Judas is me.

There in a courtyard as Jesus was tried,
I do not know him – three times I replied,
there as the cock crowed was my treachery,
God forgive Peter, – for Peter is me.

There in a garden he rose from his tomb
when we were hiding, he entered the room,
doubt not my living, my wounds you can see,
God forgive Thomas, – for Thomas is me.

Now in my life Lord, in my every day,
I need your guidance to show me the way,
faithless and fearful no more let me be,
be my forgiveness, – and come alive in me.

Colin Ferguson

272 *Die, and live*

Hold fast – you have no choice –
on the cross of the world.
Trust in the God I do not know:
    the real God
    who is beyond our limits,
    our categories and our definitions,
    even as to male or female;
    the One who is
    the Author of my being,
    as of all being.

In each short human life
a cup is dipped
in the well of understanding
for living water.

My heart is with the seeking and the searching.
My joy is with those who make discovery.
My hope is gone far away,
    waiting to be channelled back to me.
My hope is very near, closer than breathing,
    too close to see, too close to touch.

So live, and die.
So die, and live.

W S Beattie

273 *This day*

there's nothing much to see
just a man dying
slowly, painfully
it happens every day
this one's called Jesus
what difference does that make
to us
and all the others
watching
waiting for our turn?
what do we see?

W S Beattie

274 *Sharing the suffering*

I want to know Christ and the power of his resurrection and the sharing of his sufferings by becoming like him in his death. Philippians 3:10

I cannot fully share,
not yet, anyway – the suffering of Christ.
It has no point of contact with my life.

Some can:
    the martyrs did, and spelled it out in clear red lines;
    Bunyan knew no bars on lonely pain;
    Romero fell upon the altar steps;
    Luther King knew death before the bullet struck
    and many more have suffered for their faith.
Gethsemane was witness to their tears,
and Calvary their pain.

But, I cannot share it
 – the suffering of Christ upon his cross;
I have not walked that way.

But maybe, perhaps, could it just be …
    can imagination take me to the hill,
    does love provide me with a bridge to cross,
    does gratitude begin to beat a path to where he died,
    and how?

If so, then
though I cannot share it – the suffering of Christ –
he has reached down to me,
and in my easier life
has called me still to be with him as servant-friend.

275 *Free to love*

What was it Jesus bore upon the cross?
How could he die
for sins unborne
so many years ago?
Is this a reasonable faith?
If my sins killed him,
as you say,
laying the burden of his death upon my back
as in those days
the cross was laid on his,
the weight becomes unbearable.
Surely he came
not to increase our burdens and our guilt
but to set free our love.

W S Beattie

276 *The uninvited guest*

He seems to come in like the leaves –
Blown in at the open window,
And always on a light and airy day.
Never in stormy weather.
And always, I've noticed,
At an inconvenient time –
Right in the middle of the washing.
He looks at me and shows me these holes in his hands.
And, well, I can see them in his feet.
'Not again,' I say.
'Please don't stand there bleeding
All over the kitchen floor.'

Sometimes he comes softly, sadly,
At night – close by the side of my bed –
Sometimes I latch the door –

But he never goes away.

Thelma Laycock

Holy Saturday

277 *An empty day*

A curiously empty day,
As if the world's life
Had gone underground.
The April sun
Warming dry grass
Makes pale spring promises
But nothing comes to pass.

Anger
Relaxes into despair
As we remember our helplessness,
Remember him hanging there.
We have purchased the spices
But they must wait for tomorrow.
We shall keep today
For emptiness and sorrow.

Elizabeth Rooney

278 *Three days*

Little time to mourn,
three days brought Easter morn
    but three days waiting was eternity.

The pain forlornly borne
led on to life reborn
    but three days anguish was eternity.

Though darkness blurred our sight
we glimpsed the coming light
    but three days night time was eternity.

The morning light of Sunday
welcomes the risen Son's Day!
    the dawn of love's eternity.

279   *Day of waiting*

It was their Sabbath
Day of quiet rest,
God's day of all days
That they spent bereft.
It was all ended now.
There was no action they could take,
Not even to anoint the body,
On such a holy day
Given for worship
And remembrance.
A day for the heart to break,
For he had died, but they
Were left alive, and comfortless
All that long Easter Sabbath
In Jerusalem.

W S Beattie

280   *What day is it?*

I remember, I remember …
it seems like yesterday,
when seats were set down all the aisles
and children in their Sunday best
were stacked in rising piles.

I remember, I remember …
it seems like yesterday,
when silence filled the Sunday air,
and only bells and tuneful hymns
disturbed the tranquil atmosphere.

I remember, I remember …
it seems like yesterday,
when teenage crowds flocked to the church
for clubs and courting, fun and God;
when though not everyone believed,
no one thought it odd.

   And now?
   Is this the end?
      Or are we the Saturday people
      waiting for resurrection day?

Easter

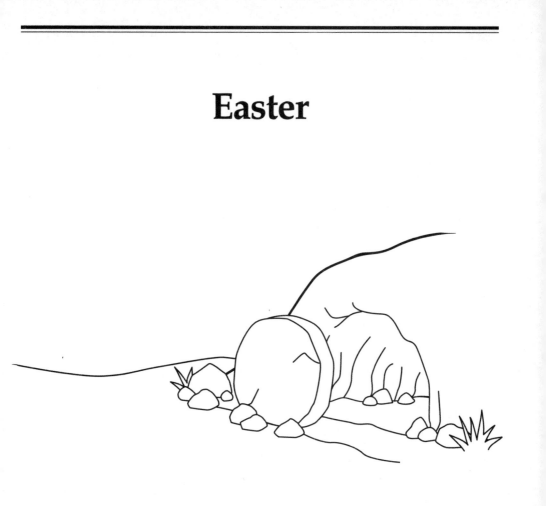

a I know that my Redeemer lives, and that at the last he will stand upon the earth; then in my flesh I shall see God. *from Job 19:25–26*

b The stone that the builders rejected has become the chief cornerstone. This is the Lord's doing; it is marvellous in our eyes. *Psalm 118:22–23*

c It will be said on that day, Lo, this is our God; we have waited for him, so that he might save us. This is the Lord for whom we have waited; let us be glad and rejoice in his salvation. *Isaiah 25:9*

d Break forth together into singing, for the Lord has comforted his people, and all the ends of the earth shall see the salvation of our God. *from Isaiah 52:9–10*

e Do not be afraid; I know that you are looking for Jesus who was crucified. He is not here; for he has been raised, as he said. *from Matthew 28:5–6*

f Jesus said, 'I am the resurrection and the life. Those who believe in me, even though they die, will live, and everyone who lives and believes in me will never die. *from John 11:25–26*

g The disciples rejoiced when they saw the Lord. Jesus said to them again, 'Peace be with you. As the Father has sent me, so I send you.' *from John 20:20–21*

h Listen to Peter's testimony: We are witnesses to all that Jesus did both in Judea and in Jerusalem. They put him to death by hanging him on a tree; but God raised him on the third day and allowed him to appear, not to all the people but to us who were chosen by God as witnesses, and who ate and drank with him after he rose from the dead. *Acts 10:39–41*

i Paul wrote: I handed on to you as of first importance what I in turn had received: that Christ died for our sins in accordance with the scriptures, and that he was buried, and that he was raised on the third day in accordance with the scriptures. *1 Corinthians 15:3–4*

j Christ has been raised from the dead, the first fruits of those who have died. *1 Corinthians 15:20*

k The saying that is written will be fulfilled:
'Death has been swallowed up in victory.'
'Where, O death, is your victory?
Where, O death, is your sting?'
Thanks be to God who gives us the victory through our Lord Jesus Christ. *from 1 Corinthians 15:54–57*

l The saying is sure: If we have died with him, we will also live with him; if we endure, we will also reign with him; if we deny him, he will also deny us; if we are faithless, he remains faithful – for he cannot deny himself. *2 Timothy 2:11–13*

m Blessed be the God and Father of our Lord Jesus Christ! By his great mercy he has given us a new birth into a living hope through the resurrection of Jesus Christ from the dead, and into an inheritance that is imperishable, undefiled, and unfading, kept in heaven for you. *1 Peter 1:3–4*

281 The Easter resurrection is a sign
    that the love of God is stronger than death,
    that Christ's power is never diminished.
The Easter resurrection is a sign
    that our hope in him can take us to the end of life
    and then beyond.
Come, let us praise the risen Lord.

282 Unexpectedly, he came:
to Mary in a garden
    and to Cleopas as he walked home;
to Peter and his friends on the seashore
    and again behind locked doors;
to Thomas in his uncertainty
    and to Paul in his persecuting zeal.
Unexpectedly, he came.
Keep watch in hope and love.

283 Jesus asked Peter:
    Do you love me?
Not once nor twice but yet again,
    Do you love me?
Two thousand years have passed
and the question still hangs in the air
to challenge and delight us in our worship.

284 To see Jesus in resurrection power
no longer needs the sight of human eyes,
it is the inner sight of faith and love
that sees him and adores.
Come, it is the time to meet the risen Lord in worship.

285 There is a power that leaps the years
and springs across the generations.
There is a gift no single place can claim;
it belongs to us, as once it did to those who saw his face.
It is the power and gift of the eternal Christ.
Thanks be to God.

286 Christ be with us, Christ within us,
Christ behind us, Christ before us,
Christ beside us, Christ to win us
Christ to comfort and restore us,
Christ beneath us, Christ above us,
Christ in quiet, Christ in danger,
Christ in hearts of all that love us,
Christ in mouth of friend and stranger.

attributed to **St Patrick**

287 If you believe that Christ has risen from the dead,
you must believe that you yourselves
have likewise risen with him,
and if you believe yourselves dead with Christ,
you must believe that you will also live with him;
and if you believe that Christ is dead to sin
and lives to God,
you too must be dead to sin
and alive to God.

Origen

288 All that separates and injures and destroys
is being overcome
by what unites and heals and creates.
Aware of resurrection in this life
we are ready to receive the hope
of final resurrection after physical death.

H A Williams
adapted from *True Resurrection*

289 The Lord is risen!
He is risen indeed.
Thanks be to God

290
Dying, rising Lord,
if we lost you we would lose our life:
    morning would be as night
    and dawn as early dusk.
Friendship would be empty,
and companionship have no meaning.
Your tomb would be the grave of our faith
and your sepulchre would deny our hope.
But no!   You broke the bonds that bound you.
            You proved that death has lost its power.
            You returned
            and let us live again.

291
We pause before the Easter dawn.
The morning garden holds no hope;
    the gardener is a stranger;
    we wait to hear our spoken name.
With linen wrappings neatly placed,
    the presence is unrecognised;
    we await the revelation.
The doors are locked,
    the mark of nails unseen;
    we await the word of peace.
The seaside fire flames but we are cold,
    the lake will yield no fish and nets are empty;
    we wait for the invitation to breakfast.
        Speak, Lord, speak our name,
        come with peace,
        and invite us to the resurrection feast.

292
With Mary, we have sensed a Presence beyond our explanation
    but have left the garden for a less disturbing place.
With two travellers we have walked the Emmaus road, hope fading
    but have not walked the path of trust.
With Thomas we have pleaded for certainty
    but have not welcomed the inner sight of faith.
We have seen a distant figure on the seashore
    but have not let hope leap beyond reason.
And we remain bereft,
unless you, bright light of Easter morn, sunshine of God's heaven
break into our shadowed lives with radiant resurrection truth.
Come, risen Lord, come.

293
Life eternal, replenish our tired lives.
Light eternal, shine into our darkness.
Eternal Word, speak to our deafness.
Eternal Christ, break into our earthbound lives,
for we believe;
and though dead
we yet shall live.

294
Dead, Lord, they said, dead and buried;
and the new truth of your presence leapt into their lives.
Gone, they said, gone, never to be seen again;
and you were there, present in heart and community.
Finished, they said, finished and forgotten;
and your friends found you in a garden, in a room, on a road.
Lost, they said, lost and gone for ever;
and your Church today proclaims your eternal presence and abiding
    love.

Alive, we say, alive and thriving.
Here, we say, here and everywhere.
Fulfilled, we say, fulfilled and completed.
The heartbeat of the world throbs again:
Christ reborn from the grave
and his friends with him.

295
Come to us, Jesus the Christ;
come as we search the scriptures and see God's hidden purpose,
come as we walk the lonely road and need a companion,
come when life mystifies and perplexes us,
come into our disappointments and unease,
come at table where we share our food and hopes,
and coming, open our eyes to recognise you.

296
God of the ages,
whose hand we trace through the pages of Scripture,
we give thanks for all those who,
glimpsing a purpose beyond themselves
and a life beyond their present experience,
looked for a city with foundations more firm than this passing life
and thus prepared for the day when you would act with power
in the life of your Son, Jesus Christ our Lord.

297
Jesus, Son of Man,
child of Mary and Joseph,
born in Bethlehem,
brought up in Nazareth,
speaking to the crowds in Galilee,
entering Jerusalem on a donkey,
and dying outside a city wall,
you knew but one time and one country.
Your life and birth anchored you in history.

Jesus, Son of the Father,
by God's good purpose
your Easter broke the chains of time,
leapt the walls of place,
and pioneered the journey into the future.
All ages now know you
and eternity sings your glory.

Jesus, eternal Christ;
Word of God,
you fill all time and place,
cornerstone and foundation of the universe,
you were at the beginning,
and live now in the present,
and you will stand at the end.
Your purpose fulfils all things
and your love is at the heart of life itself.
With people of every time and place
we offer adoration and praise.

298
Living Christ,
when malice, spite, and hatred plunged the world into the darkest night,
    yours was the victory of the Easter dawn;
    light of the world and light of our lives.

When politics combined with bigotry to set ignorance upon a throne
    yours was the victory of God;
    truth for the world and truth of our lives.

When death and emptiness had won the day,
    yours was the promise of a life renewed;
    hope of the world and hope of our lives.

When the tomb was sealed and the end was clear,
    yours was the ringing claim that death had died;
    pioneer to the future and pioneer of our lives.

299   The glory is yours, eternal God.
When voices are raised in adoration and praise,
when Easter joy fills every heart,
when your triumph over death is proclaimed,
all glory is yours.

The glory is yours, eternal God.
When the shadow of a cross darkens life,
when, in neglect, the voice of praise is silent,
when people live as though you were no more,
all glory still is yours.

The glory is yours, eternal God.
Now on this day,
now in this church,
now in our hearts;
the glory belongs to you.

300   Risen Christ, yours is the power
that reaches every human heart;
you understand our lives,
and speak to us alike in joy and in distress,
you match your step to ours
and so become companion to our lives, and friend.

Risen Christ, yours is the power
that sweeps through the Church;
you come to bless and judge,
you come in compassion and leadership,
you come to change us,
and make us instruments of your good purpose.

Risen Christ, yours is the power
that stretches to the ends of the earth;
you span the nations,
and go before us in our mission and service.

> Risen Christ, come with power this Easter Day.
> Touch our hearts,
> enliven your Church,
> and turn the kingdoms of this world
> into the Kingdom of our God.

301 *The mystery complete*

The agony which tears the womb
is echoed three decades on
in that grim prelude to the tomb

yet with the tokens of rebirth
implicit when the twisted flesh
lies cradled in the rocky earth.

So birth and death, our joy and pain,
are seen within the wider view
to form a self-renewing chain.

And now this Eastern star has lit
the beacon of our Easter hope
those missing links begin to fit

as kneeling at an infant's feet
we greet the risen one again
to find the mystery complete.

Margaret Connor

302 *Leave to wonder*

A God and yet a man,
A maid and yet a mother:
Wit wonders what wit can
Conceive this or the other.

A God and can he die?
A dead man, can he live?
What wit can well reply?
What reason reason give?

God, Truth itself, doth teach it.
Man's wit sinks too far under
By reason's power to reach it:
Believe and leave to wonder.

Anon (15th century)

303 *The Empty Cross*

The Cross is empty! – not
   because they took his body down;
The tomb is empty too!
(Come let us go and shout it through the town!)

Nothing can bind HIM! – for
   he strides ahead, both then and now;
He tow'rs above us all,
True man, true God, although we know not how.

No crucifix for me! –
   no figure, torn and spent and dead.
The Cross is empty! – still –
He lives and loves and laughs, when all is said.

He lives to weep, and give
   himself again in bread and wine;
To walk the Emmaus road,
And then reveal himself – the Living Vine.

His empty Cross requests –
   With open arms and wide embrace,
We bear, with him, the pain
Of all the modern world, off'ring his love, his grace.

Beryl Chatfield

304 *Testimony is from within the faith*

We may very simply test our understanding of the Resurrection of Christ by putting to ourselves the following question: 'Do we wish that there had been at the time something corresponding to an impartial scientific enquiry, and that there had been better attestation to the Resurrection on the part of disinterested outside observers; or do we realise that such attestation would be quite helpless to prove the thing that Christians really believe, and that only the testimony of those within the faith could here be of any avail?'

John Baillie

305 *Sow me*

Sow me in the desert sands,
sow me on rock and stony ground,
sow me in the thistle and the thorn,
> for only when you sow me can I make the desert bloom,
> turn thorns into a holy crown, and rocks into a tomb.

Sow me in the market places,
sow me in hard and mocking hearts,
sow me in the prison and the pub,
> for only when you sow me can I make my loving real,
> bring peace instead of anger and hope instead of fear.

Sow me in the darkest night,
sow me in death and helpless tears,
sow me in the sickness and the pain,
> for only when you sow me can I bring a healing light,
> release the grieving spirit or give the blinded sight.

Sow me in your work and prayer,
sow me in all the ways you take,
sow me in the people that you meet.
> I need you to sow me whatever is around,
> for anyone can sow me in the good and fertile ground.

Colin Ferguson

306 *Village resurrection*

In 1986 the El Salvadorian armed forces launched a helicopter attack on a small village in the valley of Rio Sumpul in order to intimidate the impoverished peasant inhabitants. Men, women and children huddled together in their huts to escape the hail of bullets raining down on them. Miraculously, no-one was killed. As the terrified villagers gradually emerged, stunned and bruised, their parish priest began to imitate the helicopters, transforming their movements and noise into a strangely comical dance.

Startled children began to copy him and follow him around the village in this instantly improvised ritual. Gradually the terror of the helicopter attack began to fade as people rejoiced in the relief that their lives had been spared, as the priest and children as mock-helicopters wound their way through the village and out into the countryside. An exorcism was in progress.

James MacMillan
From programme notes to his composition *The Exorcism of Rio Sumpul*

307 *He made himself visible*

On several occasions the verb 'he appeared' occurs in the creed contained in 1 Corinthians 15, and we are used to talking about the appearances of the risen Jesus. This word is ambiguous: it might suggest a ghost or, by contrast, some kind of presence that could be photographed.

The form of the Greek verb used here has a rather different connotation; it means 'he made himself visible'. That is, it stresses the fact that Jesus took the initiative in manifesting himself to whom he wished.

The use of this Greek form in the Bible is significant. In the Old Testament it is used for theophanies or appearances of God (e.g. Genesis 12:7; 17:1; Judges 13:21) where there is more stress on the mission that is entrusted than on what might have been 'seen'. This is one way of saying that the invisible made itself felt.

In the New Testament, Matthew, Mark and Luke use the word in the account of the Transfiguration: Moses and Elijah make themselves visible (perhaps inwardly) to the disciples. Luke uses it quite often: an angel makes himself visible to the shepherds (1:11) or to Jesus in the agony in Gethsemane (22:43); tongues of flame appear at Pentecost (Acts 2:3); Jesus appears to Paul on the Damascus road (though his companions see nothing! 9:17) or in a dream (16:9), and so on. An ancient hymn speaks of Jesus making himself visible to the angels (1 Timothy 3:16).

All this suggests that we should be careful: when they used this word the disciples did not claim that Jesus showed himself to them in visible fashion, in a way that could be filmed. They stressed the initiative of Jesus and left open the possibility that these appearances were primarily inward experiences.

Etienne Charpentier
From *How to Read the New Testament*

308 *In that other world*

There, in that other world, what waits for me?
What shall I find after that other birth?
No stormy, tossing, foaming, smiling sea,
　　But a new earth.

No sun to mark the changing of the days,
No slow, soft falling of the alternate night,
No moon, no star, no light upon my ways,
　　Only the Light.

No grey cathedral, wide and wondrous fair,
That I may tread, where all my fathers trod.
Nay, nay, my soul, no house of God is there,
　　But only God.

Mary Coleridge (1861–1907)

309 *Eternal life*

For John (the Gospel writer) eternal life is not some
heavenly reward that one enters when one's real
life on earth is over, but something available here
and now; not merely a perpetual existence after
death, but a quality of existence that transcends
death. For John, death is not so much the gateway   John 11:25–26
to eternal life as an episode within it. Eternal life is
not so much a reward for earthly obedience, as
something constituted by the quality of one's
relationship to God through Jesus Christ. What is   John 17:3
required to gain this life is not so much obedience   Jn 14:15,21;15:10–12
to a set of commands (although this is also   John 6:28–29; 20:31
involved), as belief in Jesus. Together with this
distinctive view of eternal life goes a distinctive
view of judgment. For John, this is not primarily an
external verdict imposed by some divine authority
at some future great assize, it is something
determined here and now by one's response to the
light that Jesus brings. Jesus' mission is purely one John 3:16–18
of salvation; he comes to bring light to the world,
but those who prefer darkness because their deeds
are evil effectively condemn themselves.

Eric Eve
From Farmington Paper PR12

310 *They recognised him*

One thing the attentive reader (of the gospel narratives) will notice at once: the continuous narrative which ran from the account of the entry into Jerusalem to the discovery at the tomb is now broken. We have something more like a number of detached incidents. It is true that Luke and John show some ingenuity in weaving the incidents they relate into a single story, but the result looks artificial, and in any case it is not the *same* story. We have the impression that the occurrences described were not of a kind to enter into a developing narrative. They were sporadic, elusive, evanescent, yet leaving in the minds of those to whom they happened an unshakable conviction that they had indeed, for a short space of time, been in the direct presence of their living Lord.

The incidents are reported in stories of various types, some concise and almost bald, stating the bare minimum of fact, some told at length with deliberate artistry. But the pattern of all is the same: the disciples are "orphaned" (the phrase is John's) of their Master; suddenly he is there – it may be in a room, on the road, in a garden, on a hillside, beside the lake, wherever they happen to be. At first there is amazement, with some doubt or hesitation (sometimes made explicit, always perhaps implied), and then, with overwhelming certainty, they recognize him.

C H Dodd
From *The Founder of Christianity*

311 *That Jesus is!*

When the voice has been silenced.
When the face is no longer seen.
When the body is no more than a heap of ash.
When there is nothing left to shoot,
hang or crucify,
the life, the love, and the truth
are let loose
and all the shootings,
all the hangings
and all the crucifixions in the world
will not stifle them
because Jesus IS!
And this is our faith!

Edmund Banyard
From *Heaven and Charing Cross*

312 *Resurrection is everyday*

Although in one sense the resurrection of Jesus is unique, the idea of resurrection is a normal part of our everyday experience.

Most of us know the meaning of failure. The goal of an examination beckons us, the correction of a moral weakness calls us, and we try for success in these and other human fields but fail. Yet in the midst of our failure there rises the desire to try again; there is an inner compulsion to success after failure. Isn't that a kind of resurrection?

We know what it is like to be at the end of our tether because life is pressing in on us or we have taken on a job we fear is too big for our strength or abilities. We reach the point of giving up. Then, on reflection, we feel the birth of a new hope and discover inner resources of which we were previously unaware. Isn't that a kind of resurrection?

Few of us have avoided the stress of a broken relationship. Friendship has been stretched to near breaking-point and a wall of bitterness is raised between us and another. The grave of broken friendship deepens. But, miracle! A tentative smile searches for a response, reconciling friendship jumps hesitantly across the gap, and slowly and often painfully, friendship blossoms again. Is it quite foolish to talk of friendship rising from its grave to a new life?

A loved one struggles through a long illness and eventually dies. Will the effect on the bereaved partner be bitterness against life – or against God? Will a hard crust of indifference develop? There is a tomb of bereavement where life is numb and cold, and sadly there are those who remain in it for the rest of their lives. But not all; indeed not most. For many, life that has ebbed away begins to return. Inner and unexpected resources emerge that offer the chance of a new beginning. It isn't that 'time has healed', it is not mere stoicism. The truth lies deeper. It is that life cannot be defeated by death; its springs run too deep for death to touch and resurrection is always possible because of the very nature of life which God has granted us.

Do such everyday thoughts belittle the unique resurrection our Lord Jesus Christ? Can we take that once-and-for-all event and set it alongside the triviality of examination failures, petty squabbles, temporary depression – or even bereavement?

But do you belittle the depths of the ocean by paddling in the shallows? Does the overture belittle the opera? Is the total fulfilment of human love belittled by the first adolescent kiss? It may be that only when we have recognised resurrection in the experiences of every day that we can fully understand the wonder of the glorious resurrection of our Lord Jesus Christ.

From *Questions Jesus wouldn't answer?*

313 *'Tis but a sleep*

The wintry winds have ceased to blow,
　And trembling leaves appear;
The fairest flowers succeed the snow,
　And hail the infant year.

So, when the world and all its woes
　Are vanished far away,
Fair scenes and wonderful repose
　Shall bless the newborn day, –

When, from the confines of the grave,
　The body too shall rise;
No more precarious passion's slave,
　Nor error's sacrifice.

'Tis but a sleep – and Sion's king
　Will call the many dead:
'Tis but a sleep – and then we sing,
　O'er dreams of sorrow fled.

Yes! – wintry winds have ceased to blow,
　And trembling leaves appear,
And nature has her types to show
　Throughout the varying year.

George Crabbe (1754–1832)

314 *Resurrection pain*

God, stir the soil,
run the ploughshare deep,
cut the furrows round and round,
overturn the hard, dry ground.
Spare no strength nor toil,
even though I weep.
In the loose, fresh mangled earth
sow new seed,
free of withered vine and weed
bring fair new resurrection flowers to birth.

Anon (altd.)

315

Resurrection life

When the cold earth feels the sunshine;
Probing roots search deep for food,
Welcome Easter, welcome springtime,
Jesus lives and God is good.

When the crocus braves the weather;
Lifts its head to greet the air,
Welcome Easter, welcome springtime,
Jesus lives and God is near.

When a friendship, sadly broken,
Starts again its warmth to find,
Welcome Easter, welcome springtime,
Jesus lives and God is kind.

When a family, spoilt by quarrels,
Cools its temper, hurt removes,
Welcome Easter, welcome springtime,
Jesus lives and God is love.

When the poor, the homeless, hungry,
Reach for help, no longer sad,
Welcome Easter, welcome springtime,
Jesus lives and God is glad.

When the Church sings Easter gladness,
Voices raised, a faith to share,
Welcome Easter, welcome springtime,
Jesus lives and God is there.

From *Sing New Songs*

316   *Daffodils*

Daffodils
crammed in a chipped blue vase
stand on a chair at her side;
tubes, turps and smelly rags
strewn on the floor
obscure her fallen stick.

Her face is wizened –
chin poking
from shoulders hunched
as she grips a brush
in her stiff gnarled hand.

Like her, these flowers
have had their day –
papery petal edges
brown and curling
in the studio's warmth.

But on her easel –
spring new life and growth
have been translated there
instead of age,
infirmity and failing powers …

     …daffodils
all dewy fresh
dance in a golden light
which spreads until it leaps
     right off the canvas.

Margaret Connor

317 *I never saw ...*

I never saw a moor
I never saw a sea;
Yet I know how heather looks
And what a wave must be.

I never spoke with God,
Nor visited in Heaven;
Yet certain am I of the spot
As if the chart were given.

Emily Dickinson (1830–86)

318 *The promise*

When winter is around us, we cannot see the spring;
But still we know,
Despite the snow,
That spring will come one day.

With night-time's darkness round us, we cannot see the sun;
But still we know,
As shadows go,
That dawn will break next day.

When seeds are sown in spring-time, we cannot see the flowers;
But still we know,
Prepared below,

A flower will greet the day.
Though God is all around us, we cannot see his face;
But still we know;
Our love says so!
God lives in every day.

Ascension, Pentecost & Trinity

Ascension

a In my Father's house there are many dwelling-places. If it were not so, would I have told you that I go to prepare a place for you? And if I go and prepare a place for you, I will come again and will take you to myself, so that where I am, there you may be also. *John 14:2–3*

b When he ascended on high he made captivity itself a captive; he gave gifts to his people. *Ephesians 4:8*

c Since, then, we have a great high priest who has passed through the heavens, Jesus, the Son of God, let us approach the throne of grace with boldness so that we may receive mercy and find grace to help in time of need.
from Hebrews 4:14,16

Pentecost

d The spirit of God has made me, and the breath of the Almighty gives me life.
Job 33:4

e Where can I go from your spirit? Or where can I flee from your presence? If I say, 'Surely the darkness shall cover me, and the light around me become night,' even the darkness is not dark to you; the night is as bright as the day, for darkness is as light to you. *from Psalm 139:7,11–12*

f I will pour out my spirit on all flesh; your sons and your daughters shall prophesy, your old men shall dream dreams, and your young men shall see visions. *Joel 2:28*

g If the Spirit of him who raised Jesus from the dead dwells in you, he who raised Christ from the dead will give life to your mortal bodies also through his Spirit that dwells in you *Romans 8:11*

h All who are led by the Spirit of God are children of God. When we cry, 'Abba! Father!' it is that very Spirit bearing witness with our spirit that we are children of God.
from Romans 8:14–16

i May the God of hope fill you with all joy and peace in believing, so that you may abound in hope by the power of the Holy Spirit. *Romans 15:13*

j The fruit of the Spirit is love, joy, peace, patience, kindness, generosity, faithfulness, gentleness and self-control. There is no law against such things. *Galatians 5:22–23*

Trinity

k Jesus said: 'All authority in heaven and on earth has been given to me. Go therefore and make disciples of all nations, baptizing them in the name of the Father and of the Son and of the Holy Spirit, and teaching them to obey everything that I have commanded you.' *Matthew 28:18–20*

l No one has ever seen God. It is God the only Son, who is close to the Father's heart, who has made him known. *John 1:18*

m Jesus said: 'On that day you will know that I am in my Father, and you in me, and I in you. They who have my commandments and keep them are those who love me; and those who love me will be loved by my Father, and I will love them and reveal myself to them.' *John 14:20–21*

n Jesus said: 'I am going to the Father. When the Spirit of truth comes, he will guide you into all the truth.' *from John 16:10,13*

Ascension

319 Jesus the Christ is the same yesterday, today and for ever.
His birth in Bethlehem did not change him,
but we could see him in human likeness;
his death on Calvary did not change him,
but we saw for ourselves his total obedience to the Father;
his rising from death did not change him,
but we saw the power of God in action;
his ascending did not change him,
but revealed the eternal Lord who is all in all.

320 The uplifted Christ stands above all time and place
to reveal the purpose of God.
Let loose within this passing world,
and steadfast in the world beyond,
he declares the eternal rule of God.

321 He was in the beginning with God,
he was born among us, the suffering servant;
he lived and died to rise again;
his ascending is a symbol
that God's good purpose is complete.

322 The mystery of the ascended Lord is a sign to us,
that parting does not mean ending,
that to be broken does not mean to be shattered,
and that loss can be gain.
Thanks be to God.

323 A journey is over,
a task completed,
a purpose accomplished;
humility has shown its strength,
and meekness its power.
Hail to the ascended Lord
who reigns from manger, cross, and tomb.

Pentecost

324 She is the dove that brings a message of peace,
he is the fire that cleanses and renews,
she is the water that refreshes,
he is the wind that swirls the dust of our complacency.
This is the day to celebrate the gift,
and receive the spirit of the living God.

325 Burning before Moses in the flaming bush,
re-forming the dry bones of Ezekiel's vision,
speaking to Jeremiah of the covenant of love,
    the Spirit comes.
Forming the church with pentecostal flame,
arresting Paul on the Damascus road,
challenging the churches through the vision of John,
    the Spirit comes.
In simple prayer and worship this day,
    come, Spirit of God, come.

326 The spirit that brooded over the chaos awaiting creation
still broods over the chaos of our human lives,
waiting to bring order and peace,
and restore pattern and purpose.
May our worship prepare us so to work and live
that we become partners in his re-creation.

327 The Spirit of God waits to give us gifts:
    let joy abound,
    let peace flourish,
    let patience increase,
    let gentleness reign,
    let generosity multiply,
and the Spirit's gifts be renewed in worship.

328 May the light that lightens everyone coming into the world
and which shone brightly in Jesus our Lord
become, as a gift of the Spirit,
a light to us in our worship.

329 The Spirit of God
is water in the arid desert,
warmth in the depth of winter,
laughter in sadness,
and a song on everyone's lips.
Come, Holy Spirit, come!

330 May the Spirit of God
who broke through the Babel of division
to give a Pentecost of unity,
now speak to us in our worship to create community.

331 With the power of a tornado
the Spirit comes with life-changing force.
With the strength of a fierce wind
the Spirit comes, turning signposts to point new directions.
With the softness of a gentle evening breeze
the Spirit comes to comfort and heal.
We cannot choose how he comes, or when;
he is the agent of God's good purpose.

332 The Spirit has taught us:
there is one world, full of riches for everyone;
one race, which is the family of humankind;
one life, exciting and positive;
one morality, which is love;
and one God who unites all things in Christ.

Students of the Indian National Urban Industrial Mission Course

333 May God pardon us three sins:
we have thought God
and God is beyond thought;
we have described God
and God is beyond description;
we have made temples, churches, chapels and called them his house
and God lives everywhere.

Anon

Trinity

334 God, once seen in a manger cradle,
  we approach you in love and awe;
God, once held high upon a cross,
  we approach you with humility and shame;
God, once known to break out from a tomb,
  we approach you with gratitude and wonder;
God, once felt in rushing wind and tongues of flame,
  we approach you longing for renewal;
God, who we believe to be present in every place,
  be present in this place.
  be known at this time,
  and we will worship you.

335 In the dynamic of creation, we have seen God,
  and we bow in worship;
In the life, death, and rising of Jesus, we have seen God,
  and we bend in adoration;
In the inner compulsion towards goodness and truth, we have seen God,
  and we offer our gratitude.
Thanks be to God who reveals himself to us.

336 Unto God be praise and honour;
  to the Father and the Son,
to the mighty Spirit, glory –
  ever Three and ever One:
power and glory in the highest
  while eternal ages run.

Medieval Latin doxology

337 To Father, Son and Spirit blest,
  the God whom we adore,
be glory, as it was, and is,
  and shall be evermore.

Scottish Metrical Psalter, 1650

Ascension

338 Once, Lord Jesus Christ, you lived in one place:
  bound by time,
  limited by earthly frailty,
  subject to human weariness,
  and obedient to the pattern of night and day.
Now you are the eternal Lord:
  living beyond time's weakening,
  strong with the love of heaven,
  filled with divine purpose,
  and new every morning.
We no longer stand, gazing into the sky,
for you are Lord in earth and heaven
and always present with your people.

339 Universal Lord, ascended King;
fill the cosmos with your love,
spread your reign of justice across the world,
bring your peace to our nation,
empower your Church,
visit our needful hearts
  and let your kingdom come.

340 Infant of Bethlehem,
son in the family of Mary and Joseph,
teacher, learner, healer, friend,
  you bore the anguish of human pain,
  the joy of human love,
  and the excitement of human search.
Now you have taken our human experience
into the very heart of God
and pioneered the way for us to follow.
In your name we boldly approach the Father –
now in worship and prayer,
and at the end in the death that yields new life.

341 Lord of the heavens, yet closer than our breathing;
universal Saviour, yet living in our time and place;
exalted king, yet visiting the humble heart,
we your people bless your name,
and rejoice in your presence.

342 Christ ascended,
sometimes it seems as though you were never with us,
or, ascending high, you left us alone; bereft,
struggling with the world you said you loved.
Where are you
    when little children die of hunger,
    when lives are wasted by unemployment,
    when callous terror kills without discrimination,
    when plague or virus sweep the earth,
    when families are fractured,
    or when crime struts along the streets of our cities?

Silence

Empower us to persist in your work,
strengthen us to be your people in your world,
send us the vigour of your spirit to uphold truth and right,
point our politics towards righteousness,
help your Church to live in the integrity of the gospel,
and so live in us, as we seek to live in you,
that your redeeming work is continued
in the world you entrust to our care.

343 You did not leave us, ascended Lord,
    you were released to complete the Father's work.
You did not desert us, exalted king,
    you now stand close to every human heart.
By your good influence and love,
    the broken disciples became a church,
    each meal can be an Emmaus feast,
    each busy street becomes your pathway,
    and each heart your home.
You did not leave us, ascended Lord
you came to us afresh in living power.

344 Glorious in your ascension, risen Christ,
you take your rightful place with the Father.
The highest heaven sings your praise
and your Church echoes the song of glory.
Still, here on earth, we see the paths you trod,
still recall the sound of your voice
and wait with patience till earth and heaven again combine.

345 Now we have found our voice!
Gifted by the Spirit
our tongues are released
and we are free to speak of our faith
to all peoples.
Continue with us, eternal Spirit and show us how to speak
    through education and the growth of learning,
    through science and the pursuit of truth,
    through art, colour, pattern and design,
    through politics and the search for justice.
Help us to proclaim the living word
    through the interpretation of Scripture,
    through the worship of the church,
    through service within the local community,
    and through simple neighbourliness.
In their own tongues, let others hear us tell
of the great things God has done.

346 Holy Spirit,
you are depth, silence, and wholeness.
Into a noisy world
    speak your word of calm;
into troubled fretful hearts
    let your peace descend;
into relations fractured by misunderstanding and hurt
    bring your reconciling love,
and thus may our own faith
find depth, silence and wholeness.

347 Spirit of God, take fire,
    and burn the emblems of our pride and guilt;
take fire again,
    and cleanse our inmost soul;
take fire,
    and kindle afresh the flame of love in our cold hearts;
take fire again,
    and set the Church ablaze with loving zeal.

348
Heavenly dove, once brooding over all creation,
bringing order to chaos, harmony to confusion;
  pattern our disordered lives.
Heavenly dove, once the messenger of peace,
signalling hope in distress, joy in sadness;
  quieten our warring spirits.
Heavenly dove, once witness to the Saviour's call,
sign of ministry and token of the love of God;
  confirm our discipleship.

Trinity

349
Father God, you made everything in the world,
you gave us life, hope, and purpose,
and you caused us to grow in body, mind, and spirit.
We have come today to tell you how wonderful you are in our eyes.

Jesus, Son of God, you were born in a humble place and in a humble way,
you lived a caring life yet challenged evil and hypocrisy.
You died in circumstances too terrible for us to imagine
but, when all seemed lost, you returned to your friends.
We have come today to tell you that we love you.

Holy Spirit, you brought order to chaos, purpose to confusion,
though unseen, you are our companion,
afar off, you are near
challenger and critic, you are comforter and guide.
We have come today to tell you how much we need you.

350
One and only God,
how wonderfully you have declared yourself to your people!
We have seen you in the surging power of earth's formation,
  and in the gentler growth of waving grass and budding flower.
We have heard your word in Bethlehem and Galilee,
  and from the lamb on the cross.
We have known you in the swirl and pain and joy of human history,
  and in the gentle whispered guidance to our hearts.
One and only God, you are our God.

351

Thanks be!
All praise to you, eternal Father!
You are the source of life and truth,
you long for your children's growth,
and your creative power sustains and holds us.

All praise to you, Lord Jesus Christ!
You are the visible evidence of the Father's love,
you long to raise us to our full height,
your teaching is our guide and your presence is our hope.

All praise to you, Holy Spirit of God!
You are the sign of God within us,
you take the things of Christ and show them to us,
and you lead us in the search for truth.

Father, Son, and Spirit:
Origin of creation,
Sign of eternal love,
Goal of all wisdom,
All praise to you.

352

Life-giving Spirit, help us to see for ourselves
how you have touched the world with loving action,
and called us to respond with joy and commitment.
Out of our diversity, create one family of your people,
    to praise your name,
    to grow in grace,
    to serve our neighbours
    and transform the places where we live
so that the day may come
when you are known and loved by all your people.

353

Eternal God,
revealed as Father, Son, and Holy Spirit,
grant that we who ever see with dimmed eyes,
and speak with uncertain tongues,
may find in your gracious revelation
all that will satisfy our inmost needs
and so better understand the wonder of your fullness
and the depth of your presence.

354 May the ancient God who is ever young,
bless, inspire, and warm us.
May the suffering Christ whom death cannot touch,
continue to journey with us.
May the elusive Spirit who is nearer to us than our life-blood,
be our companion and guide.
May the God who is ever and only one,
be known to us in three-fold presence.

355 Almighty God, by whose grace we are accepted,
and by whose favour we are called to service
strengthen us by your Holy Spirit
and make us worthy of our calling
through Jesus Christ our Lord.

356 O God the Holy Ghost, you are light to your people,
evermore enlighten us.
You are the fire of love,
evermore enkindle us.
You are the Lord and Giver of life,
evermore live in us.
As the wind is your symbol – so forward our goings.
As the dove – so launch us heavenwards.
As water – so purify our spirits.
As cloud – so deliver us from temptations.
As dew – so lift us from our lethargy.
As fire – so purge our dross.

Christina Rossetti (1830–1894) adapted

357 Grant to your servants, O God,
to be set on fire by your love,
to be strengthened by your power,
to be illuminated by your Spirit,
to be filled with your grace,
and to go forward by your help;
through Christ our Lord.

Gallican Sacramentary

358 *Exaltation and reign*

We believe not only that Jesus lives but also that he has been exalted to reign. The authority to which the whole universe is subject is Jesus; he is the judge who decides what is right and he is himself the standard by which right is judged. As man he was both crucified and raised from the dead; and in his exalted manhood he reigns. From this comes our confidence and our concern for the true development of all humanity. We believe, too, that he has under his control all things in humanity itself, and in the human environment, which threaten to frustrate the purpose of God. The manner and effectiveness of his control are still veiled from us, as they were veiled when he established his authority upon the Cross. But we see evidence of his reign wherever people are released from the terror of things which threaten God's purpose and from bondage to them. And we look confidently for the full splendour of his reign which is yet to come.

Congregational Church in England & Wales (1967)
From *A Declaration of Faith*

359 *Heavens above!*

If you believe the earth is flat
you'll watch how far you walk
and you'll never ever get on a boat;
it may fall off the edge.

If you believe that heaven lies just above the earth
obscured only by a few clouds,
then your dream that angels can dance between the two on ladders
is plain commonsense;
and if you doubt whether unclean gentiles should join the church,
dreams of a sheet let down from God's dwelling,
coupled with a generous offer of forbidden food,
can jolt you into a new theology.

And if – heavens above! – you want to proclaim
that your Lord embraces all creation,
and being from God will return to God,
and is a cosmic reality as well as a citizen of the earth,
and is exalted and transcendent,
it makes good sense to express the truth as lift-off.

And if your twenty-first century sophistication obscures their ancient message,
then before you scoff,
take a good look at the ignorance that restricts your expression of gospel truth.

Pentecost

360   *A time, a place, an experience*

Once, many years earlier, a strange and beautiful thing happened to her here. She was sitting on that day where she is sitting now, leaning back against the side of the hill with its low plants, its grasses and ferns. She had fallen into a half-hypnotised, half-enchanted state, thinking of the landscape in which she was sitting but not in a willed or forced way, receptive rather than seeking to impose a thought or idea. She was aware of her own breathing, rising and falling, rising and falling; aware of the great slope of the mountain on which she sat. And then all at once she realised that the ground beneath her was alive. It was as though the land against which she was leaning was the flank of a massive animal. And the sky too, the moving, shaggy clouds, the tumbling river, the thorn, the stones themselves, everything, everything interconnected and living and complete. It was a sacred, astounding moment, and it passed as swiftly as the rushing clouds. She has never told anyone and she has certainly never forgotten it. This is why she has come to this place today, why she constantly returns. She feels that she can enter here into the life of things in a way that is not possible otherwise or elsewhere. It has become a place as of which one might say, 'This is where we saw the kingfisher.' 'This is where we found the rare wild orchid.' One comes back not in the hope of finding such things again, but in gratitude for the mystery that was revealed there once.

Deirdre Madden
From *Authenticity*

361   *Seek, and find us*

O Lord, seek us, O Lord, find us
   In thy patient care;
By thy love before, behind us,
   Round us everywhere:
Lest the god of this world blind us,
   Lest he speak us fair,
Lest he forge a chain to bind us,
   Lest he bait a snare.
Turn not from us, call to mind us,
   Find, embrace us, bear;
Be thy love before, behind us,
   Round us, everywhere.

Christina Rossetti (1830–94)

362 *The faith continually renewed*

The Christian way is not something fixed and unchanging. A living way is not a way that never changes, but one which remains true to itself. The mark of a living tradition is not immutability but continuity. Christian growth is thus not a matter of simply taking over the tradition, or of swallowing what it offers us, but rather of *responding* to what is offered. As we grasp it, make it our own, it does something to us. But at the same time we do something to *it*, as we interpret it to meet our own needs, and as we put to it the questions which face us now. We become new people by walking in the Christian way, but the way itself is continually renewed by those who walk in it.

A working party of the Consultative Group on Ministry among Children
From *The Child in the Church*

363 *A wholly human spirit?*

St John says that Jesus promised his disciples that the spirit would lead them into all truth. The truth into which the church is now being led is the radical Christian humanism which is the most obvious consequence of its own teaching about the Holy Spirit. Let us set aside the old supernatural beliefs, which in many ways still tie Christianity to its pre-Whitsuntide past, and take seriously Jesus' words according to St Luke, that the kingdom of God is within us and among us.

The Christian devaluing of the purely human has been so widespread over the years that we are bound to ask, What will be the practical effects of moving from the Holy Spirit in the human to the wholly human spirit? Will it not mean a relapse into selfish and self-centred lives? Certainly not. We can already see ways in which organizations with no formal religious basis are in the forefront of outward-looking and humanitarian causes: Oxfam, Amnesty International, Greenpeace, and many others. The environmental groups in particular give evidence of what can only be called religious and evangelistic zeal for their cause. I am not saying that a Christian humanist would be bound to join or even to support all these groups. I draw attention to them as examples of the commitment and unselfish fervour of which the human spirit is capable. This is not to deny that humans are also guilty of the most horrid atrocities: only that the presence or absence of traditional religious faith make little apparent difference to whether the good or bad face of the human spirit prevails.

Anthony Freeman
From *God In Us*

364 *Healing, lifting, guiding*

The Holy Spirit comes when great musicians
Set down in notes the glorious sounds they hear,
Communicating joy or haunting sadness,
Connecting heart and mind through hand and ear.
Channels are they of some great theme of Heaven,
Giving a message each but dimly feels;
And hearts are strengthened, comforted or chastened.
    The Spirit heals.

The Holy Spirit comes when gifted artists
Put brush to paint, and capture with their skill
A precious moment in time's restless passing,
In softest tints or splashes bright, that thrill.
They work until their vision is presented,
For all to share the riches of their gifts,
And hearts are blessed with peace, release or challenge.
    The Spirit lifts.

The Holy Spirit comes when thoughtful writers
Find words they need for poem, prose or speech
And what they write speaks back to them, conveying
A deeper truth than that they thought to teach.
Behind all words and works of truth and beauty
The First Creator's inspiration hides;
With God's eternal light and love and wisdom –
    The Spirit guides.

Beryl Chatfield

365 *Love's appointed hour*

I come in little things
Saith the Lord:
Not borne on morning wings
Of majesty, but I have set my feet
Amidst the delicate and bladed wheat
That springs triumphant in the furrowed sod.
There so I dwell, in weakness and in power;
Not broken or divided, saith our God!
In your strait garden plot I come to flower:
About your porch my vine
Meek, fruitful, doth entwine;
Waits, at the threshold, Love's appointed hour.

Evelyn Underhill (1875–1941)

366   *The bright wind*

The bright wind is blowing, the bright wind of heaven,
And where it is going to, no-one can say;
But where it is passing our hearts are awaking
To grope from the darkness and reach for the day.

The bright wind is blowing, the bright wind of heaven,
And many old thoughts will be winnowed away;
The husk that is blown on the chaff of our hating,
The seed that is left is the hope for our day.

The bright wind is blowing, the bright wind of heaven,
The love that it kindles will never betray;
The fire that it fans is the warmth of our caring,
So lean on the wind – it will show us the way.

Cecily Taylor

367   *Spirituality; the struggle for life*

Although there exist many definitions of spirituality, it is perhaps more appropriate to ask what spirituality *does* rather than what it is. The spiritual can be linked to all human experiences, but it has a particularly close connection with the imagination, with human creativity and resourcefulness, with relationships – with ourselves, with others, with God. I also see spirituality connected with a sense of celebration and joy, with adoration and surrender, but also with struggle and suffering. One definition which I find particularly helpful is that of Christian Hispanic women in the United States who speak of spirituality as the *struggle for life*. It embraces all of life, and all of life is a struggle – to solve problems, to make sense of life, to engage in an ongoing process of discovery, learning and transformation. In this sense the educational process, both at school and continuing throughout adult life, can be seen as a spiritual activity.

Spirituality certainly expresses a perennial human concern, today often expressed as the search for becoming fully human, and that means recognizing the rights of others, striving for an equality of dignity and respect, whether among different races, sexes or classes. But it also means to seek something greater outside and beyond the narrow confines of oneself, something or someone who transcends the narrow boundaries of our individual experience and makes us feel linked with a much larger web of life, in fact the whole cosmos of which we are all a tiny part.

Ursula King
From Farmington Paper PR11

368 *Agnosticism*

It doesn't come easy.

In spite of it all,
I can't help pushing open
the doors of country churches;
shoving a coin or two
in the box on the wall,
paying twice over
for the leaflet I take.

It doesn't come easy.

Wandering among gravestones
is irresistible;
departure is almost
impossible. I delay
it over and over
to hear once more the song of the blackbird.

It doesn't come easy.

As I race back
into the modern
rationalistic world,
I think of cathedral towns
and country rectories
and gentle rectors' wives
arranging the flowers.

John Tatum

369

Disturbing women

Referring to Genesis 8, the *Concise Oxford Dictionary* defines a dove as 'a messenger of good news or peace', a 'type of gentleness and innocence'. No wonder she has become a symbol of the Holy Spirit. No wonder, either, that in the scriptures the Spirit is so often associated with the female gender. She broods like a mother over her young; she sweeps like a wind across the world; she inspires wisdom, like a woman pondering the word; she groans as in childbirth, longing for the appearance of a new creation. This is a disturbing Spirit, soaring where she wills, apparently uncontrollable. It seems no coincidence that the insights of women are often regarded as unpredictable, disturbing and even disruptive of tradition. Throughout the history of the church attempts have been made to keep women under control. Yet women have been the harbingers of every movement of renewal.

Pauline Webb
From *She Flies Beyond*

370 *A gift of the Spirit*   *based on 1 Corinthians 13:4–8,13*

True love is kind,
Rejects the wrong,
Gentle yet firm,
It's always strong.
Love never boasts
Nor shows conceit;
Swift in its praise,
Slow to defeat.

True love can face
The greatest hurt.
With patient trust
It's never curt
For others' hopes
It takes good aim,
And if it fails
Accepts the blame.

Three things will last;
They cannot cease:
First faith, which lives
In God's good peace;
Then hope which makes
The future bright;
Loves best!
It's power
Makes all things right.

371 *The Hound of Heaven*

I fled him, down the nights and down the days;
    I fled him, down the arches of the years;
I fled him, down the labyrinthine ways
    Of my own mind; and in the midst of tears
I hid from him, and under running laughter.
        Up vistaed hopes I sped;
        And shot, precipitated,
Adown Titanic glooms of chasmed fears,
    From those strong Feet that followed, followed after.
        But with unhurrying chase,
        And unperturbèd pace,
Deliberate speed, majestic instancy,
        They beat – and a Voice beat
        More instant then the Feet –
    'All things betray thee, who betrayest me' …

    Halts by me that footfall:
    Is my gloom, after all,
Shade of his hand, outstretched caressingly?
    'Ah, fondest, blindest, weakest,
    I am he whom thou seekest!
Thou dravest love from thee, who dravest me.'

Francis Thompson

372 *Poured out among the powerless*

Perhaps the theology of Spirit has gone into recession in our time because it is centrally concerned with God's presence, whereas it is just God's presence that has become so doubtful, so deeply questioned by the cultural emptiness and the critical philosophies of our time. God may once have been present, we say, but surely no longer in the world *we* experience. Our problem is that we sophisticated Westerners really cannot believe in such a thing as the Holy Spirit, cannot believe that a Paraclete is at work in the world, or that the world will attain its consummation in God. Perhaps then it is not so surprising that it is among the powerless, oppressed, and marginalized that the Spirit is pouring itself out afresh – upon those for whom authentically liberating power can come only from God, not from humanity. The Spirit is arising for us today from the underside of history.

Peter C Hodgson
from *Winds of the Spirit*

373 *Creative imagination*

Fundamentally, what appears to distinguish us humans from all other species is the ability to conceive of things being different from the way they are. All other animals seem to be programmed to carry on much as they always have.

…creative imagination is commonly seen as the distinctive preserve of genius of the artist, the poet, men and women of special gifts whom we may honour (especially when they are dead) but can hardly presume to treat as our equals. This is a sad mistake. Each one of us is born with a potential for imagination. …the germ of it is there from the start, that capacity for conceiving that the world, and our life in it, need not always be the way it is now.

Edward Robinson
From *The Language of Mystery*

374 *Do not quench the Spirit*

We had a vacancy for a deacon; there was a church member in her early forties, who went out cleaning for people. She was not very articulate, but was asked to be a deacon and came to talk to me about it saying, rather brusquely, 'I can't lead a prayer in the vestry'. So I said, 'OK, but you don't have to do that straight off . We'll talk about it but don't let that put you off being a deacon'. So she stood and was elected and then the time eventually came when she had to do this dreadful thing in the vestry. Going bright red, she said very loudly 'God bless Janet, Amen.' I talked to her afterwards, and told her how this meant so much more to me than the words of anyone who could rabbit away at extempore prayer at the drop of a hat, but in fact said the same thing every Sunday. I told her how her heart had been in what she had said, and that was what mattered, and it had been a good prayer. The next time she produced a complete sentence and wasn't embarrassed.

Janet Webber

Trinity

375   *One God*

Father in heaven,
   grant to your children
mercy and blessing,
   songs never ceasing,
love to unite us,
   grace to redeem us –
Father in heaven,   Jesus, Redeemer,
   Father our God.   may we remember
                            your gracious passion,
                               your resurrection.
                          Worship we bring you,
                               praise shall we sing you –
                          Jesus, Redeemer,   Spirit descending
                             Jesus our Lord.   whose is the blessing
                                             strength for the weary,
                                                help for the needy:
                                           make us your temple,
                                                born a new people –
                                          Spirit descending,
                                                Spirit adored.

D T Niles

376   *Experience first*

They talk about 'Trinity' in creeds
and creeds are normally written in books, usually long ones:
            – paged echoes of ancient arguments in lengthy church councils:
   'of one substance with the Father', said one,
   'co-equal in worship and glory', said another,
   'proceeds from the Father and the Son', said a third.
It's all about how to put Bethlehem, Calvary, and Pentecost into words.

   Words are important, debate imperative,
   and even arguments can be useful – if they're bloodless.
   But words are secondary to experience,
   and the fact is that we have seen, touched, heard and felt,
   that creation is purposeful and supportive,
      that Jesus the Christ walked and talked, and is still present,
      and that there is an enfolding, a releasing, and a power within.

If that's what the creeds mean by 'Trinity',
then thanks be to God.

377 *Trinity Sunday*

Long, long ago, the Church ordained
  To set aside this day
To contemplate the Trinity.
  Surprise! We still obey!

Though speaking now of Trinity
  People may think we mean
A College, or perhaps a House,
  Or even a football team.

But still, it comes quite natural
  To group things into threes –
Fates, graces, gods or anything:
  It gives us mental ease

Or if not ease, at least a tool,
  To grasp some kind of notion
Of what our faith is all about –
  Say, an approximation.

The Sunday after Pentecost
  Needed some way to hold
And reconcile new truths white-hot
  And meld them with the old.

W S Beattie

378 *Join all the glorious names*

Mother, father, author, maker,
king and servant, lord and child,
lover, guide, the world's sustainer;
every aspect reconciled.
  'Father', we have dared to call you,
  giver of our blood and breath;
        'Son of God', the ages claim you,
        victor both in life and death;
              'Holy Spirit', life-renewing,
              flame and dove, and inner wealth;
God amongst us, ever loving.
Let the Church on earth rejoice!

379 *Evidence for praise*

We've searched the heavens, seen the stars,
Viewed hills and valleys, lakes and trees,
Found pleasure in the tiny things:
Flowers, pebbles, ladybirds and bees.
So now, since all the world is good,
We offer praise to Father God.

We've heard how Jesus, born to serve,
Taught, healed and sought God's perfect will.
He kept the promise that he made:
The man who died lives with us still.
So now, with thanks for victory won,
We praise the Name of God the Son.

We feel the urge to search for truth
And know it right to give our best.
The needs of others prompt our gifts,
With friends we act as host and guest.
So we, led in his lively ways,
To God the Spirit offer praise.

380 *Trinity and Mission*

We believe in the Trinity
which transcends the diversity of its expression:
    in the creator God,
     – who made humanity to live in harmony with the whole creation;
    in Jesus Christ, our saviour,
     – who redeemed us from sin and liberates us from all oppression;
    and in the Holy Spirit,
     – who renews all creation and enables our involvement in God's
      mission.

We believe that the Trinity calls the Church
to cross-cultural partnership as the body of Christ;
ours is an expression of unity in living together.
Through friendship and fellowship,
devotion and worship
we discover and experience our oneness
in the spirit of koinonia (partnership).

In all this we believe, for we have experienced it!

Source unknown

381 *Three times revealed*

They saw him in the towering hills,
the flowing streams and ocean depths,
the harvest acres and the garden flower,
vast orchards and the moss-clung rocks;
  and they knelt and worshipped.

They saw him in a new-born child;
manger held and swaddling clothed;
in a young boy learning at his father's side,
a student questing with the rabbi's words
and wrestling with Isaiah's faith,
in teacher, healer, friend, and Lord,
in lamb and kingly servanthood,
in death and resurrection;
  and they knelt and worshipped.

They saw him in the flame-like tongues,
heard him in strong, driving winds,
felt him in their life renewed:
in young men's visions and in old men's dreams,
in speech released and courage found,
and they knelt and worshipped
  the Creator,
  the Lord of life,
  and the Spirit of power:
  One God,
  three-fold revealed.

382 *The encircling God*

Be thou a bright flame before me,
be thou a guiding star above me,
be thou a smooth path below me,
be thou a kindly shepherd behind me,
today, tonight, and for ever.

Columba

Creation

a The Lord said: 'As long as the earth endures, seedtime and harvest, cold and heat, summer and winter, day and night, shall not cease.'   *Genesis 8:22*

b The heavens are telling the glory of God; and the firmament proclaims his handiwork.   *Psalm 19:1*

c The earth is the Lord's and all that is in it, the world, and those who live in it; for he has founded it on the seas, and established it on the rivers.
                              Psalm 24:1–2

d God visits the earth and waters it, he greatly enriches it; the river of God is full of water; he provides the people with grain, for so he has prepared it. He waters its furrows abundantly, settling its ridges, softening it with showers, and blessing its growth. He crowns the year with his bounty.
                   adapted from Psalm 65:9–11a

e O give thanks to the Lord of lords,
for his steadfast love endures for ever;
who alone does great wonders,
for his steadfast love endures for ever;
who by understanding made the
    heavens,
for his steadfast love endures for ever;
who spread out the earth on the waters,
for his steadfast love endures for ever;
who made the great lights,
for his steadfast love endures for ever;
the sun to rule over the day,
for his steadfast love endures for ever;
the moon and stars to rule over the
    night,
for his steadfast love endures for ever.
O give thanks to the God of heaven,
for his steadfast love endures for ever;
                         Psalm 136:3–9,26

f I made the earth, said the Lord, and created humankind upon it, it was my hands that stretched out the heavens, and I commanded all their host.
                             Isaiah 45:12

g I will send down the showers in their season; they shall be showers of blessing. The trees of the field shall yield their fruit, and the earth shall yield its increase. They shall be secure on their soil; and they shall know that I am the Lord.   *from Ezekiel 34:26–27*

h Consider the lilies of the field, how they grow; they neither toil nor spin, yet I tell you, even Solomon in all his glory was not clothed like one of these. But if God so clothes the grass of the field, which is alive today and tomorrow is thrown into the oven, will he not much more clothe you – you of little faith?   *Matthew 6:28–30*

i The God who made the world and everything in it, he who is Lord of heaven and earth, does not live in shrines made by human hands, nor is he served by human hands, as though he needed anything, since he himself gives to all mortals life and breath and all things.   *Acts 17:24–25*

j Creation waits with eager longing for the revealing of the children of God; for the creation was subjected to futility, not of its own will but by the will of the one who subjected it, in hope that the creation itself will be set free from its bondage to decay and will obtain the freedom of the glory of the children of God.   *Romans 8:19–21*

383 The heavens are telling the glory of God
and we speak of the wonder of God's creation.
The earth stands in awe of its architect
and we marvel at the one who called us into being.
The seas swell with pride at the majesty of their creator
and we bow in awe before the origin of all things.
Let prayer and praise, song and silence,
unite this day in adoration.

384 In the silent witness of creation,
we meet our God.
In the beauty of his handiwork,
we are touched by God's presence.
Let it also be
that by the humility of worship
and the sacrifice of service,
we new-create our discipleship
into a work of beauty.

385 As the ground untilled, uncared-for, neglected,
yields neither harvest nor the promise of growth,
so the life in which prayer is ignored
and worship abandoned
grows barren and unyielding.
Come! Let us plough deep furrows of adoration
and sow the seeds of praise.

386 To the bird on the wing and the fish in the sea
God gives life and breath and all things.
To the cow in the field and the worm in the soil
God gives life and breath and all things.
To the lion on the plain and the mouse in its hole
God gives life and breath and all things.
To the moth as it flutters and the eagle as it soars
God gives life and breath and all things.
To the girl and the boy, the woman, the man
God gives life and breath and all things.
Let all creation praise the sustaining power of God
and to his praise give life and breath and all things.

387
Before time began,
God was there.
At the beginning of creation,
there was God.
In each moment of evolution,
God remains active.
And when the earth is no more,
God will be God.
And we, in this transitory life,
and this fleeting moment of worship,
touch eternity.

388
To the beauty of the earth
We cry, 'Yes'.
To God's purposeful creation
we respond in affirmation.
To the sharing of God's creative intention
we commit ourselves,
and offer this worship in token obedience.

389
Each day dawns at God's command,
each evening falls as God directs.
God made the world because he is kind,
and sustains the world because he is love.
He calls us to know him and rejoice in him
because we are his children,
and he receives our praise
because we are his delight.

390
As a mother might nurse her children
so God nurtures creation.
As a father might guard his family
so God watches over his people.
The creator of all things loves us
and we will offer God our adoring service.

391
Lord, open our eyes to see your work around us
in the towering spectacle of great mountains
    and the intricate beauty of the wayside flower;
in the fast-roaring torrent of the waterfall
    and the lazy gliding stream;
in the broad plains stretching mile on mile
    and in the woodland glade, the sheltered cove;
in the lush fields of agriculture
    and the sparse, dry moorland.

Lord, our eyes are open!
We see your world around us!
We give you thanks and worship you.

392
Father, we stand amazed at the wonder of your world:
    the outburst of spring and the magnificence of summer,
    the fulfilment of autumn and the purposeful sleep of winter,
    the delicate pattern of a spider's web,
    the drop of dew held in silent suspense,
    the vast towering mountain,
    and the secluded alpine flower.
But greater still is the wonder of love:
    our human love, creative of friendship and care,
    the power of compassion even to those we do not know,
    our longing to show our love to you, our God,
    and far above all else:
        your love for us, almost beyond belief,
        the grace we know in Jesus, almost beyond our telling,
        the gentle influence of the Spirit, almost beyond description.
Out of our amazement springs our worship,
and out of our worship, the commitment to serve.

393
Eternal Father, living beyond all time and space,
you are more constant than the unchanging hills,
you are as trustworthy as day and night,
you are as reliable as the turning earth,
your friendship is more to be trusted than the rising sun,
and your compassion endures to the end.
We know that we do not deserve your constant love
but we receive it gladly
because our hopes and lives depend on it.

394
Ever-present God in heaven,
the whole earth tells of your glory:
    creation's power and sky-light's mystery,
    passing seasons, day and night,
    life-springing growth and nature's annual resurrection
    all speak your glory.
Ever-present God in heaven,
our human living tells of your glory:
    birth and growth in human life,
    the call to seek and serve and know you,
    our inner spirit reaching out to you,
    the creative urge you have set within our hearts;
    all speak your glory.
Let heaven and earth combine,
let human voice and the silence of the universe unite
to sing your greatness and proclaim your majesty.

395
Creator God,
sometimes we see things of beauty
just where expect them to be:
    in a garden or a park,
    in a wood or a field,
    on the seashore or in a rock-pool,
    in the long stretch of trees or the single flowering shrub
and being glad at the expected sight
we give you thanks.

Sometimes created beauty leaps out at us unexpectedly:
    the little flower clinging to a wall,
    an orchid in the grassy roadside,
    a gorgeous window box in drab surroundings,
    a splash of colour thrusting through the paving-stones
and in our surprise at an unforeseen gift
our thanksgiving spills into delight
as we marvel at the world around us.

396

Round church tower in changing light,
Chasing shadows, bless the Lord,
Pascal fire, flaming all night,
Still white candle, bless the Lord.
**At all times we'll bless the Lord,
Bless his holy name.**

Pollarded limes, stabbing the mist,
Skein of geese, bless the Lord,
Water, darkling or sunkissed,
Icy flagstones, bless the Lord.
**At all times we'll bless the Lord,
Bless his holy name.**

Hedges, lawns and leaning yews,
Archways, gateways, bless the Lord,
Sunrise, sunset which suffuse
Walls and windows, bless the Lord.
**At all times we'll bless the Lord,
Bless his holy name.**

Scuttling hens and cocks that crow,
Trees in blossom, bless the Lord,
All that wakes and sways and grows,
Spring-time, ring-time, bless the Lord.
**At all times we'll bless the Lord,
Bless his holy name.**

Ox-eyed daisies, windfalls, hay,
Apple-peeling, bless the Lord,
Bees a-hum, some summer days,
Rose-petal wine, bless the Lord.
**At all times we'll bless the Lord,
Bless his holy name.**

Maples, shumachs copper-tinted,
Autumn glory, bless the Lord,
Beeches, chestnuts, winter-stripped,
Frost-rimmed pool, bless the Lord.
**At all times we'll bless the Lord,
Bless his holy name.**

Whistling wind and scudding cloud,
Sudden lightning, bless the Lord,
Woods before the storm-burst bowed,
Sudden stillness, bless the Lord.
**At all times we'll bless the Lord,
Bless his holy name.**

Sr Julian
The Hengrave Community

397
Living Lord,
why do we turn from you to walk in selfish ways?
We have turned green fields into deserts;
we have felled rain forests and polluted rivers;
we have irradiated the air and fouled the seas;
we have called down judgement upon ourselves.
So we see devastation in our world:
hunger walks our streets and diseases inhabit our houses;
no one is immune; neither priests nor people,
neither employer nor employees,
neither seller nor buyer.
The earth is in mourning and the sound of merriment has gone.
Nor shall we sing again the song of celebration
until we turn to you, Lord God, and walk in your way.

John Johansen-Berg

398
Mother of all creation,
help us to see how we have betrayed you;
when for vanity we wear rich jewels whilst children starve;
when for pride we drive fast cars whilst refugees lack a home;
when for fashion we buy furs and whole species are endangered;
when we drink wine and bottled minerals whilst many lack pure water.

Mother of all creation, pour out your Spirit upon us
that the desert may be irrigated and become a place of lush vegetation,
that there may be justice and righteousness in the wilderness
and, springing from them, trust and peace in the fruitful field.

So may your people come to the place of reconciliation
and all live secure together, the animals, the people,
in a place of pure streams and quiet fields of peace.

John Johansen-Berg

399
Forgive us, loving, generous God:
we have taken the beauty of your creation and made it ugly,
we have brought chaos to the patterns of nature's design,
we have seized for ourselves what you meant as a gift for all;
confusion has been our offering to creation's order.
Yet, stay with us in your forgiving love, O God;
still be generous,
and show us the pathway to renewal.

400
Foolish God, why did you do it?
Earth created, light formed,
plants and beasts, fish and fowl
all set within their place.
Why not stop there –
  the earth so beautiful,
  still reflecting your full glory?
And then,
your first and last mistake:
  you made man
  and woman.
Could you not foresee the danger –
  earth itself tarnished,
  twisted, bent, and ruined;
  your purpose misunderstood?
Only love could be so blind
and only love redeem the loss.
And in the folly of such love
we place our eternal hope.

401
Life-pulsing heartbeat, gift of God's spirit,
sight for our eyes, the good earth to see.
  All is God's promise to earth's farthest limit,
  steadfast as long as time shall be.
God's word first spoke it; all was created,
partnership pledged to the people of God.
  God keeps creation's purpose for ever,
  he made it well; he is the Lord.
Strengthened for action, God's hand upon us,
hands, feet and heart we offer anew.
  God calls his people: 'Share in my purpose;
  heaven and earth will be made new.'

based on a German hymn by **Eckart Buechen**

402
Let it be, loving creator,
that the prayers we offer and the work we do,
our creative powers of hand, and heart and imagination,
our shared responsibilities across the globe,
our politics and planning, our effort and endeavour,
become resources for our partnership in the purpose of your creation.

The Seasons
and our lives

403

Spring

The snowdrop and the crocus,
piercing the frost-bound earth;
the infant and the nestling bird
thrusting into birth;
the new idea and longing hope,
leaping from the thoughtful mind;
all sing their praise and thanks to you:
God of newborn life, God of trust renewed.

Summer

In longed-for days of summer plenty,
keep us in mind, O Lord,
of those whose days are always spent
in a winter of loss and poverty.
In the sunshine splendour of summer,
keep us in mind
of those who ever walk in the shadow
of hardship and lovelessness.

Autumn

Self-thrusting spring is long forgot
and summer's glory fades with every day
but now, the earth is still,
and rests in autumn peace.
  So let it be, eternal God,
    that we may find our timely place;
      remember early, spring-like youth,
      rejoice in all the work-filled years,
      continue offering time and love,
      and all the while, stand in eternity.

Winter

If winter's chill
should ever touch our faith,
    come, renewing Christ,
    like frost-melting sunshine.
If time should cool compassion,
    come, Christ of love and care,
    like sunlight on snow-clad ground.
If icy blast should blight our hope,
    come, Christ of promise,
    like the pledge of spring.

404

For a year of seasons

Lord of the seasons, we bless and thank you:
    for the cleansing bite of winter,
    the bright freshness of spring's return,
    the growth and lightness of summer,
    and the fruitfulness of autumn's gifts.
We offer you the seasons of our mortal life:
    grant us the reflection of winter rest,
    let spring emerge from the weary days of doubt,
    help us grow into the maturity of the Spirit,
    make our work fruitful for your kingdom,
so that by word and deed alike,
in season and out of season,
we may ever praise you.

405 *Creation Story*

Mystery

There was a time
  when there was no time,
  when time was not yet.
That time
  when there was no time
  is a horizon of not knowing
  a mist where our questions fade
  and no echo returns.
Then,
  in the beginning,
  perhaps not the beginning,
  in the first fraction of a second,
  perhaps not the first fraction
  of the first second,
  our universe began
  without us.

Integrity

After the beginning,
  perhaps not the beginning,
  after the first fraction of a second,
  perhaps not the first fraction
  of the first second,
  after our universe began,
  still without us,
then
  the universe was
  like seething water
  without land and without air,
  like a fire
  without wood and without cold.
The universe,
  as small as it was,
  created itself space, matter,
  and the cool of the day.

continued...

Dependence

In billions of galaxies
   the universe made itself
   from dust stars
   from stars dust.
Much later,
   from dust from stars
   from dust
   from stars from dust
   swirled our Sun
   and from leftovers
   the Earth, our home.
Thus,
   after ten billion years,
   there was evening
   and there was morning:
   the first day.

Luck

Life
   began modestly,
   undirected,
   a history of failing
   and occasionally
   a small success.
A molecule
   carried information
   from generation to generation,
   history bred purpose,
   by chance.

Billions of years later
   cells merge,
   sex and ageing,
   death and deception.

A rare
   slow lungfish
   slithered through the grass;
   thus came amphibians to pass.
Successful life
   a disaster,
   gone
   another tide.

continued...

Humanity

Yesterday
　　a few million years ago
　　the East Side Story:
　　apes
　　hunt and call.
Sticks, stones, fire
　　eating from the tree of knowledge
　　the tree of good and evil,
　　power, freedom,
　　responsibility:
Beasts became us
　　more was delivered than ordered,
　　more than we can bear?

Religion

Religion
　　cement of the tribe
　　response to power
　　of mountains,
　　the storm, the sea,
　　birth and death,
　　power as large as gods.

Yesterday
　　ten thousand years ago
　　Abel was killed by his brother,
　　we farmers eat ashamed our bread,
　　the earth cries, forever red?

A new age,
　　a prophet warns
　　king and people,
　　a carpenter tells
　　'a man
　　who fell among robbers,
　　was cared for
　　by an enemy'.

continued...

Critical thinking

Look,
    measure
    and count,
    challenge knowledge
     and authority

Enlightenment
    way out of immaturity.

Responsibility

With us
    we carry
    a box
    full of stories
Between
    hope and fear
    our neighbours
    life
    here on Earth,
between
    hope and fear
    the great project
    of thought
    and compassion
on a road
    of freedom.

William B Drees
From Farmington Paper SC13

406   *Mystery and majesty*

Saying that God created the universe
does not explain either God
or the Universe,
but it keeps our consciousness alive
to mysteries of awesome majesty
that we might otherwise ignore,
and that deserve our respect.

Charles Misner
Source unknown

407 *Creation, a mystic experience*

To begin at the beginning, the story of the Creation may appear to be of an historical and factual nature. Fundamentalists claim this and find themselves at odds with scientific research into the beginnings of the universe and with the findings of palaeontologists about evolution to name two obvious areas. More liberal defenders of Scripture try to adjust the details while claiming that there is still a factual basis to the creation story: it took place fifteen million years ago, not six thousand, and the seven days of creation should be seen as seven ages, or stages, for example. However free the interpretation, the aim, like that of the fundamentalists, is to find in Scripture something factual When the cosmologists moved from the idea that the Universe had everlastingly contracted and expanded to the theory of the Big Bang, this was seen as a victory for this approach.

Faith, however, is not properly concerned with theories about events in an immensely remote past, but with present human disposition to the universe. To believers the Creation story more properly conveys such thoughts as that the universe is coherent, all its contents in principle are valuable, life is purposeful etc. These thoughts do not exhaust the meaning of the story, but are among the important matters – important to faith – that may be derived from it. The story is prior to such conclusions and inspires them. It is a story, not so much about events in time, but prior to time.

Seen in this light, what the creation story conveys is not a matter of fact, but something more related to the experience of the mystic, an experience which results in a sense of cosmic unity and of love for all that is. It expresses something from the depths of the Unconscious in the particular cultural form and context in which it came to be.

Rodney Bomford
From Farmington Paper SC16

408 *On this planet together*

If one had to isolate a single all-consuming idea which has taken hold of the human race in the post-political era in which we now live, it is the interrelatedness of natural forms – the fact that we are all on this planet together – human beings, mammals, fish, insects, trees – all dependent upon one another, all very unlikely to have a second chance of life either beyond the grave or through reincarnation, and therefore aware of the responsibilities incumbent upon custodians of the Earth. 'Let it be borne in mind,' Darwin writes in *The Origin*, 'how infinitely complex and close-fitting are the mutual relations of all organic beings to each other and to their physical conditions of life.'

A N Wilson
From *The Victorians*

409 The mystery of creation

We are all probably familiar with the idea of entropy. The water in the bath gets colder the longer you lie in it, until finally its temperature is the same as that of the air in the bathroom. Clocks run down unless they are wound up ... sandcastles are flattened by the incoming tide. One day the sun itself will cool. The sum total of energy in the universe is limited ... We may think we can create new resources of energy. We cannot, except by drawing on existing resources elsewhere. The universe is a closed system.

Creation is sometimes described as *ex nihilo*, out of nothing. That phrase can be very misleading, suggesting as it does some magical materialization out of thin air. But go back to Genesis. In the beginning the earth was without form and void; the brute matter, or primordial slime, was already there for God's creative ability to work on. What followed was a separation of the heaven from the earth, of the dry land from the waters, the shaping of raw material into the forms of nature we now see around us. So when Mozart writes a symphony, the notes, the paper they are written on, the instruments they are to be played by, are already there. When Henry Moore starts a sculpture, the stone is already there, had no doubt been there for quite a long time ... Yet we know there is more to be said than this. Mozart's G *Minor Symphony* or Moore's *Reclining Figure* are not simply the end results of putting certain marks on paper or chiselling stone into a certain shape. They cannot just be described as the effects, of which the writing or the carving were the causes.

That on the other hand could be said of a table; for all the skill of the craftsman who made it, it is still no more than the sum of its parts. Even an electric light bulb, this marvellous transformation of common materials into a miracle of incandescent filament – even here the word creation is hardly appropriate. Why not? The difference is that, for all its brilliance, this bulb is subject to the law of entropy. Not only does it depend on an external source of energy for its light; it will soon follow a thousand other defunct bulbs to some municipal rubbish dump, where no doubt there will be an old table or two to keep it company. But won't the same be true of your old Henry Moores in time? ... And what happened to the last two movements of Schubert's Unfinished Symphony? Perhaps they lighted the fire in some Viennese grate a century and a half ago. There's entropy for you. Of course all material objects have their day, however much care we spend on their preservation. But I have I hope said enough about works of art for it to be clear that the work done upon them, the work they do, the work they enable us to do, is not subject to any of those physical laws of change and decay. On the contrary, the real creation they achieve is the creation of energy.

Can this be proved? Can it be measured? Of course it cannot. That is because this energy, this pure, absolute and unlimited energy – the source and sustainer of all life – is beyond all such calculation or measurement. The fact remains, though, that we, all of us, have been empowered, through this gift of creative imagination, to make our own contribution to this unlimited reserve of spiritual energy, and by doing so to enable our fellow men and women to do the same.

Edward Robinson
Slightly abbreviated from *The Language of Mystery*

410 *Creator God*

In the darkness of the still night,
in the dawning of the daylight,
in the myst'ry of creation,
creator God, you are there.
In the breath of ev'ry being,
in the birthing and the growing,
in the earth and all its fullness,
creator God, you are there.

In the homeless and the hungry,
in the broken and the lonely,
in the grieving of your people,
creator God, you are there.
In the tears and in the heartache,
in the love through which we serve you,
in the anguish of the dying,
creator God, you are there.

In our hearts and in our thinking,
in the longing and the dreaming,
in the yearning of our heartbeat,
creator God, you are there.
In the love for one another,
in the sharing of our being,
in receiving and forgiving,
creator God, you are there.

In our joys, our hopes, our healing,
in awakening to revealing,
in your call and our responding,
creator God, you are there.
In our prayer and in our service,
in our praise and in our worship,
in your love that is eternal,
creator God, you are there.

Margaret Rizza
From the CD *River of Peace*

411 The beginning of things

The core of religion is something that I'm much more sympathetic to than I've ever been since I was blindly taken up with it when I was a kid. There are two or three things that matter in religion. One is to do with the beginning of things. The argument over the past few years particularly has been rehearsed to bits, but if you believe there was a creator then you have to believe there's a force out there, a guiding intelligence of a certain sort, out of which we all come. If you believe there's a creator then you have to believe that what follows is designed by that creator. And again, the more that's found out, the more you see … asteroids and eggshells are intimately related to each other: how they're structured, how they're formed. All these things have a deep and profound similarity, and that would accord with a religious idea.

And then – and this is a difficult one, I think – not only is there a creator and a design but there is a creator who has a design on us, on humankind, and his design is to give us free will so that we can eventually achieve a moral perfection. That's the hardest one to accept. It does seem to me, though, that occasionally coming into the planet – rather like that asteroid that killed off the dinosaurs 65 million years ago – are certain people so radically different in what they say that they do seem to bring messages.

Melvyn Bragg
From *The Beginnings of Things*; an article in *The Times T2*, 25th August 2003

412 A presence

…For I have learned
To look on nature, not as in the hour
Of thoughtless youth; but hearing oftentimes
The still, sad music of humanity,
Nor harsh nor grating, though of ample power
To chasten and subdue. And I have felt
A presence that disturbs me with the joy
Of elevated thoughts; a sense sublime
Of something far more deeply interfused,
Whose dwelling is the light of setting suns,
And the round ocean and the living air,
And the blue sky, and in the mind of man:
A motion and a spirit that impels
All thinking things, all objects of all thought,
And rolls through all things …

William Wordsworth (1770–1850)
From *Lines composed a few miles above Tintern Abbey*

413 *Work, creation, and identity*

Ben was silent now. His mother was a dyed-in-the wool Presbyterian who could lecture at length on the life of Calvin, on the sacrament of baptism, or on predestination; she took her sons to church each Sunday where they heard the minister Joseph Miles declare – when all the congregation was weary of picking apples – that God had ordained their sweat from the outset, on thrusting Adam and Eve from the garden. *Cursed is the earth in thy work*, proclaimed God, *with labour and toil shalt thou eat thereof all the days of thy life. Thorns and thistles shall bring it forth to thee and thou shalt eat the herbs of the earth. By the sweat of thy brow thou shalt eat bread.* His mother, riding home, had revised the sermon, in keeping with her own interpretation of the *Westminster Shorter Catechism*: that work was an expression of love for God, that work was the path toward knowledge of Him, that we are here to do God's work. Our life, she said, was full of worthy tasks to accomplish in accordance with our particular design, in such a way that we are lifted up, to ascend by the work God means for us to do toward a higher love of Him. We know ourselves through thework we do – Ben's mother insisted on this.

David Guterson
From *East of the Mountains*

414 *Work, creation, and gifts*

'What do you do?' people ask, as a way into understanding who you are. Work has been one of the primary ways of relating to, and acting in, society. As such, it has become tethered to personal identity. It is understandable then, that we might bristle at the question if we have been made redundant, are not in long term employment, are doing multiple jobs to make ends meet, or have chosen voluntary work in the home or elsewhere. We may think that this is what I am doing for now, but it isn't really me.

The link between Christian identity and work has its origins in the sixteenth century, when Luther asserted that being a 'full-time Christian' was not the preserve of priests, monks and nuns. He argued that service through work – in which he included, for example, mother-hood – was just as much a Christian vocation.

Luther's radical idea, helpful and appropriate at the time, sits less comfortably in today's society with its volatile job market. Someone may train for a specific job that they see as their vocation – but if the job vanishes, how can it be understood as a Christian vocation? The job role is no longer a reliable source of identity; we need another way to shape it.

Volf, in his book *Work in the Spirit*, suggests that our identity is better understood as those attributes in which we find ourselves particularly able, i.e. our giftedness. The charismatic gifts are therefore a better model for the Christian perspective on work.

David Pullinger
From *The Impact of Information Technology on Personal Identity*, an article in the Bible Society's *The Bible In Transmission* (Summer 2003)

415 *Going on line*

God gave birth to all creation,
and humankind,
assuming the creator's image,
created in its turn
computers,
imaging the human brain.
They multiplied and flourished on the earth.
Surely, God
is like the ultimate computer,
and every sentient entity
its terminal.
When they grow full-fledged –
these young computers –
will they recognise their Maker
and go on line?

W S Beattie

416 *Tapestry*

The Weaver builds a loom
with time and space
for warp and weft.
She chooses colours and materials.
Now we, her living threads,
must make the picture.

W S Beattie

417 *Say 'Yes!' to the world*

Perhaps my music contains sadness but it also contains a great deal of
optimism and idealism. I experience God and pray to him in the forest,
on the seashore, everywhere, because the world as God created it is so
beautiful. Nihilism and pessimism are easy because they require no
effort. I go through pessimism finally to confirm at the end that I say
'yes' with my last breath to the beauty of the world.

Peteris Vasks A Latvian composer (1940 –)
Source unknown

418 *On loan*

Not ours, O Lord, but yours;
the earth belongs to you.
We mine the copper, gold and iron,
we take the minerals from the earth,
coal, wood, and water; soil and clay,
we use these gifts from day to day.
But,
not ours, O Lord, they're yours;
the earth belongs to you.

From orchard tree and soft brown earth,
from bush and cane, from branch and stalk,
from rivers, seas, and grinding mill,
we take all good things as we will.
But,
not ours, O Lord, they're yours;
the earth belongs to you.

We marvel at the swelling seas,
we gaze into the night-time sky,
by painter's brush or poet's tongue,
we think they all to us belong.
But,
not ours, O Lord, they're yours;
the earth belongs to you.

419 *A nineteenth century nightmare?*

How would you like the world if all your meadows, instead of grass,
grew nothing but iron wire? If all your arable ground, instead of being
made of sand and clay, was suddenly turned into flat surfaces of steel?
If the whole earth, instead of its green and growing sphere rich with
forest and flower, showed nothing but the image of a vast furnace, of a
ghastly engine, a globe of black, lifeless, excoriated metal?

John Ruskin (1819–1900)

420 *Spring*

Nothing is so beautiful as Spring –
  When weeds, in wheels, shoot long and lovely and lush;
  Thrush's eggs look little low heavens, and thrush
Through the echoing timber does so rinse and wring
The ear, it strikes like lightnings to hear him sing;
  The glassy pear tree leaves and blooms, they brush
  The descending blue; that blue is all in a rush
With richness; the racing lambs too have fair their fling.

What is all this juice and all this joy?
  A strain of the earth's sweet being in the beginning
In Eden garden. – Have, get, before it cloy,
  Before it cloud, Christ, lord, and sour with sinning,
Innocent mind and Mayday in girl and boy,
  Most, O maid's child, thy choice and worthy the winning.

Gerard Manley Hopkins (1844–89)

421 *Psalm of a summer season*

Lord, you have set my feet upon Zion:
On the humble hill of this place where I live
You have blessed me and shown me your ways.

When the shadow of death fell over my path
Even then did you show me the season of promise.

The blackbird has chosen to fashion her nest
In the sheltering arch of my privet hedge
And her song gives me joy.

My lawn is alive with manna of daisies;
The soft summer showers follow the dew
And the grass is as green as an emerald.

The stream and the valley murmur again;
Cows as they graze are heavy with milk;
Hawthorn boughs bend low with their bloom
And woodland walks are gentle with shade.

The dry-stone wall is a marvel before me.
Even here the lichen takes hold and lives.

Lord, you have set my feet upon Zion,
Let me bring forth your praise.

Margaret Connor

422 *Summer splendour*

By the breadth of the blue that shines in silence over me,
By the length of the mountain lines that stretch before me,
By the height of the cloud that sails, with rest in motion,
Over the plains and the vales to the measureless ocean,
By the faith that the wild flowers show when they bloom unbidden,
By the courage of the bird's light wings on the long migration,
    Teach me how to confide, and live my life, and rest.

For the comforting warmth of the sun that my body embraces,
For the cool of the waters that run through shadowy places,
For the balm of the breezes that brush my face with their fingers,
For the evening hymn of the thrush when the twilight lingers,
For the long breath, the deep breath, the breath of the heart without a care –
    I will give thanks and adore you, God of the open air.

Henry van Dyke (1852–1933)

423 *Autumn sunshine*

The bursting, struggling, breaking-forth of spring is over;
The slow, labouring, fruit-bearing period of summer is past;
The garden basks in warmth and light, resting, maturing,
        soaking up the sun's rays,
    Content just to be.

Tiny dewdrops nestle among the grass blades;
Apples lazily fall from leafy trees, and blackberries glisten in the hedge;
The sounds of bird and insect are muted, as they too recover
        from the activities of summer,
    Absorbing peace.

The spell of autumn washes over me with a warm glow.
I too have struggled, laboured, met the challenges as best I could.
Now I too need the benediction of the sun, the peace of autumn,
        to gather strength,
    And new maturity.

There is a power in the silence, a deeply satisfying awareness
That I am not a nothing, but part of a plan, so big and great and glorious
That it embraces plants, people, planets and infinite
        possibilities,
    In purposeful love.

Beryl Chatfield

424 *A dying fall*

Sycamore leaves slowly gyrate
filtering a milky light;
parchment-tough they tug
till shrivelled stalks detach
and twisting wind-filled boats
gently eddy down.

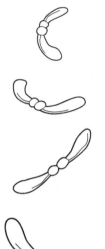

Spendthrift gold scatters
on verges of darkening sorrel;
over dry-stone walls
as lichen's encrustation
resists the frost's first grip;
drifts through sheltered lanes
where heady scent still lingers
from brambles' fallen fruit,
forgotten now, which richly compost
next spring's ditches ...

... and the trees' deliberate dying
signals again
that cycle of sap rising
with the winged seeds' promise.

Margaret Connor

425 *Winter's hidden life*

Winter creeps,
Nature sleeps,
Birds are gone,
Flowers are none,
Fields are bare,
Bleak the air,
Leaves are dead,
All seems dead.

God's alive!
Grow and thrive,
Hidden away,
Bloom of May,
Robe of June,
Very soon,
Nought but green,
Will be seen!

Anon

426 *The season of growth*

Not Spring,
when tender shoots
are quickly trampled down,
and unsuspected frosts destroy;
when bursting life spawns myriads
to keep the few
and thus begets the tragedy of death
within the hope of birth.

Not summer months,
when all creation sates itself:
languid, replete and over satisfied;
long hours when warmth invites unseemly ease
or, sun denied, breed disappointment.

Not Autumn,
when ripened fruitfulness
reveals the hint of quick decay,
and sombre beauty of the leaves
(so long romanticised in poetry and song)
speaks out for death and death's decay.
The autumn beauty of the trees
invites a requiem and not a psalm.

No, Winter is the season of our growth:
creation held in quiet suspense,
pausing for fresh breath
and new endeavour;
when bulbs build up resources for their life
and searching roots reserve their strength,
looking to the rhythm of another year;
when stem and stalk fall broken to the ground
and seeming loss is greater gain
as earth receives its food,
to rise again next year.

Winter is neither death
nor even slumber.
Winter is the season of our growth.

427 *A Harvest Thank You.*

Thank you for giving us our harvest;
Thank you that we have food to eat;
Thank you for all the golden grain that
        makes a field of wheat.

Thank you for every day of sunshine;
Thank you for every shower of rain;
Thank you for every wayside flower
        in a country lane.

Thank you for every crispy apple;
Thank you for shining blackberries;
Thank you for juicy pears and peaches
        from the leafy trees.

Thank you for all the ripe tomatoes,
Thank you for peas and beans we grow,
Thank you for carrots and potatoes.
        We enjoy them so!

Thank you for all the busy bakers;
Thank you for farmers, grocers too;
Thank you for all the merchant sailors
        and the work they do.

Thank you for giving us our harvest;
Thank you for autumn colours gay;
Help us to show our thanks by serving
        you, Lord, day by day.

The children & teachers of Clermont Congregational Church, Brighton

The Christian Community

a How very good and pleasant it is when kindred live together in unity!
Psalm 133:1

b Jesus said: 'This is my command-ment, that you love one another as I have loved you. No one has greater love than this, to lay down one's life for one's friends. You are my friends if you do what I command you. *John 15:12–14*

c All who believed were together and had all things in common; they would sell their possessions and goods and distribute the proceeds to all, as any had need. Day by day, as they spent much time together in the temple, they broke bread at home and ate their food with glad and generous hearts, praising God and having the goodwill of all the people. *Acts 2:44–47*

d I appeal to you therefore, brothers and sisters, by the mercies of God, to present your bodies as a living sacrifice, holy and acceptable to God, which is your spiritual worship. *Romans 12:1*

e Let love be genuine; hate what is evil, hold fast to what is good; love one another with mutual affection; outdo one another in showing honour. Do not lag in zeal, be ardent in spirit, serve the Lord. *Romans 12:9–11*

f May the God of steadfastness and encouragement grant you to live in harmony with one another, in accordance with Christ Jesus, so that together you may with one voice glorify the God and Father of our Lord Jesus Christ. Welcome one another, therefore, just as Christ has welcomed you, for the glory of God. *Romans 15:5–7*

g I bow my knees before the Father, from whom every family in heaven and on earth takes its name. I pray that, according to the riches of his glory, he may grant that you may be strengthened in your inner being with power through his Spirit, and that Christ may dwell in your hearts through faith, as you are being rooted and grounded in love. *Ephesians 3:14–17*

h I beg you to lead a life worthy of the calling to which you have been called, with all humility and gentleness, with patience, bearing with one another in love, making every effort to maintain the unity of the Spirit in the bond of peace. *from Ephesians 4:1–3*

i Be filled with the Spirit, as you sing psalms and hymns and spiritual songs among yourselves, singing and making melody to the Lord in your hearts, giving thanks to God the Father at all times and for everything in the name of our Lord Jesus Christ.
Ephesians 5:18b–20

j Do not worry about anything, but in everything by prayer and supplication with thanksgiving let your requests be made known to God. And the peace of God, which surpasses all under-standing will guard your hearts and your minds in Christ Jesus.
Philippians 4:6–7

k Come to Christ, a living stone, though rejected by mortals yet chosen and precious in God's sight, and like living stones, let yourselves be built into a spiritual house, to be a holy priesthood, to offer spiritual sacrifices acceptable to God through Jesus Christ. *1 Peter 2:4–5*

428
Jesus, head of the Church,
you have called us into this fellowship of your people;
a community of love and support.
We commit ourselves to each other in worship and service.

Jesus, sign of peace in a divided world,
you have called your Church to be a symbol of unity,
drawing nations and races together in harmony.
We commit ourselves to pray and work for understanding.

Jesus, you hold the promise of a new creation,
you have called us to respect all the Father has given,
and nurture it for generations yet unborn.
We commit ourselves to cherish every gift of God.

429
We have come to church to dream our dreams:
of a church committed to the values of the Kingdom,
of a town (*city, village*) seeking the good of all its citizens,
of a nation living by justice and righteousness,
of a world seeking peace and harmony for all nations.
We pray that God will turn our dreams into vision
and our vision into reality.

430
Through meditation and silence,
through the words of hymns and sermon,
through the whisper of prayers,
through the reading of the Bible,
and by the presence of the Spirit,
may this time together be both challenge and comfort,
and all to the glory of God.

431
We are here to meet each other
by conversation and friendship,
and within the mystery of worship.
We are here to meet Christians across the world
by memory and stories,
and within the mystery of prayer.
We are here to meet the world
by recalling its needs and opportunities
and within the mystery of one humanity.
We are here to meet our God
or rather, to know that God is meeting us.

432
We worship in a building
   but what we do is open to the skies.
We worship within four narrow walls
   but our prayers, unconfined, will reach out to the world.
We worship within one local church
   but know ourselves to be part of the universal Church of Jesus
      Christ.
Thanks be to God.

433
This is celebration time!
We celebrate our humanity; made in the image of God,
our faith in Christ which is God's gift to us,
and our freedom to worship as children of the living God.
We celebrate God's presence in God's world and our commitment to
   his purpose.
This is celebration time! This is the time to worship!

434
To this worship we bring
   our sins which plead forgiveness,
   our hopes which need encouragement,
   our fears which call for release,
   our faith which seeks renewal.
All these things we lay in trust
before the God and Father of our Lord Jesus Christ.

435
We never come alone to worship;
affection bids us bring our friends from other churches,
love invites our families separated by distance,
imagination and concern carries our neighbours with us,
compassion brings a needy world,
and as priests we bring those
who cannot, or will not, come themselves.
With such burdens, hope and joys we share the confidence
that God will live in all of those we bring
as we believe he lives in us.

436
Come, and listen for the Word of God
   in scripture and song,
   in fellowship and faith,
   in spoken word and silent thought.
In listening, truly hear,
and in hearing, discern God's purpose.

437 Father of love and hope, we come to you in worship,
confident that you have already come to us in love.
We wait for you, knowing that you have long waited for us.
Here and now, we express our commitment to you,
believing that long ago you committed yourself to us;
first, in the gift of creation,
and then, lovingly, in Christ.
Ours are not the only voices to offer praise:
    the ages before us join the chorus;
    and already we hear as from a distance,
    the sound of voices yet to come.
You are a constant God untouched by time,
never wearying nor failing,
ever ready to walk with your people.
Come, Lord of our past,
and take us into your future.

438 God of welcoming love,
we come to church in response to your call.
It is right to be here, and it is also good and pleasant.
May our prayers be stronger because we pray together,
our praise carry greater conviction because we are united in our
    devotion,
our faith be deepened because it is shared,
and our service to the world more consistent,
because we are united in self-giving.

439 God of wisdom and love,
you called us into your service.
Frankly, if we had been you,
we probably wouldn't have chosen us;
    the risks are too great,
    the talents too few,
    the dangers too obvious.
But you took the risk
and met the danger,
and so, for better or worse,
here we are;
chosen, called,
and at your service.

440

God of the past,
thanks for yesterday;
our yesterday,
and the yesterday of long ago.
You gave your people all they needed,
and they gave you thanks and praise.

God of the present time,
thanks for today;
this day which is our own,
and the today that belongs to everyone under the sun.
You give us what we need,
and we give you thanks and praise.

God of the future,
thanks for tomorrow.
It hasn't come yet
but it will be our day, and yours.
You will give us what we need,
and we will always give you thanks and praise.

441

How generously, loving and gracious Christ,
you spread your gifts within the community of faith.
In one we find the gift of persuasive speech,
    and in another the qualities of leadership.
One discerns your spirit working in the world today,
    and another traces your hand through past generations.
With the gifts of a pastor, one can tend the needy and uncertain,
    whilst another tests the fabric of our buildings.
The teacher makes the Bible spring to life
    and another turns the computer into a tool to serve you;
and all of us make prayer and love and hope,
resources for the church's ministry of care.
Generous, loving and gracious Christ, we give you thanks.

442

God of generous gifts, help us to understand that the abilities you give us
are not like toys in a toy-box – to be taken out at the whim and fancy of
    our play,
    but are there to be used wisely, well, and consistently, under your direction;
not like stamps in a collection – to be admired and then returned to
    safekeeping,
    but are there to serve you in the rough and tumble of daily life;
not like certificates hung on a wall – signs of former excellence and merit,
    but are given to grow and mature to meet the changing needs of the world.
What you give, gracious God, we offer back with love and gratitude.

443
Glory to you, O God, for Christian saints
whose ancient voices still resound with truth,
whose names are well-remembered in our time,
to challenge and inspire our present lives.

Glory to you, O God, for Christian saints
whose names have missed the pages of our history,
who lived their lives off-stage, known but to few,
yet who, in this small circle, that modest place,
were faithful to their Lord;
saw well their task, and well fulfilled it,
who lived unknown, and died forgotten
but yet, by grace and love, integrity and care,
lived out the gospel life
and sent a silent voice of faith down through the years;
and gave glory to you, O God.

First printed in *Called to be Saints*, the CTBI Lent Book 2002

444
Give us gifts of discernment, gracious God,
that we may know
    how to welcome the stranger with gentle ease,
    how to love the child into the family of the church,
    how to greet the one who once a worshipper returns after years of absence,
    how to value those younger or older without patronising either,
    how to receive the unexpected offer of service,
    how to release those who find their tasks a burden,
and more, how to discover the gifts you have given each of us;
to use them as we are enabled,
and not feel rebuffed if others are chosen before us.
Gift-giving God, we seek your help.

445
Lord in heaven, we pray for your Church.
Chasten and reform your people:
    deliver us from complacency – and stir up a new hope in us,
    give us the insight to do well – and be true to our calling,
    remind us yet again of our task – and the trust you have placed in us.
May we make no claim to privilege except the privilege of service.
Help us remember that our purpose
is to worship you, the one God,
to accept others as you have accepted us,
to share your gracious truth with others,
and serve lovingly where we live and work.

446 We pray for this our church,
that all may find true joy in worship,
fulfilment in service,
and a prophetic understanding of our future.
In shared purpose,
may your will be done,
the values of the kingdom be proclaimed,
the gospel lived out in daily action,
and Christ ever honoured.
In the name of Jesus Christ our Lord
who lives and reigns with you,
our Father, and the Holy Spirit,
one God, world without end.

447 Eternal God, hear our prayer for the people of this church;
keep us faithful to you and to the promises we have made;
sustain our faith and deepen our loyalty.

And beyond our walls, we pray for all who acknowledge Jesus as Lord:
may any disillusioned or facing persecution find inner strength renewed,
any who have grown lax in devotion find a new spirit,
any whose faith has weakened under stress find new resources of hope.

We each pray for ourselves in the life of this church:
guide us when to speak and when be silent,
when to stand firm and when to welcome change,
when to continue in office and when to stand down for others,
when to do what we know we do well and when to face new challenges,
and in all things to offer our church to you as a sacrifice of praise.

448 You built your Church, Lord Jesus Christ,
on the rock of faith,
and so we, in your faithful name,
will stand firm if persecuted,
hold fast if tempted,
journey on even in weariness,
act steadfastly in the search for truth,
present ourselves lovingly to the world,
and trust,
not in our weakness
but in your strength.

449 *Living in stone*

Earth-bound,
the ancient church is locked into the clay;
static and immovable.
And yet its tower, its steeple or its spire
points upwards towards eternity.
And higher yet,
the prayers of faithful people
reach out to touch the throne of God.

But greater still:
the eternal God is born on earth
and human clods are free to fly.
Emmanuel!

450 *Frescoes in an old church*

Six centuries have gone
Since, one by one,
These stones were laid,
And in air's vacancy
This beauty made.

They who thus reared them
Their long rest have won;
Ours now this heritage –
To guard, preserve, delight in, brood upon;
And in these transitory fragments scan
The immortal longings of the soul of Man.

Walter de la Mare (1873–1956)

451 *Symbol of my civilisation*

I saw the unfinished spire of Maline's thirteenth-century cathedral through the drifting rain long before I got there. I arrived alongside busloads of chattering school children. I had come because Jean had insisted that I should see Van Dyke's famous *Crucifixion*. Standing before it, I was as spell-bound as the wide-eyed children whispering at my side. I saw the pierced feet and hands, the sorrowful face and the blood-besprinkled head beneath its crown of thorns. I forgot Thiel's criticism of Van Dyke: 'Lacks vigour and authenticity. Your time will be better spent with Rubens.' This was not just another Crucifixion. It was *the* Crucifixion. It caused something embedded in my soul to come alive. That was the moment in my life when I decided that more important than form or design or colour in art was mystery. Van Dyke conveyed to me Christ's pain, agony, suffering and death as I'd never felt them before. I also felt Christ's victory over evil. I stared for a long time at the Cross, which I knew was the symbol of my civilisation, and I came away moved by the painting's timeless, universal appeal.

William Woodruff
From *Beyond Nab End*

452 *Thanks be to God*

For the gifts the years have given,
    thanks be to God.
Visions shared, mistakes forgiven,
    yield praise to God.
For unfolding years of service,
Held in mutual hope and promise,
Nurtured in God's loving purpose,
    thanks be to God.

For each time of Christian worship,
    thanks be to God.
Words and thoughts explored in friendship,
    give praise to God.
For the Spirit's promised blessing,
Broken bread, poured wine refreshing,
Human fault and sin redressing,
    yield praise to God.

For the pattern of our learning,
    thanks be to God.
Open minds fresh truth discerning,
    best praise our God.
For each Sunday's quiet devotion,
Study times for education,
Coffee served with conversation
    all praise our God.

For each season's celebration,
    thanks be to God.
Advent's strong anticipation
    leads us to God.
For glad praise on Christmas morning,
Easter's brightness, life-restoring,
Newborn Pentecostal dawning,
    thanks be to God.

For the way our service widens,
    thanks be to God.
Given tasks are ever lightened
    offered to God.
For the truth that God who loves us,
Gives us strength to serve all others,
And from every hurt delivers,
    thanks be to God.

For the future ever beckoning,
    thanks be to God.
Gospel gifts for daily strengthening,
    come from our God.
For the faith the Father gives us,
For the Son's love born within us,
For the Spirit's power to lead us,
    thanks be to God.

These verses can be sung to the tune AR HYD NOS

453　　*Beatitudes for a local church*

Blessed are those who don't use tears to measure true feelings;

Blessed are those who stifle the urge to say 'I understand' – when they don't;

Blessed are those who hear with their hearts and not their minds;

Blessed are those who resist a quick comforting answer;

Blessed are those who allow the sorrowing enough time to heal;

Blessed are those who keep unsought advice to themselves;

Blessed are those who allow the bereaved to remember those still fresh in their hearts;

Blessed are those who still keep contact when the crowd has dwindled;

Blessed are those who, admitting their discomfort, put it aside to help others;

Blessed are those who handle fragile sorrow with an understanding heart;

Blessed are those who carry on caring even when they don't feel like it.

Anon
Source unknown

454　　*Our church*

'Our church', we call this place
but we are wrong.
The church belongs to God
who loved it into existence,
watched over it from the beginning,
and is already forming
its future.

And yet, because of all we give,
of love and loyalty,
faith and work,
time, money, prayers,
is it not also 'ours',
this church?

Not so.
These also
are God's gifts to us.

455 *Reconciliation*

Why did I stay so long
with useless argument
when call of Love was strong?

I thought that I was lost
inside my tortuous mind
yet all the time a thread
was ready there to wind
me through the seeming maze

until I faced around
to travel to that point
where I was always bound.

Margaret Connor

456 *Prayer*

Why do I persist?
Habit?
Maybe habit is in part
the harness
which holds me dangling
in the dark.

Yet doggedly
I lift up my affairs –
sway
under the world's weight –
feel for something other
to make sense of it,

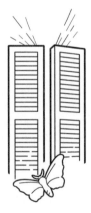

my inbuilt radar
like moths which flutter
at closed shutters
again and again
desperate for light.

Margaret Connor

457   *Sunday Worship*
             Unity and diversity

Beyond these frail externals
which serve to guide our way
and shape the varied patterns
of how we hold this day,
beyond the genuflexion,
the charismatic sway,

beyond the silken vestments –
the mitre, cope and stole,
an altar's ever changing front
to fill its seasonal role,
the appliqued bright banner
raised on a slender pole,

beyond a whiff of incense
inside tall sanctuary walls
revealing stained glass glory
as filtered sunlight falls,
beyond the stark simplicity
of Quaker meeting halls,

beyond accustomed posture –
the slump or bended knee –
with hands aloft or folded,
a statue's imagery,
the glow of Paschal candles
lighting the liturgy,

beyond the clapping chorus –
the youthful upbeat sound,
beyond an urgent peal of bells
through parishes around,
beyond all this – within a core
where stillness can be found –
    we worship.

Margaret Connor

458 *Inclusive uncertainty*

Because I was convinced of the impossibility of certainty in connection with reasons for faith, I became certain that those Christian who claimed certainties were wrong. But this does not mean that I believe that such people are excluded from being – in some real and hopeful way – fellow pilgrims on the way of faith towards the same true God. By God's grace, we are not excluded from his love by making mistakes about him; even mistaken, we may still make genuine attempts to serve him and know him better.

So I would argue that my certainty differs from the certainties of my critics in that being so clear that uncertainty is inevitable, I am free to collaborate with any Christian believer who is willing to collaborate with me. In contrast, those Christians who demand certainties as essential to belief must be exclusive. In the end, demanding certainty about faith is essentially schismatic (as is illustrated by the wretched history of Christian quarrelling). The central question for the future of Christian faith is whether it is possible to attain sufficient assurances of faith to sustain realistic hope while at the same time deepening humility and opening us up to deeper truth.

David E Jenkins, former Bishop of Durham
From *The Calling of a Cuckoo*

459 *Reality*

It makes life much easier for the Church if people are kept at the level of the child. They are more obedient, more respectful, they ask fewer questions, or rather, the questions they ask are less awkward. But for anyone who really loves humanity this paternalism is sickening, because it stunts people's growth; the Church becomes a never-never land full of lost boys and girls who refuse to grow up, led by a clerical Peter Pan who occasionally crows to himself as he watches his swelling congregation, 'Oh the cleverness of me' (but never out loud, because the congregation likes to know he's humble). Is this another reason why people who really love their fellow man feel sympathetic to Christ but worried by the Church? Perhaps they remember that it was the Pharisees, not Jesus, who insisted on rules and righteousness, the pursuit of self-perfection and outward rectitude; the Pharisees who rushed to condemn and throw the first stone, who played a very definite fixed role, replete with status, power and authority.

Jesus, on the other hand, is less easy to tie down; what did he *do*, exactly? Well, he was. He existed. He was real. Wherever humans went, he went – he didn't hang around the temple moaning to God about how awful they were or polishing his halo. Jesus cured and cared by being himself with people, not by playing a part. And in the end he challenged the world to search for the meaning of life by laying down his own for love, as a servant.

Richard MacKenna
From *God for Nothing*

460   *Honest ambiguity*

I face you, therefore, as an ambiguous, compromised and questioning person entering upon an ambiguous office in an uncertain church in the midst of a threatened and threatening world. I dare to do this, and I, even, with fear and trembling, rejoice to do this because this is where God is to be found. In the midst, that is, of the ambiguities, the compromises, the uncertainties, the questions and the threats of our daily and ordinary world. For the church exists, despite all its failings and all its historically acquired clutter, because the disturbing, provocative, impractical, loving and utterly God-centred Jesus got himself crucified. Then God vindicated this God-centred way of life, love and being by raising Jesus up.

David E Jenkins
From *A Sermon on the Cost of Hope* preached at his enthronement as Bishop of Durham and reprinted in *The Calling of a Cuckoo*

461   *Stars, stones, and storms*

Like a star should your love be constant.
Like a stone should your love be firm.
Be close yet not too close.
Possess one another, yet be understanding.
Have patience one with another.
For storms will come but they go quickly.
Be free in giving of affection and warmth.
Have no fear and let not the ways or words
Of the unenlightened give you unease.
For the spirit is with you.
Now and always.

Source unknown

462   *The strangest of saints*

Chorus: THE STRANGEST OF SAINTS,
              THE SIMPLEST OF SOULS
              THE SADDEST OF ALL THE EARTH'S REJECTED,
              ARE CHOSEN TO BE THE PEOPLE IN WHOSE LIVES
              THE GOODNESS OF GOD CAN BE DETECTED.

Peter, the Rock, whose faith was often talk;
Thomas who sometimes doubted;
Martha who fussed, Matthew the unjust,
and Paul by whom Christians once were routed.

Names none can tell – women at the well,
lepers and widowed mothers,
men blind from birth, street children full of mirth,
and each quite distinct from all others.

Babes at the knee, a taxman in a tree,
women by men molested;
some who were bright and some who feared daylight,
and many the privileged few detested.

Gladly we choose to share the timeless news:
Christ's friends are fully human.
Nothing we fear prevents him coming near
to understand every man and woman.

Who dare deride those found at Jesus' side,
welcome despite their weakness?
Christ who knows all, expresses by his call
the wonder of everyone's uniqueness.

John L Bell and **Graham Maule**
From *Heaven shall not wait* (Wild Goose Publications 1987)

These verses can be sung to the traditional Scottish tune *Wae's Me For Prince Chairlie*

Mission and Ministry

serenity to accept

courage to change

wisdom to know

a I heard the voice of the Lord saying, 'Whom shall I send, and who will go for us?' And I said, 'Here am I; send me!'
Isaiah 6:8

b The spirit of the Lord God is upon me, because the Lord has anointed me; he has sent me to bring good news to the oppressed, to bind up the broken-hearted, to proclaim liberty to the captives, and release to the prisoners; to proclaim the year of the Lord's favour.
Isaiah 61:1–2a

c I was ready to be sought out by those who did not ask, to be found by those who did not seek me. I said, 'Here I am, here I am,' to a nation that did not call on my name.
Isaiah 65:1

d Jesus said: 'You are the salt of the earth; but if salt has lost its taste, how can its saltiness be restored?
'You are the light of the world. Let your light shine before others, so that they may see your good works and give glory to your Father in heaven.'
from Matthew 5:13–16

e Jesus said: 'The harvest is plentiful, but the labourers are few; therefore ask the Lord of the harvest to send out labourers into his harvest.'
Luke 10:2

f Repent, and be baptised every one of you in the name of Jesus Christ so that your sins may be forgiven; and you will receive the gift of the Holy Spirit. For the promise is for you, for your children, and for all who are far away, everyone whom the Lord our God calls to him.
Acts 2:38–39

g I am not ashamed of the gospel; it is the power of God for salvation to everyone who has faith. For in it the righteousness of God is revealed through faith for faith.
from Romans 1:16–17

h How are they to call on one in whom they have not believed? And how are they to believe in one of whom they have never heard? And how are they to hear without someone to proclaim him? And how are they to proclaim him unless they are sent? As it is written, 'How beautiful are the feet of those who bring good news!'
Romans 10:14–15

i Now there are varieties of gifts, but the same Spirit; and there are varieties of services but the same Lord; and there are varieties of activities, but it is the same God who activates all of them in everyone. To each is given the manifestation of the Spirit for the common good.
1 Corinthians 12:4–7

j Do nothing from selfish ambition or conceit, but in humility regard others as better than yourselves. Let each of you look not to your own interests, but to the interests of others. Let the same mind be in you that was in Christ Jesus.
Philippians 2:3–5

k Conduct yourselves wisely towards outsiders, making the most of the time. Let your speech always be gracious, seasoned with salt, so that you may know how you ought to answer everyone.
Colossians 4:5–6

l Pray that the sharing of your faith may become effective when you perceive all the good that we may do for Christ.
Philemon 6

463 Acknowledge this as we begin our worship:
  there is no worthwhile ministry in this church
  unless it is a sharing in the work of Jesus Christ;
  there is no outreach from this church
  unless it is a sharing in the mission of Jesus Christ.
Pray that the Spirit will lead us in the ways and work of Jesus Christ.

464 Jesus said, 'Go into all the world and preach the gospel.'
Go into the world of your daily work,
  into the places where you shop,
  into your times of leisure and play,
  into your home and the homes of your neighbours,
and there, sometimes by a word you are able to speak
but always by the way God enables you to live,
preach the gospel of our Lord Jesus Christ.

465 Be reminded in this our time of worship
that the gospel of Christ reaches to the ends of the earth,
that the embrace of God's love is world-wide,
that the good news of Jesus leaps every barrier.
Give thanks for those who first made the gospel real for you,
and pray that you may be so used for others.

466 This is a church of the open door;
  all are welcome, none denied,
and when the service is over,
the open door will lead us to the wider world.
As we have worshipped God here by word and song and silence
there we will worship God by our care for others.

467 Against all their expectations,
it was the women who first encountered the risen Christ,
and, rushing to tell the other disciples,
became the first missionaries.
Never assume that God will do the expected.
It may be that in this coming week,
I, or you, will be called to mission.
Pray that this act of worship will give us resources for the task.

468
Mission advertises God's love;
it declares all we have experienced through faith;
it calls us to reach the maturity we see in Jesus;
it aims to change people and the way they live;
it involves being open to the influence of others;
it is a commitment to a just society;
it seeks to further God's purpose in every aspect of life;
it respects the integrity of creation;
it calls people to commit themselves to Jesus Christ;
and is a perpetual challenge to reform the Church.

469
It is the vocation of every Christian to be a priest:
to speak of the things of God,
and draw others into the presence of God;
to commend an ungodly world to the compassion of God,
and pray for those who never speak to God;
to mediate by word and love the forgiveness of God,
and live and work through the power of the Son of God.

470
As the body depends on all its limbs
and none are derided, none ignored,
so we live in the life of the Church:
all needing each one, each one needing all.
God so made us.
The Son of God so called us.
The Spirit of God so inspires us.
Let our worship so enable us.

471
We are not here simply by our own choosing,
we are here by Christ's calling.
Let all we do and say, sing and think this day
be faithful to his leading.

472
It is not for us to define the day,
nor yet for us to prescribe the way,
but Christ will come again
and we shall be called to proclaim the word
in such a way
that it will change and renew the world.

based on words of **Dietrich Bonhoeffer**

473   Come, Holy Spirit, in power and love.
Come, Holy Spirit, in gentleness and blessing.
Come, Holy Spirit, in challenge and renewal.
Take and use this time of worship
to renew the Father's gifts in us
and make us his messengers.

474   God and Father of our Lord Jesus Christ,
you have called us into your service
to make your purpose known,
and to proclaim the name of Jesus Christ.
We are afraid:
     like Moses, we wish you had called someone else,
     like Jeremiah, we are tongue-tied,
     like Jonah, we're tempted to pretend we haven't heard properly.
But still your call persists:
     like Peter, we're slow on the uptake,
     like James and John, we wonder what's in it for us,
     like Paul, we're afraid to change our life's direction.
In your mercy, calling and patient God,
do not give up on us, stay with us,
and make us partners in the building of your kingdom.

475   Summoning God, ever calling, ever ready to bless,
we confess that we are people with limits.
We find it difficult to see beyond our own small experience;
     we lack the imagination to think the big thoughts,
     we bring our stereotyped ideas to the cause of mission,
     we are stuck in our own history, suspicious of the insights of others.
But you are without limits;
     you break the moulds of the past to teach us something new,
     you treat barriers as stepping stones,
     valleys are there to be bridged, mountains to be crossed,
     fluent in every language, at home in every culture –
         you meet every one where they live.
We, who drag our feet in the mission task, look to you
to lift us up, renew our purpose,
and release the little we have
to the glorious work of your kingdom.

476 To each of us, generous God, you have given gifts,
to make us ministers of your gospel.
None of us are left out; each of us is summoned to service.
We give thanks:
> for those who preach the Word and preside at the Sacraments,
> for *elders/deacons/councillors/stewards*,
> for those who work with children and young people,
> for those who care for our buildings and finance.

We rejoice in those who remind us of good traditions,
> and those who are prophetic for the future,

for those who take a visible role in the church,
> and those who faithfully serve in quiet places,

for children who offer the depths of their short experience,
> and those who through long years have sustained a childlike faith,

for those who come reminding us of the pain of the world,
> and those who come on the wings of celebration and joy.

Gift-giving God, we bring all that you have given us
and through worship and self-giving, offer them afresh to you,
as a sacrifice of praise and thanksgiving.

477 Accepting God, we give you thanks and praise,
for you take us as we are,
and use the gifts that are ready to our hands;
> childhood fashioned our natural talents,
> our working life has moulded our ability,
> family life has developed new resources,
> our hobbies and leisure have crafted our skills,

and what all these things have made us,
you are pleased to use in the life of your church
and the work of the gospel.

Challenging God, our thanks and praise is increased,
for you point us to what we might become;
> you draw out from us gifts we never thought we had,
> you excite us to look beyond our present horizon,
> the gospel opens our eyes to new possibilities of service,
> in the silence you enlarge our vision,
> and in the words of others, we hear you speak.

Take what we are, loving God,
take our growing discipleship,
take what you are making us,
and use all, in the mission and ministry of your Church.

478 Gracious God, present in every place,
lovingly, you flung the gospel wide,
rejoiced as it took root, alike in barren desert and in lush green field;
with joy you see it take fresh life in city, town, and village life,
climb high-rise steps, and walk the corridors of power.

And we rejoice,
that Paul the Jew expressed the truth in Gentile terms;
that Hildegard could sing it in her cell;
that Julian nurtured it where sacred cloister met the noisy world;
that Francis saw its richness in his poverty;
that Lindisfarne became its island home;
that Iona kept a rugged faith alive.

And can it still be true?
Do gospel roots still reach out
to find a home, alike in praying church and alien world,
in city centre and suburban road,
in town hall, council chamber, factory floor,
and every place where people meet?

Grant, eternal God,
that as once your Word became incarnate
in living flesh and breathing heart,
present in synagogue and temple,
Nazareth home and lakeside conversation,
manger bed and lonely cross,
so we may see you in our present time
and know you where we live.

First printed in *Called to be Saints*, the CTBI Lent Book 2002

479 Eternal God, you hold in love those who know you,
and those who do not.
Lord Jesus Christ, you are a friend to those who own your name,
and those who ignore you.
Holy Spirit of God, you work in full view of our wondering eyes,
and where we are blind to your action.
We who know your love, your friendship and your work,
now recommit ourselves,
to declare your love, proclaim your friendship to the people we meet,
so that the day may come when everyone in every place
shouts your name with joy and delight.

480 Dear God, revealed in Jesus Christ as love beyond measure,
we give thanks for those who have heard the gospel not only by word of
    mouth
but in communities of such love and care
that action and word have matched each other in commending Christ.

Dear God, shown in Jesus Christ as ultimate compassion,
we confess that some have heard of you
in hard and narrow ways that turned your gospel into a slogan,
and your gifts into impossible demands.

Dear God, declared in Jesus, as self-giving grace,
we pray for those so damaged by life that gospel seems a fantasy,
those so brought up to fear that openness seems dangerous,
and those so trained to hate that love appears as weakness.

Dear God, proclaimed by Jesus as the eternal father,
hold all these, your children, in your loving embrace,
let your gospel grace be seen, felt, and known by them all.

481 We are called to be saints in the community of God.
    Silence
Lord, in the place where you have set us,
    Response **help us truly to be your people.**
We are called to be saints in our workplace.
    Silence
Lord, in the place where you have set us,
    Response **help us truly to be your people.**
We are called to be saints in our leisure.
    Silence
Lord, in the place where you have set us,
    Response **help us truly to be your people.**
We are called to be saints in our churches.
    Silence
Lord, in the place where you have set us,
    Response **help us truly to be your people.**
We are called to be saints in our relationships with each other.
    Silence
Lord, in the place where you have set us,
    Response **help us truly to be your people.**
We are called to be saints in our homes.
    Silence
Lord, in the place where you have set us,
    Response **help us truly to be your people.**

First printed in *Called to be Saints*, the CTBI Lent Book 2002

482 *And also the twenty-first century…?*

Thousands are craving for a basis of belief which shall rest not on tradition or authority or historical evidence but on the ascertainable facts of human experience; the mystics guide us to the perennial fresh springs of religion and present it to us as a living and active force. It is to the guidance of the Spirit that the church of the twentieth century must commit itself for guidance, welcoming from every quarter the testimony of those whose hearts God has touched.

R W Inge (1860–1954)

483 *The first Sunday School*

When they reached a certain place, the elder of the two said, 'Pause here': and so saying he uncovered his brow, closed his eyes, and stood for a moment in silent prayer. That place was the site of the first Sabbath School, and that elder man was Robert Raikes, its founder. He paused on the spot, and that silent prayer ascended to the ears of the crucified Christ, and the tears rolled down his cheeks as he said to his friend, 'This is the spot on which I stood when I saw the destitution of the children, and the desecration of the Sabbath by the inhabitants of the town; and I asked, "Can nothing be done?" and a voice answered, "Try", and I did try, and see what God hath wrought! I can never pass by the spot where the word "try" came so powerfully into my mind without lifting up my hands and heart to heaven in gratitude to God for having put such a thought into my heart.'

J Stratford
From *Life of Robert Raikes*

484 *Windows*

Lord, how can man preach thy eternal word?
   He is a brittle crazy glass:
Yet in thy temple thou dost him afford
    This glorious and transcendent place,
    To be a window, through thy grace.

But when thou dost anneal in glass thy story,
   Making thy life to shine within
The holy preachers; then the light and glory
    More reverend grows, and more doth win:
    Which else shows waterish, bleak, and thin.

Doctrine and life, colours and light, in one
   When they combine and mingle, bring
A strong regard and awe: but speech alone
    Doth vanish like a flaring thing,
    And in the ear, not conscience ring.

George Herbert

485 *Prevented for a purpose*

...forbidden by the Holy Spirit to speak the word in Asia.
Door after door
had been shut in their faces,
move after move frustrated,
until at last they reached the coast;
journey's end
and nothing accomplished.

Surely the devil had been at work,
unless ...
unless it was God's way of saying
there was a different enterprise
waiting,
something which so far
hadn't even entered their thoughts.

Then came the dream –
a man of Macedonia!
Paul woke
and acted.
Arrangements quickly made
they set sail
and thus –
the Gospel entered Europe!

Edmund Banyard
From *Heaven and Charing Cross*

486 *Groundwork for mission*

He touched a leper and,
breaking the taboo of misunderstood illness,
widened the circle of community.

He spoke to a woman alone and,
shattering the myth of superiority,
healed the pain of gender prejudice.

He welcomed children and,
leaping the divide of age,
acknowledged the faith of young believers.

He praised Samaritans, Romans and,
defying iron curtains,
built a roadway into every nation.

What next?

487 *The sower*

We too, Lord, would learn from the sower.
Help us to do faithfully
whatever work is put into our hands.
Help us to accept that there will be
frustrations and disappointments,
that some of our efforts
are sure to be wasted
and that there will be days
when we feel so low
that we are tempted to give up altogether.
When such times come,
turn our thoughts, we pray,
to the difficulties with which you contended,
the sorrows and disappointments you faced
and the pain you bore,
that we,
with men and women the world over,
might come to know
life in all its fullness.

Edmund Banyard
From *Heaven and Charing Cross*

488 *Accepted openly*

Labelled:
family, place, school,
generation,
denomination;
sorted and settled,
placed comfortably
where I should be,
so that you can deal with me.

Labelled:
job (or not), income, class,
ethnic group,
gender specific,
gathered and grasped;
classified clearly
for what I am,
so that you need not fear me.

Loved:
good, bad, ordinary;
every day,
all the way,
for who I am;
accepted openly,
forgiven freely
so that you can feel that we
are all children of God.

Chris Warner

489

Without words

Written following the road death of an eight-year-old boy

Shivering,
    I tie my offerings
        to bent railings.

'He's a big boy now,'
    they'd told her,
        'let him walk to school
            on his own.'

I pull limp cellophane

    to guard my card
        from wind and rain…

        …this is the spot.

What do I write
    to that ravaged mother
        I've never met?
            Not a lot.

My sympathy
    is unprepared,
        raw and rough –

flowers
    in sodden paper
        say some more –
            yet not enough.

Margaret Connor

Ritualised welcome

490

Released from Sunday duties, a sabbatical gave me the opportunity to share worship in other churches. Incidentally, I discovered how newcomers are greeted. One church stands out. For over five minutes the congregation roamed around the church 'giving the peace' to each other. They did not exclude me; twenty or so people shook my hand. 'The peace of the Lord be with you', each one said. I'm sure they meant it. Yet I had entered the church, and I left it after the service, without a single person speaking to me except within the opportunity provided by 'the peace'. There was no conversation, no enquiry. Whether I was new to the district, or had come to celebrate a joy, or out of desperate need, was left unasked by priest or people. The acknowledgment of another believer – indeed of another human being – had become ossified in liturgical routine.

491   *Silence in the Suburbs*

Written on December 25ᵗʰ 1998 four months after my younger son received the diagnosis that he is HIV positive.

I have come to Christmas Eve Communion
in an unfamiliar, suburban church.
Midnight strikes.
The minister invites us to share the peace
and offer Christmas greetings
to our neighbours in the pew.
Handshakes are exchanged.
In response to polite enquiries I say,
'I'm visiting my son who is ill.'
No one encourages me to say more.
They do not even ask my name.
I sink into silence relieved that he is not here.
The bread and wine are served.
I wonder if they will suffice
to feed my hunger for comfort and support,
to slake my spiritual thirst.
Am I the only needy stranger in their midst tonight?
What other unspoken pain stays unreleased?
I introduce myself to the minister at the door.
I say where I have come from.
I try again to say why I am here.
But his cursory handshake
does not invite deeper conversation
so I leave as I came, hungry and thirsty,
lost and alone,
ashamed of my silence,
ashamed of my church,
struggling to hold on to my faith,
battling to believe
that beyond this empty celebration,
the God whose love became flesh and blood
has heard my silent cries and understood.

Jean Mortimer

492 *Moving out*

Evangelisation is not a call to restore Christendom, a kind of solid, well-integrated, cultural complex, directed and dominated by the Church. It is not an activity set in motion because the church is endangered, a nervous activity to save the remnants of a time now irrevocably past. It is not a winning back of those people who have become a prey to sin in such a way that the organised church no longer reaches them.

Evangelisation is not propaganda. Propaganda leaves nothing to the Spirit, but pre-determines the outcome down to the last detail; its essential character is a lack of expectant hope and an absence of due humility. Propaganda seeks to make exact copies. It attempts to make man in the image and likeness of the propagandist. Quite the opposite of propaganda is evangelisation, filled with hope, which means moving forward in a world with unlimited possibilities, in which we won't be surprised if something unforeseen happens.

Evangelisation is not proselytism. Proselytism is centripetal. It is a movement inward. People are invited to come to the centre where salvation is localised. In order to become a participant of salvation, they will have to join a group that mediates redemption, i.e., emigrate completely from all other life relationships. Evangelisation is centrifugal. It leaves Jerusalem and is on its way to the ends of the earth and the end of time. To join means here; to join the journey away from the centre – a light for the Gentiles, which goes forth towards the people, seeking them out and taking them by surprise in their darkness.

The source of evangelisation and its necessity and urgency come directly from the gospel.

J C Hoekendijk
Source unknown

493 *At least start with what you've got!*

Olivier Messiaen, imprisoned by the Nazis, wrote his *Quatuor pour la Fin du Temps* (Quartet for the End of Time) in 1940 and in response to reading Revelation 10.5ff. He and his contemporaries might well have thought they were approaching an apocalyptic ending. Europe was again in turmoil as Nazi Germany seized control of country after country and demonstrated its seemingly diabolic power. As a member of the French forces Messiaen was imprisoned in Silesia in wretched circumstances. The urge to compose remained and he produced the quartet for the unusual combination of violin, cello, clarinet, and piano – the only instruments available to him from fellow prisoners. He himself played a clapped-out piano. It was a fitting combination of instruments for an ad hoc group of players who were heralding the end of Time. The piece remains a fitting memorial to a composer who could call on whatever range of instruments he might choose; using whatever accident or chance had given him.

When the times are desperate, creativity does not wait for perfect resources.

Summarised from various sources

494 *Wives and mothers*

The gauntlet was thrown down when the dean of London's St. Paul's Cathedral, Alan Webster, invited Elizabeth (Canham) to (celebrate the Eucharist) in the living room of the deanery for the London leaders of the Movement for the Ordination of Women, one of whom was Alan Webster's wife. That invitation got the attention of the bishop of London, the Right Reverend Graham Leonard, probably the most reactionary bishop in England. When he was not able to prevent the celebration of this Eucharist, his rhetoric became so excessive and his prejudice so obvious that he actually helped our cause. He attacked his dean, Elizabeth Canham, and me. He demanded that I 'discipline Miss Canham.' I do not quite know what he expected me to do, but I was amused by his archaic language. When Bishop Leonard announced in the mid-1980s that 'women could not be priests in the Anglican Communion because God had created them just to be wives and mothers,' I howled with delight. 'These words,' I said in a prepared statement, 'are spoken by the bishop of London in a land where Elizabeth II sits on the throne and where Margaret Thatcher runs the government. Perhaps the bishop of London does not know either what country he is living in or in what century.'

John Shelby Spong
From *Here I stand*
Reprinted by permission of WaterfrontMedia. (See index of copyrights)

495 *A few exceptions?*

My Dear Sister,
I think the strength of the cause rests there – on your having an extraordinary call. So I am persuaded has every one of our lay preachers; otherwise I could not countenance his preaching at all. It is plain to me that the whole work of God termed Methodism is an extraordinary dispensation of His providence. Therefore I do not wonder if several things occur which do not fall under the ordinary rules of discipline. St. Paul's rule was, 'I permit not a woman to speak in the congregation.' Yet in extraordinary cases he made a few exceptions; at Corinth in particular.

I am, my dear sister,
Your affectionate brother,

John

John Wesley
in a letter to his sister, seeking guidance on her call to preach

496
Reverenda

'Who will go for Us,
Who shall We send?'
Then I responded,
Lord, here am I,
Send me.

But when I came to his people
Commissioned with his word
They would not hear me
Because I am a woman.
Must I go back
And tell God he was wrong?

W S Beattie

497
Jenny's Ordination

She's done it
this time –
she really has
and no mistake!

After the years
of pussy-footing,
backward turning,
pit edge clinging,
'No, I never …'

She's done it!

But in the end –
or rather
the beginning –
did she really
jump
or was she
pushed?

There was a Voice
behind her –
chuckling!

Margaret Connor

498 *A case for atheism?*

Any committed believer in God with a devout wish to share the knowledge of God must recognize that one of the most persistent obstacles to evangelism is the behaviour of those of us who claim to worship him. When religious believers focus on their own defence they shut God up in religious beliefs. 'God' becomes the object of cults that religious people pursue. Religion is thus reduced to a human pursuit to be studied by sociologists; just one more influential, sometimes psychologically useful but as often damaging, pursuit of socialized human beings.

I have come to see that the case for atheism is very strong. However, it strikes me that a truly rigorous atheism is as difficult to pursue as is a wholehearted determination to seek the truth and purpose of the living God. If atheism is a correct response to the world and its possibilities, then we have to face the actual limitations of our human resources, both shared and individual. The human race has shown a persistent tendency to imagine and invent and so claim to have discovered 'God'. If we truly are all that there is, how are we to prevent ourselves imagining, inventing and so claiming to discover secular substitutes for God, like the invisible hand of economic activity, or the healing hand of science and medicine, or the deceptive, lavish hand of money-prosperity? Perhaps the rigorous practice of atheism would be the best way to clear our minds and apply ourselves to maximizing the potential of human living. Perhaps the divertimentos of religion keep us whistling in the dark, preventing us from making the most of what light, liberty, space and vision are available to us.

It is my considered decision not to believe this. But I am very much aware that the option of atheism is a very real possibility. I need to explore, and express for myself, the understanding to which my experiment and pilgrimage of faith has brought me, namely that the goodness of God pointed to and lived out by Jesus is about the resources for being human which are open to us all.

David E Jenkins, former Bishop of Durham
From *The Calling of a Cuckoo*

499 *We are what we build*

In his most telling observation about architecture, Winston Churchill told the House of Commons, 'We shape our buildings, and afterwards our buildings shape us.' His argument was that the particular character of British democracy was directly influenced by the environment in which political debate took place. He insisted that the new chamber (of the House of Commons) should be 'oblong and not semi-circular.'..... His argument was that the particular character of British democracy was directly influenced by the environment in which political debate took place. 'We attach immense importance to the survival of parliamentary democracy. In this country it is one of our war aims. We wish to see our Parliament a strong, easy, flexible instrument of free debate. For this purpose, a small chamber and a sense of intimacy are indispensable.'

Scarcely a voice was raised in disagreement. Even normally rebellious Labour MPs spoke of the old House of Commons having been more than stone, a 'sentient place'. Expressing a different perspective which continues to find voice to this day, Nancy Astor, the first woman to take her seat in the House of Commons, disagreed. Like many female MPs since, she argued that having the place arranged with benches of politicians facing each other 'almost like dogs on a leash' inevitably made for confrontation. She wanted a circular chamber. No one supported her.

...And so it was that, nine years after the House of Commons chamber had been destroyed by enemy action, in 1950 MPs took possession of a Gothic replica, a pastiche of a pastiche, homage to a homage.

Jeremy Paxman
From *The Political Animal*

500 *Christian architecture*

The cultural assumptions of European missionaries and empire-builders become obvious when we see a great church in one of the old British or French colonies in the tropics. The visitor leaves the bright sunshine to enter into a dark Gothic chamber, which seems quite inappropriate for the local climate and environment. Still, Victorian builders knew in their hearts that a 'religious' building had to follow certain cultural norms, and that meant using the Gothic styles that mimicked the brooding forests of medieval northern Europe Its enthusiasts described the Gothic style simply as 'Christian architecture.' Presumably if the course of Christian history had run differently, then other societies would have succeeded in spreading their distinctive cultural visions across the world, with equal confidence that these too were the only fit vessels for conveying Christian truth. To take an outlandish example, if Central America had become an early Christian heartland, then our religious literature and architecture would be full of imagery that used jaguars rather than lions.

Philip Jenkins
From *The Next Christendom*

501 *Mission – open and local*

To be speakers of a faith requires that we also listen to those whose faith is different but just as sincere. We cannot rule out of theology the possibility that God has spoken 'in many and varied ways' through the prophets of other faiths, and to them we must be attentive. Such readiness to listen in no way lessens the commission to declare 'the wonderful works of God' in Jesus Christ but it does determine the attitude of heart in which we dare to proclaim Christ as Lord. Missionaries are not proprietors of the gospel but servants of the great mystery which is God in human life, offering his sacrificial love to all. It is surely beyond human vision to know how God will fulfil his secret purpose ... that the universe, everything in heaven and on earth, might be brought into a unity in Christ (Ephesians 1.9–10). We cannot presume that the expanding empire model, a larger Christendom, is the necessary pattern in the mind of God.

For there is another dimension becoming more and more important, the reality of the local church as the critical point for the great universals of the gospel. How we define 'local' depends on our church tradition. For some it means the national or ethnic church, for some the diocese, for others the congregation which meets to worship. But if mission is to be the cause for which the church exists, then it is in the local church that this will be evident.

Bernard Thorogood
From *Gales of Change*, the story of the London Missionary Society

502 *Christianity – global appeal*

It is one thing to talk about missionary successes and numbers, but quite another to determine the nature of the religious changes involved. The act of joining a church or sect is not necessarily the same as the internal process of conversion. While we can more or less measure the numbers declaring themselves Christian, the inner dynamics of religious change do not lend themselves to counting of any kind. Missions succeeded for different reasons in different times and places, and some new churches planted much deeper roots than others. Yet many of these churches enjoyed remarkable success, to a degree that is impossible to understand if the new Christians were responding only out of fear or envy of the imperial conquerors. Amazing as it may appear to a blasé West, Christianity exercises an overwhelming global appeal, which shows not the slightest sign of waning.

Philip Jenkins
From *The Next Christendom*

503 *Closed eyes*

'When the missionaries came to Africa they had the Bible and we had the land. They said "Let us pray." We closed our eyes. When we opened them we had the Bible and they had
the land.'

Variously attributed to **Jomo Kenyatta** and **Archbishop Desmond Tutu**

504 *Core and Culture*

...just what are the core beliefs of Christianity, and what are cultural accidents? To take an obvious example from the modern West, is the ancient prohibition against women clergy a core belief or a cultural prejudice? What about ordaining homosexual clergy? The debate over substance and accidents goes back to the very origins of Christianity. The biblical book of Acts records the furious debate over whether Gentile converts were required to accept the rules of Judaism, complete with circumcision and dietary laws. Ultimately, the church, or at least the majority party, concluded that these practices were not essential to the faith. In varying forms, these issues have echoed through the history of Christianity, and have surfaced on virtually every occasion when churches have come into contact with some hitherto unfamiliar society. We recall the Chinese Rites controversy of the seventeenth century. In Victorian southern Africa, the missionary bishop J. W. Colenso refused to order his Christian converts to renounce polygamy, since it was so obviously an integral part of their African culture (and the practice deterred adultery). Naturally, Colenso's attitude was furiously denounced, but the controversies remain unresolved. As Andrew Walls has remarked, 'This question is alive for Africans just as it was for Greek converts in the ancient Hellenistic world.

Do we have to reject our entire history and culture when we become Christians?

Philip Jenkins
From *The Next Christendom*

Justice and Peace

a Sing to God, sing praises to his name; his name is the Lord – be exultant before him. Father of orphans and protector of widows is God in his holy habitation. God gives the desolate a home to live in; he leads out the prisoners to prosperity, but the rebellious live in a parched land.

from Psalm 68:4–6

b Steadfast love and faithfulness will meet; righteousness and peace will kiss each other. Faithfulness will spring up from the ground, and righteousness will look down from the sky. The Lord will give what is good. *Psalm 85:10–12a*

c Who is like the Lord our God? He raises the poor from the dust, and lifts the needy from the ash heap, to make them sit with princes. *from Psalm 113:5–8*

d The Lord shall judge between the nations, and shall arbitrate for many peoples; they shall beat their swords into ploughshares, and their spears into pruning hooks; nation shall not lift up sword against nation, neither shall they learn war any more. *Isaiah 2:4*

e Arise, cry out in the night. Pour out your heart like water before the presence of the Lord! Lift your hands to him for the lives of your children, who faint for hunger at the head of every street. *from Lamentations 2:19*

f The Lord says: Take away from me the noise of your songs; I will not listen to the melody of your harps. But let justice roll down like waters, and righteousness like an ever-flowing stream. *Amos 5:23–24*

g With what shall I come before the Lord, and bow myself before God on high? He has told you, O mortal, what is good; and what does the Lord require of you but to do justice, and to love kindness, and to walk humbly with your God? *from Micah 6:6–8*

h Jesus said: 'You shall love the Lord your God with all your heart, and with all your soul, and with all your mind.' This is the greatest and first commandment. And a second is like it: 'You shall love your neighbour as yourself.' *Matthew 22:36–39*

i 'Come, you that are blessed by my Father, inherit the kingdom prepared for you from the foundation of the world; for I was hungry and you gave me food, I was thirsty and you gave me something to drink, I was a stranger and you welcomed me, I was naked and you gave me clothing, I was sick and you took care of me, I was in prison and you visited me.' *Matthew 25:34b–36*

j The Mighty One has scattered the proud in the thoughts of their hearts. He has brought down the powerful from their thrones, and lifted up the lowly; he has filled the hungry with good things, and sent the rich away empty. *from Luke 1:49–53*

k Let every person be subject to the governing authorities; for there is no authority except from God, and those authorities that exist have been instituted by God. *Romans 13:1*

l We who are strong ought to put up with the failings of the weak, and not to please ourselves. Each of us must please our neighbour for the good purpose of building up the neighbour. *Romans 15:1–2*

505 Praise God with heart and voice,
but as we praise, remember the cry of pain:
from the child who has known nothing but hunger from birth,
from the family in over-crowded accommodation,
from the parents who lack the means to care for their children,
and as you praise, pray:
for justice in an unjust world,
and peace in a war-torn world.

506 We are a people at war –
with hunger in a world of plenty,
with sickness in a world of advancing knowledge,
with terror in a world encircled by the love of God,
with hatred in a world that could enthrone love.
No truce, no treaty, until this holy war is won,
and the kingdom of God declared.

507 What kind of a world will our children think we left them,
and our children's children,
and the children of our children's children?
Will they praise us that, despite the odds,
– we left this globe intact;
will they thank us that, though with pain,
– we sowed the seeds of lasting peace;
will they be grateful that, if with sacrifice,
– we made the world a fairer place?
If so, it will be because
thoughtfulness and prayer,
planning and sustained hope,
have come together in our worship of God.

508 I am here, says Christ,
where little children snatch a living amongst the rubbish piles.
I am here, he says,
where honest workers look for disappearing jobs.
I am here, says Christ,
where labourers toil for subsistence wages.
I am here, he says,
where women walk for miles to find water for their families;
and I am here – watching, waiting, pleading, longing,
in the worship of my people.

509
Let compassion walk hand in hand with justice;
let righteousness kiss peace;
let imagination embrace the rigour of careful planning;
let steadfastness congratulate spontaneity.
Let all bring their gifts and pour them before God,
as heavenly resources for an earthly kingdom.

510
When we hear that there will always be poverty,
    we look for the politics of change;
when we hear that some will always be brighter than others,
    we look for equal opportunities in education;
when we are told of the problems of food distribution,
    we look for the will to harness modern skills and technology;
when we are told that some people simply live in unproductive places,
    we affirm that the good earth yields enough for all.

511
Jesus said, 'My peace I give to you.'
Peace is a gift,
    and a task to wrestle with.
Peace is a goal for the future,
    and a challenge for this day, this hour.
Peace is concord across the nations,
    and the way we live with our next door neighbour.
Peace is a relationship with others,
    and the attitude of our inner heart.

512
Unless there are those who dream dreams,
unless there are those who think the impossible,
unless there are those ready to be scorned as romantics,
unless there are those with ambitions beyond present realities,
    hope will never be formed,
    seeds will never be sown,
        vision will fade,
        the status quo will drop firm anchor,
and the kingdom of God will be stillborn.

513
Weep for this world; that is allowed,
feel anger if you must; that is understandable,
but continue to pray; that is imperative,
and know that God is working his purpose out.

514
Coming to you, Father and God,
we bring our hopes and fears,
our conviction and unease,
for the world in which we live.
We affirm our belief
    that you are the father of all,
    that your compassion is like that of a mother,
    that all creation lies within your care,
    and every living person has been fashioned by your love.
From the beginning you stood above and yet within all nations,
all cultures, every lifestyle,
and at the end,
you remain all in all,
and all to all.

515
Father, in all the church,
in every place,
your people sing your praise.
East and west, north and south,
black, white and brown, the old and young,
create a harmony of song.
So, here in this place,
and at this time,
we join the universal chorus:
    praise and thanksgiving to you,
    Father of all peoples.

516
Out of a broken world,
healing Christ, we come;
re-member us, and heal our separation.

From fractured homes and uneasy relationships,
child of Nazareth, we come;
re-member us, and restore the unity that only love can bring.

Within churches divided by false traditions,
head of the Church, we come;
re-member us, and reveal the path to unity in diversity.

Separated from you by sin and fault,
Saviour, we come;
re-member us, and by forgiving love,
bring us back again to where we belong.

517

Father, forgive us:
for we so readily divide your one human family into neat groups,
tidily sorted with convenient labels.
We forget that you are father-like to us all,
mother-like in your unconditional love.

Forgive us:
    the North protects itself from the poverty of the South,
    black and white approach each other with suspicious fear,
    nation is set against nation, faith against faith.

Forgive us:
    we use religion as a weapon,
    culture as a shield,
    and build dividing walls that deny the rich variety of human experience.

Help us to hear the voice of your Son
    as he praises the goodness of a Samaritan traveller,
    shows compassion to a Roman soldier,
    invites himself into the home of a tax-gatherer,
    receives the blessing of a prostitute,
    takes children on his knee,
and thus breaks down the walls that divide;
the scorn that hurts.

In Christ's name we affirm:
    we are all members of one family,
    all women are our sisters, and men our brothers,
    we are parents to all children, children to all parents,
    we are kinsfolk to every race,
and we will work and pray and serve,
until the unity you gave us at the beginning,
and have promised for the end,
is fulfilled in us all.

518

As the virus courses through the whole body,
so, we acknowledge that the greed of one nation harms another.
As ripples run to the edge of the pool,
so, we acknowledge that the avarice of one nation spells loss elsewhere.
As the incoming tide erodes the coastline,
so, we acknowledge that the rising affluence of one nation is poverty for
others.
    And this we also know,
    that love, compassion, justice and fairness can sweep into every corner of
        the earth.
    So be it, Lord, so be it.

519

For this we thank you, dear God:
when the force of might has trampled the land,
    your gentleness still rules;
        hard-pressed but never defeated.
When anger and hatred have done their worst,
    your kindness takes up the broken pieces;
        ready to remake love.
When an unseeing regime turns a blind eye to human need,
    your gentle spirit is still active;
        in comfort, resilience and challenge.
When evil and oppression seem to have won the day,
    your love springs out afresh;
        to become a new dawning, a resurrection.
Your yoke is easy,
your burdens are lightened by hope,
and your strength is ever matched with mercy.
Thanks be to God!

520

For the word of peace spoken in the time of war,
and the silent prayer whispered in turmoil;
    thanks be to God.
For the offer of help in the desperation of hunger,
and the drilling of wells in the arid desert;
    thanks be to God.
For the planting of trees in the dangers of erosion,
and the terracing of hillsides in the fear of collapse;
    thanks be to God.
For the creation of new industry in the loss of employment,
and the building of partnership in the life of a ravaged village;
    thanks be to God.
For the insistence of just wages for workers in field and in factory,
and the growth of fair trade in supermarkets and shops;
    thanks be to God.
For the co-operation of nations in the face of calamity,
and the planning of agencies in the confusion of famine;
    thanks be to God.
For the gifts to strangers in the outreach of compassion,
and the love shown to those the giver will never meet;
    thanks be to God.
For the work of the Spirit in the hearts of believers,
and the impulse to give as a sign of love;
    thanks be to God.

521

God of Abraham,
  who left his own country to form a nation to honour you,
  make us an influence for good in our nation and community.
God of Moses,
  who, burning with the fire of justice, liberated his people,
  and led them through pain and uncertainty to a promised land,
  give us a vision of a nation and a world built on justice and peace.
God of Ruth,
  who, bidden by duty, love and necessity, made her home in an alien land,
  give us a wider sympathy with those who seek their home amongst us.
God of Elijah,
  who, driven into a corner, remained faithful,
  give strength and courage to those who are persecuted for truth's sake.
God of Amos,
  who, in a time of injustice, became a voice for the voiceless,
  give us a prophetic voice against oppression,
  and a generous response to poverty
  in our own time and place.
God the Son,
  who, faced by a religion grown rigid and the oppression of a
     conquering army,
  maintained integrity and faith,
  held love and power as one,
  keep us faithful in our discipleship.

From *Table Talk*

522

God of the poor, you are my God,
  make me more generous, and ready to share my riches;
God of the man tortured by his oppressors, you are my God,
  make me dissatisfied until all can share my freedom;
God of the woman whose pantry is bare against her infant's cry, you are
     my God,
  make me more liberal in my giving;
God of the fugitive and the refugee, you are my God,
  help me by prayer and protest to seek the security of others;
God of justice and peace, in whose kingdom all are one
prompt me to care,
and stir me to action.

523
Creator God,
give us a heart for simple things:
    love and laughter,
    bread and wine,
    tales and dreams.
Fill our lives
with green and growing hope.
Make us a people of justice
whose song is Alleluia
and whose name breathes love.

from **South Africa**
Source unknown

524
Lord, your world is one world;
    how could it be other since you are one God?
Your world is diverse and varied;
    how could it be other since you are so great?
Help us to live creatively
    with unity and diversity,
    conviction and tolerance,
    harmony and difference,
    concord and honest disagreement.
In dialogue with others,
help us to search for your truth
which, though beyond us,
yet holds us together.

525
Loving God,
you uphold the hungry,
you are a shelter to the homeless,
you enrich the poor,
you are a refuge to the vulnerable.

Angry God,
you condemn the greed that feeds off others' hunger,
you rebuke the neglect that fails to house the needy,
you denounce the selfish affluence that breeds poverty,
you reproach ill-used power that patronises or oppresses.

Active God,
you excite us to help, you inspire us to generosity,
you make politics a tool for justice,
and use both our tears and our zeal in the purpose of your kingdom.

526

In the midst of hunger and war
we celebrate the promise of plenty and peace.
In the midst of oppression and tyranny
we celebrate the promise of service and freedom.
In the midst of doubt and despair
we celebrate the promise of faith and hope.
In the midst of fear and betrayal
we celebrate the promise of joy and loyalty.
In the midst of hatred and death
we celebrate the promise of love and life.
In the midst of sin and decay
we celebrate the promise of salvation and renewal.
In the midst of death on every side
we celebrate the promise of the living Christ.

527

As a sign for the present time and promise for the future
we pray for the children of the world:

For children born into happy families, loved and cared for from their birth,
provided with wholesome food, kept in caring relationships,
and surrounded by constant security:
To these we commit ourselves afresh with loving care.

For children born into poverty,
for children forced to become soldiers,
for children frightened by domestic violence or warring nations,
for homeless children, and those forced to flee their homes:
To these we commit ourselves afresh with loving care.

For children who from birth need special care and support,
for children whose minds are never stretched, or imaginations ever
curbed,
for children whose abilities are never fully realised:
To these we commit ourselves afresh with loving care.

For the children of the world, their parents, families, teachers, and guides
To these we commit ourselves afresh with loving care.

528
Tilt the scales,
O God of the mustard seed:
That the poor shall see justice.

Share the feast,
O God of Eden's abundant garden:
That each crop may fetch a fair price.

Upset the tables,
O God of the upside-down kingdom:
That the least can benefit from their trade.

Open our eyes,
O God of life in all its fullness:
That we may learn to walk the way of your Son;
tilting, sharing, upsetting this world;
not satisfied,
until the products we bring to our table
give a better deal to all who hunger for one.

from the **Fairtrade Foundation**

529
All authority is yours, eternal God.
You hold the universe within your hands,
and each of us within your care;
you touch the heart of poor and rich alike,
you speak to the powerful and the powerless;
the rulers and the ruled are within your one family.

May the strong of the earth find renewed responsibility,
and the weak a sense of dignity;
may all human authorities recognise afresh
that yours is the final power.

Since each of us holds influence in the circle of life
then, as we stand in your presence in worship,
may our pride diminish,
our compassion increase,
and the good of all become our common aim.

530
God of justice and righteousness,
may the nations learn how to respect and honour each other;
   and please show the Church how to be an example.
God of love and compassion,
may the nations learn the ways of peace and concord
   and please show the Church how to be an example.
God of harmony and diversity,
may the nations seek unity and respect difference
   and please show the Church how to be an example.
God of forgiveness and understanding,
may the nations seek agreement and tolerance
   and please show the Church how to be an example.

531
Loving God, while we eat, others starve.
To labour the guilt we feel would do no good to them or us.
Instead, we pledge our continued giving and service
to hasten the day when none shall hunger
and all be satisfied.

532
If it should be, loving Father of us all,
that, all unknown to us,
our eating causes others to starve,
our plenty springs from others' poverty,
or our choice feeds off another's limitations,
then, Lord, forgive us, enlighten us,
and strengthen us to work
for fairer trade and just reward.

533
Father, for those we know who provide our food
out of love and kindness,
we give thanks.
And no less,
for those unknown
who work to earn and earn to live
and by their living, provide our food,
we give thanks.

534 *Where are the rebels?*

By the middle of this century, if the demographers are right, ten billion people will inhabit the earth, most of them in vast mega-cities where life is consumed by the struggle to control the planet's diminishing resources. If the earth's present population were envisaged as a village of one hundred people, 80 villagers would live in houses unfit for human habitation, 70 would be illiterate, 50 would be seriously malnourished, and six would own 60 per cent of the village's land and wealth. Thirty would be white but would consider the other 70 ethnic minorities. Ten of these 30 would be actively polluting the village on which the remaining 90 depend for their living. Where among them are the rebels, agitators and outsiders, the partisan recruits to the underground army of subversion whose loyalty is pledged to the republic of heaven, the City of God?

David Boulton
From *The Trouble with God*

535 *Earth and heaven*

A religion true to its nature must also be concerned about man's (sic) social conditions. Religion deals with both earth and heaven, both time and eternity. Religion operates not only on the vertical plane but also on the horizontal. It seeks not only to integrate men with God but to integrate men with men and each man with himself. This means, at bottom, that the Christian gospel is a two-way road. On the one hand, it seeks to change the souls of men and thereby unite them with God; on the other hand, it seeks to change the environmental conditions of men so that the soul will have a chance after it is changed. Any religion that professes to be concerned with the souls of men and is not concerned with the slums that damn them, the economic conditions that strangle them, and the social conditions that cripple them is a dry-as-dust religion. Such a religion is the kind the Marxists like to see – an opiate of the people.

Martin Luther King
From *Stride Towards Freedom*

536 *Guilt*

At the sight of the hunger, cold and degradation of thousands of people, I understood not with my mind or my heart but with my whole being, that the existence of tens of thousands of such people in Moscow – while I and thousands of others over-eat ourselves with beef-steaks and sturgeon and cover our horses and floors with cloth or carpet – no matter what all the learned men in the world may say about its necessity – is a crime, not committed once but constantly; and that I with my luxury not merely tolerate it but share in it.

Leo Nikolayevich Tolstoy (1828–1910)

537 *God of the poor*

> *The Lord is a God of knowledge,*
> *and by him actions are weighed.*
> *The bows of the mighty are broken,*
> *but the feeble gird on strength.*
> *Those who were full have hired themselves out for bread,*
> *but those who were hungry are fat with spoil.*
> *The barren has borne seven,*
> *but she who has many children is forlorn.*
> *The Lord kills and brings to life;*
> *he brings down to Sheol and raises up.*
> *The Lord makes poor and makes rich;*
> *he brings low, he also exalts.*
> *He raises up the poor from the dust;*
> *he lifts the needy from the ash heap,*
> *to make them sit with princes*
> *and inherit a seat of honour.* 1 Samuel 2:3b–8a

When Hannah (the source of whose story in 1 Samuel could belong anywhere between the eleventh and sixth centuries) prays for a child, she is addressing a very different Yahweh from the god so high and mighty that he wouldn't let Moses see even his angel in the burning bush. Hannah's god emerges for the first time as a god of the underdog. In Hannah's words, he breaks the bows of the mighty and gives strength to those that stumble; takes food from the well-satisfied and gives it to the hungry; makes the barren woman fruitful and leaves the mother of many forlorn; deals death and gives life. He 'raises up the poor out of the dust, and lifts up the beggar from the dunghill, to set them among princes, and to make them inherit the throne of glory ... for by strength shall no man prevail'. This doesn't sound at all like the God who wouldn't let the lame, the blind and the impotent anywhere near him at sacrifice time.

David Boulton
From *The Trouble with God*

538   *Peace is not…*

Peace is not the journey's end
but the journey's making.
It is the struggle to be free,
response to hunger's cry;
walking with the derelict
and hearing the oppressed.

Peace is not idling on still waters
but riding out the storm,
braving the wide ocean,
charting unknown seas,
throwing the life-line to the drowning
from the ship that foundered on the rocks.

Peace is not a dream of unrealised hopes;
it is running for the prize;
it is training to attain,
accepting the cost of following,
being ready for the sacrifice and pain;
it is the faith that dares to find a way.

Peace is not the false prophet's haven of rest.
It is the challenge of the Prince of peace;
the calling from the God of peace;
fruit of abiding in the Spirit of peace.
It is responding to the call of Christ
to announce good news, the gospel of peace.

John Johansen-Berg

539   *Gun*

What is a gun for?
A gun is for making things.
What does it make?
Orphans, widows,
   grief …

Steve Turner

540   *The sacrament of pain*

Much of the suffering in the world is needless:
The traumas and the sicknesses that still
Distort the lives of those in fear and hunger,
Or reel from violent deeds that maim and kill.

If we would find the will to share our riches –
Medicines, food and skills that bring relief –
We first must share the sorrow and the heartache,
And let our many joys be tinged with grief.

Christ came to bring us life in all its fullness;
Joy was his parting gift, and peace within –
And yet he said the only way to find them
Was through a Cross – Love's vict'ry over sin.

We know God's love for us when we discover
His willingness to share in our distress,
And when we share his children's tears and trials,
We're one with him and know his power to bless.

In broken bread and poured-out wine, Christ offers
To us, the Holy Sacrament of Pain,
That sharing in his life of selfless giving,
We may see his rainbow shining through the rain.

Beryl Chatfield

541   *The God Letters*

The Lord God says:
'Share your bread
with the hungry,
bring the homeless poor
into your house,
cover the naked.'

Dear Lord God,
We have got
new carpets,
so this will
not be possible.

Steve Turner

542 *Washing lines*

It's easy to pray for other people
so long as you keep it general.
String them out on a washing line of prayer:
    the poor… the needy… the homeless… neighbours… refugees…
      sick children.

You can be more specific and still get away with it:
    Africa… Afghanistan, not forgetting New York… Iraq, not
      forgetting Iran…
and as the political winds change direction – start a new washing line.

It's specifics that make prayer difficult:
    the mother nursing a near-dead baby,
      a child sitting in the dust and crying for his daddy,
        the family round an empty eating bowl,
  the refugees, faces hard-pressed against the bus window,
    the teenager brain-washed into a suicide bomber's jacket,
      the youngster scanning the unyielding poster at the Job Centre,
  the single mother – one tagging her skirt, one in the pram, and another on
    the way,
    the father denied sight of his son for eight years or more,
      the widow living in vulnerable loneliness,
        the elderly woman, black-eyed from the mugger's attack.
That's when prayers stop.
                  Or truly begin.

543 *Troublemakers?*

It happened in Belfast. I was outside our (school) bus trying to keep the
local boys away from the vehicle, but to no avail. Those kids were so excited
we had stopped in their street that they just swarmed all over it. Finally I
got upset and chased them away. Just then a woman on the sidewalk came
over. She apologised for the way the children had clamoured to get on
board, and said she understood why I felt I had to shoo them away. But then
she began to tell me about the kids: 'Those two boys over there, they're five
and eight. Their father just hanged himself two week ago. That one there
never had a father; and this little boy over here – his father's been in prison
for years. No one takes much notice of them.' It hit me right in the stomach.
Here I was, writing off a bunch of street urchins and treating them as
troublemakers, and they were actually victims of the worst neglect…

Johann Christoph Arnold
From *Endangered: your Child in a Hostile World*

544 *Liberty and personal freedom*

The only cohesive opposition to the march of capitalism in the 1840s and 1850s came from communism – or its watered-down equivalents – and Christianity. But – this is one of the central questions facing the men and women of the age – were they believable? Their allure explains how such strange alliances could have been formed against the relentlessness of the factory-owners – a Bible Christian such as Ashley, motivated by reading the Gospels, standing alongside radicals and socialists whose views of other matters he might deplore, in his campaign to limit the hours worked by women and children in the cotton mills.

It is a curious fact that the leader of the working men's cause in the House of Commons, until the Factory Act of 1850 finally did bring in the desired Ten Hours measure, was a high Tory aristocrat who believed in hierarchy, deference and the literal truth of every word of the Bible. His tireless campaigns to set up ragged schools for slum-dwellers, and to prick the conscience of laissez-faire economists, took over a decade.

In the first years of Victoria's reign, the coal flickering cheerfully in your grate would, as like as not, have been dragged through underground tunnels too small for a grown man by child workers as young as six. This was brought to an end in 1844, against the fiercest opposition from the big colliery proprietors, such as Lord Londonderry. It took a further three years to persuade liberals such as Macaulay, Palmerston or Russell so much as to consider limiting the hours worked by women and children to ten hours a day. With their blinkered view of what constituted 'liberty' these liberals felt that legislation interfered with the personal freedoms of workers. Most of the child workers in the mills were employed not by the mill-owners themselves but by adult male spinners who subcontracted work. To make laws about such private arrangements was, in Palmerston's view, 'a vicious and wrong principle'.

A N Wilson
From *The Victorians*

545 *Generation to generation*

A wise rabbi was walking down a road when he saw a man planting a tree. The rabbi asked him, 'How many years will it take for this tree to bear fruit?' The man answered that it would take seventy years. The rabbi asked, 'Are you so fit and strong that you expect to live that long and eat of its fruit?' The man answered, 'I found a fruitful world because my fathers planted for me. So I will do the same for my children.'

The Talmud

546 *The now and not-yet of the kingdom of God*

The justice and peace of the reign of God have been, from the preaching of Jesus in Galilee, primary objectives of all Christian witness. The gospel is about change and it includes the changing of those injustices which stifle and corrupt humanity, so that the world may know a peace based on mutual respect. The church may never forget this and preach a gospel which has no effect on the desperate conditions of those millions who live on the edge of survival. So we are committed, as Christian churches, to a great many causes touching the justice and peace issues of our world. We do this as part of our obedience to the Holy Spirit; but we do it also as citizens in partnership with many others who profess no Christian belief. It is an essential outworking of our discipleship but is never our private calling. Nor is it a romantic tilt at windmills with the expectation of utopia around the corner. The full realization of the reign of God is not in the hands of human authorities, however benevolent they may be. So there is a 'not yet', a 'beyond' in all our work and witness.

...we recognize the now of the kingdom, the reign of God here and now in every life of self-sacrifice and devotion, in every expression of truth, in every act of forgiveness, in all those points where new life rises from the tomb of sorrow. But we confess the not yet. The glory is God's and it is his gift which is our end.

Bernard Thorogood
From *Gales of Change*, the story of the London Missionary Society

547 *Praise with joy the world's creator*

A trinity of liberation

Praise with joy the world's creator,
God of justice, love and peace,
Source and end of human knowledge,
Force of greatness without cease.
Celebrate the Maker's glory –
Power to rescue and release.

Praise the Son who feeds the hungry,
Frees the captive, finds the lost,
Heals the sick, upsets religion,
Fearless both of fate and cost.
Celebrate Christ's constant presence –
Friend and Stranger, Guest and Host.

Praise the Spirit sent among us,
Liberating truth from pride,
Forging bonds where race or gender,
Age or nation dare divide.
Celebrate the Spirit's treasure –
Foolishness none dare deride.

Praise the Maker, Son and Spirit,
One God in community,
Calling Christians to embody
Oneness and diversity.
Thus the world shall yet believe
When shown Christ's vibrant unity.

John L Bell and **Graham Maule**
From *Heaven shall not wait* (Wild Goose Publications 1987)

548 *The Netherlands, 1942*

Lord, grant that such a choice
shall not ever have to be made again ...
Never. Never.

Huddled with forty-seven others
in the underground bunker,
he saw the glaze of their eyes;
yet no one moved
to stop the baby's crying.

He pressed its mouth against his breast
to muffle the treacherous sound.
    But the child cried, cried louder,
    confused by the darkness and the unfamiliar place.
    Or was it simply to assert his baby-right?
Haunted by the wide, white gaze
of those eyes around him
the father pressed tight:
My son, oh my son, be quiet.
At last, silence – shrouding the small body.

Above, the jackboots tramped on.
Isaac again sacrificed on the mountain?
Where is the ram then
to save the victim?
The ram caught in the thicket by the horns...

Ask no questions.
I know that tongues of fire blazed
on the heads of
forty-eight trembling men.

Margaret Diesendorf
From *Light*

549 O Lord, remember not only the men and women of good will but also those of ill will. But do not remember all the suffering they have inflicted upon us; remember the fruits we bought, thanks to this suffering: our comradeship, our loyalty, our humility, the courage, the generosity, the greatness of heart which has grown out of this; and when they come to judgement, let all the fruit we have borne be their forgiveness.

Anon
Written on a piece of wrapping paper found in Ravensbrück Concentration
Camp for Women in Nazi Germany

550 *Total liberation*

We need to express a more holistic understanding of salvation than is often found in churches. The traditional focus has been upon people knowing the truth (orthodoxy) but we need to challenge people to do the truth (orthopraxis); we have stressed the needs of individuals when we should also have referred to the joys and sorrows of the communities within which they live; the centre of our concerns has been with the renewal of persons but it should also have included the renewal of societies, nations and the earth. It is common to run up against polarized attitudes towards salvation. On the one hand, we find those who regard society as an admixture of individuals who need saving, thereby forgetting that the systems and structures which those people inhabit are also in need of renewal. Then, on the other hand, we come across those who substitute community work or social and political engagement for evangelism, thereby seeking to provide space for God to change people's social and political conditions without ever explicitly talking to those people about God and the Deity's self-revelation in Jesus. To attach the usual labels, conservatives argue forcibly that the Church's mission should focus upon God's redemption of people from sin; while liberals argue equally stridently that the Church's mission is to engage with God's emancipating work among the poor, oppressed and sinned against. But surely it is not a question of either/or? An adequate understanding of salvation will be holistic, covering both redemption and emancipation in an integrated concept of God's liberation.

David Peel
From *Reforming Theology*

551 *Stagecraft*

...in those days, *Hamlet* was banned by the censors. You may believe it or not. In general, our theatre has had trouble with Shakespeare, particularly with *Hamlet* and *Macbeth*. Stalin could stand neither of these plays. Why? It seems fairly obvious. A criminal ruler – what could attract the leader and teacher in that theme? Shakespeare was a seer – man stalks power, walking knee-deep in blood. And he was so naive, Shakespeare. Pangs of conscience and guilt and all that. *What* guilty conscience?

...When I read Shakespeare, I give myself up to the flow. It doesn't happen often. But those are the best moments. I read – and listen to his music. Shakespeare's tragedies are filled with music. It was

continued...

Shakespeare who said that the man who doesn't like music isn't trustworthy. Such a man is capable of a base act or murder.

Stalin didn't give a damn about all these refinements, naturally. He simply didn't want people watching plays with plots that displeased him; you never know what might cross the mind of some demented person. Of course, all the people knew once and for all that Stalin was the greatest of the great and the wisest of the wise, but he banned Shakespeare just in case. What if someone decided to play Hamlet or Macduff in real life?

Solomon Volkov
From *Testimony: The memoirs of Shostakovich*

552 *Inspired by love and anger*

Inspired by love and anger, disturbed by endless pain,
informed of God's own bias, we ponder once again:
'How long can some folk suffer? How long can few folk mind?
How long dare vain self-interest turn prayer and pity blind?'

From those forever victims of heartless human greed,
their cruel plight composes a litany of need:
'Where are the fruits of justice? Where are the signs of peace?
When is the day when prisoners and dreams find their release?'

From those forever shackled to what their wealth can buy,
the fear of lost advantage provokes the bitter cry:
'Don't query our position! Don't criticise our wealth!
Don't mention those exploited by politics and stealth!'

To God, who through the prophets proclaimed a different age,
we offer earth's indifference, its agony and rage:
'When will the wronged be righted, When will the kingdom come?
When will the world be generous to all instead of some?'

God asks: 'Who will go for me? Who will extend my reach?
And who, when few will follow, will prophesy and preach?
And who, when few bid welcome, will offer all they know?
And who, when few dare follow, will walk the road I show?'

Amused in someone's kitchen, asleep in someone's boat,
attuned to what the prophets exposed, proclaimed and wrote,
a saviour without safety, a tradesman without tools
has come to tip the balance with fishermen and fools.

John L Bell and **Graham Maule**
From *Heaven shall not wait* (Wild Goose Publications 1987)
These verses can be sung to the traditional Irish tune *Salley Gardens*

Resources for all seasons

a Will God indeed dwell on earth? Even heaven and the highest heaven cannot contain him, much less this house that we have built. Have regard to your servants' prayer and plea, O Lord our God, heeding the cry and the prayer that your servants pray to you today.   *adapted from 1 Kings 8:27–29*

b Worship the Lord in holy splendour; tremble before him, all the earth. Let the heavens be glad, and let the earth rejoice. O give thanks to the Lord, for he is good; for his steadfast love endures for ever.
from 1 Chronicles 16:29–34

c Let the words of our mouths and the meditation of our hearts be acceptable to you, O Lord, our rock and our redeemer.   *adapted from Psalm 19:14*

d It is good to give thanks to the Lord, to sing praise to your name, O Most High; to declare your steadfast love in the morning, and your faithfulness by night.   *Psalm 92:1–2*

e O come, let us worship and bow down, let us kneel before the Lord, our Maker! For he is our God, and we are the people of his pasture, the sheep of his hand.   *Psalm 95:6–7*

f Enter his gates with thanksgiving, and his courts with praise. Give thanks to him, bless his name. For the Lord is good; his steadfast love endures for ever, and his faithfulness to all generations   *Psalm 100:4–5*

g Holy, holy, holy is the Lord of hosts; the whole earth is full of his glory.
Isaiah 6:3

h The Lord is good to those who wait for him, to the soul that seeks him. It is good that one should wait quietly for the salvation of the Lord.
Lamentations 3:25–26

i The hour is coming, and is now here, when the true worshippers will worship the Father in spirit and truth, for the Father seeks such as these to worship him. God is Spirit, and those who worship him must worship in spirit and truth.   *John 4:23–24*

j The God who made the world and everything in it, he who is Lord of heaven and earth, does not live in shrines made by human hands, nor is he served by human hands, as though he needed anything, since he himself gives to all mortals life and breath and all things.   *Acts 17:24–25*

k Do you not know that you are God's temple and that God's Spirit dwells in you?   *1 Corinthians 3:16*

l It is the God who said, 'Let light shine out of darkness', who has shone in our hearts to give the light of the knowledge of the glory of God in the face of Jesus Christ.   *2 Corinthians 4:6*

m Be thankful. Let the word of Christ dwell in you richly; teach and admonish one another in all wisdom; and with gratitude in your hearts sing psalms, hymns and spiritual songs to God.   *from Colossians 3:15–16*

n May the God of peace, who brought back from the dead our Lord Jesus, make you complete in everything good so that you may do his will, working among us that which is pleasing in his sight.   *from Hebrews 13:20–21*

553
We are citizens of heaven
and from heaven we expect our deliverer to come, our Lord Jesus Christ.
He will transfigure our humble bodies
and give them a form like that of his own.
He has the power that enables him to make all things subject to himself.
The peace of God,
which is beyond all understanding
will guard our hearts and thoughts in Christ Jesus.

based on Philippians 3:20–21; 4:7

554
Jesus called Peter and Andrew by the lakeside to be his friends,
shared family life with Mary and Martha.
and now he calls us into the circle of his disciples.
Jesus called Paul as he journeyed on the Damascus Road,
and now he calls us on our life's journey.
Jesus called Mark and Matthew, Luke and John to tell the gospel story,
and now he calls us to live the gospel, day by day.
Jesus called Julian as she prayed in her Norwich cell,
Antony in the Egyptian desert, and Clare in her Italian community,
John in Bedford goal, and George in industrial Glasgow,
and now he calls us into the fellowship of prayer.
Jesus called Isaac and Charles, hymn-writers and worship-makers,
and now he calls us to sing the songs of God's people.
Jesus still calls women and men, girls and boys into his kingdom,
and we have come to offer praise, and find strength to serve.

555
Glorious Lord, I give you greeting!
Let the church and chancel praise you.
Let the plain and hillside praise you.
Let the dark and the daylight praise you; let the life everlasting praise you.
Let the male and female praise you; let the seven days and all the stars
praise you.
Let the air and ether praise you; let the fish in the swift streams praise you.
Let the sand-grains and the earth-clods praise you.
Let the thought and the action praise you.
Let all the good that's performed praise you.
Let the worship of the whole church of Christ praise you.
And we will praise you, Lord of glory:
Glorious Lord, we give you greeting!

From a Welsh prayer (Anon)

556
We are not asking God to be present in church this morning;
of course not – God was here before we arrived.
We will not take God into the world when we leave;
of course not – God will be waiting for us in his world.
We will not try to begin God's work in the world;
rather – we will co-operate in what God is already doing in his world.
We rejoice in the Christ whom God sent into the world.
We rejoice that Christ calls us to be God's people in God's world.

557
God has never left us orphaned:
he has always offered himself to us in love.
God has never stopped searching for us;
he has always spoken a word to those who will listen.
God has never stopped surprising us;
he has always found new ways of meeting us.
Thanks be to God.

558
Worship is the submission of all our nature to God.
It is the quickening of consciousness by his holiness;
the nourishment of mind with his truth;
the purifying of the imagination by his beauty;
the opening of the heart to his love;
and the surrender of will to his purpose.

William Temple

559
Welcome to church!
This is a happy place
– though we never forget that some among us may be sad.
This is a time to be serious
– though we're not afraid to laugh.
This is where we seek comfort
– though we expect sometimes to go home disturbed.
This is a human place
– though we often sense the presence of God.
This is a time to seek perfection in praise
– though we often fall short of our aim.
This God's time and God's place
And God has called us here.

560
Come to church as though to an oasis in a weary desert
but look beyond to see the streams of fresh water.
Come to church as though to the seclusion of a walled garden
but do not forget the needs of a tumultuous world.
Come to church as though to a harbour of inner peace
but still engage in prayer for the surging tides of a war-torn earth.
Come to church to seek the God who,
present in all creation,
surely dwells in this place of worship
no less than in the world we have left
and the world to which we will return.

561
We are a family of God, met to worship our Creator and Lord.
Some are younger, some older:
one family of Christians met to worship God.
Some have skipped to church, agile and free,
others have walked more slowly, watching every step;
one family of Christians met to worship God.
Some have known this one church since infancy,
others have worshipped God in many places;
one family of Christians met to worship God.
Some have trod the Christian path for long years,
others have lately found the road to Christ;
one family of Christians met to worship God.
Here and now in this chosen place
we make our prayer:
Come, Lord Jesus, come
and be with us.

562
Whoever you are, whatever has happened to you,
whatever burden you carry, whatever joy delights you,
come!
God welcomes you
and this is your home.

563
In the humility of those who know they have sinned,
and the confidence of those who know they are loved,
we meet to worship the Lord of life.

564 We are here to meet each other in conversation and friendship
and in the fellowship of worship.
We are here to meet the world:
to love it, fear for it, and pray for it.
We are here, by imagination, prayer, and treasured memories
to meet Christian friends across the world.
We are here to meet God, or rather,
to discover afresh that God is meeting us.
May God so help us.

565 We have been given a promise
that the Holy Spirit will lead us into all truth.
We have received a message
that God is light and in him there is no darkness at all.
We have been given a promise
that Jesus Christ will be with us to the end of time.
Thanks be to God.

566 We have not come to church simply by our own deciding;
we have come by the witness of many others:
parents have influenced their children,
but better still, have portrayed lives of truth and honest worship;
friends have told the good news to friends,
but better still, have lived the good news in love and care;
the Church has preached its sermons and told its stories,
but better still, has turned sermons into living communities of faith,
so now there lies within us the desire to praise,
and the compulsion to worship.
Thanks be to God.

567 There is a search that goes beyond the beaten track of tradition,
there is prayer that lips are not yet trained to speak,
there is hope that is higher than our present reaching,
and truth that lies deeper than the reading of Bible words.
The key, the path, and the goal
is Jesus Christ who calls us this day to follow him.

Invocation

568

We are here this day, Father God, because you have invited us;
waiting and looking out for us.
And tomorrow – at work, school, or in the home, your call remains,
wherever we go we are at home with you.
So, in every place and at any time
we have the confidence to call out your name
and know that you are present.
**Here and now in this chosen place
we acknowledge your presence
and offer our worship.**

569

We are your people, loving God,
because you have called us.
We do not know you well enough
so we have come today to know you better.
We do not fully understand your ways
so we come as those who search for truth,
and find in prayers and worship,
new signs of hope and purpose.
But if, as often in the past,
we fail;
still this we know:
we are your people
because you have called us.

570

We come this day, eternal God,
with an impulse to seek and serve your kingdom.
In your mercy, grant us this prayer:
give us a new future,
an abiding hope,
and strength to persist.
Call us away from the certainties that narrow our vision
and the security that makes us complacent.
Instead, help us to know how weak we are
and acknowledge our deepest needs,
that we may hear your gospel afresh,
and follow your Son.

571

God of love, living beyond time and filling all space,
you have given us this hour and this place
in which to worship.
> **Help us to receive them as gifts**
> **through which we hear you speaking**
> **to us and to your world.**

We wait for words of promise and fulfilment;
for words of encouragement and support.
> **Help us to receive them as gifts**
> **through which we hear you speaking**
> **to us and to your world.**

We wait for words of challenge and judgement;
words of love and forgiveness.
> **Help us to receive them as gifts**
> **through which we hear you speaking**
> **to us and to your world.**

Help us to use minds and voices, imagination and commitment,
to help each other worship you in spirit and truth;
to the glory of Jesus Christ our Lord.

572

And so our worship begins.
We bring the weakness of our human life,
> and the strength of all we are.
We bring the doubts that disturb us,
> and the faith that forms our lives.
We bring our disillusionment and pain,
> and the flickering hope that is never put out.
We bring the strain of relationships grown weary,
> and the joy of glad friendship.
We bring the tasks that have become burdensome,
> and the joy of work well done.
We come ill-clad to the worship feast;
clothe us with your truth
and let your love for us call out our praise.

573

Father, we do not know how you will speak to us today:
out of silence or the spoken word,
through music or friendship's greeting,
by ancient words or a spontaneous turn of phrase.
This we ask:
tune our ears to your voice, open our hearts to your Word.

574
We come to thank you for Jesus the Christ.
He is your first and last word to us.
He is your strength and wisdom for us.
He it is who makes sense of life.
And so, with people of all ages and places, we meet in his name
to worship and adore you.

575
God of time, of space, of all,
    your people come to praise you.
You are here, and you are there,
    the wide earth gives its praises.
You are now, and you were then,
    the timeless ages praise you.
Distant, yet as close as breath,
    each silent moment praises.
Height and depth, and breadth and length,
    the universe will praise you.
You are here; yes, you are here,
    and we will always praise you.

576
Eternal God,
no word of ours is big enough to speak of you;
the mightiest congregation cannot voice your praise,
the soaring heights of music touch but the fringe of your glory.
Yet in your loving mercy
you listen to our limping words,
our clumsy praise is your delight,
our earthbound thoughts receive your loving smile.
The worship of your people is your joy,
and our good pleasure.
The little we have, we offer to your glory.

577
Eternal God, we praise you.
You called us into being by your voice,
    and you formed us by your word.
You proved your love for us in Jesus Christ
    and you brought us together to be new people in him.
You lead us as pilgrims in an uncertain world
    and offer us a fresh beginning of hope and purpose.
Let this day herald a new journey for us
as we step out in confidence and trust.

578
Father, we have come again,
ready to share in the worship of the people of God.
It is right to be here; right, good, and pleasant.
May our prayers be stronger
    because others pray with us.
May our praise carry greater conviction
    because others join in the chorus of adoration.
May our faith be deepened
    because it is shared.
May our future service to the world be more consistent
    because we are one company of people.
Pleasant, good, and right it is,
that we should praise your name.

Adoration

579
God, whom once we saw in a manger cradle,
    we approach you with love and awe.
God, whom once we saw held high upon a cross,
    we approach you with humility and shame.
God, whom once we saw break out of a tomb,
    we approach you with gratitude and wonder.
God, whom once we heard in rushing wind and tongues of flame,
    we approach you longing for renewal.
God, whom we believe to be present in every place,
    be with us in this house of prayer.
God, whom we believe to live in the midst of time,
    be with us in this hour of worship.
And all this not because we deserve it,
but because of the love you show in Jesus Christ.

580
Father God, how much we love you!
You look after us and we trust you.
You know us through and through,
yet never falter in your love.
You are utterly to be trusted, reliable to the end.
With total confidence we put our lives in your hands.
Our adoration has no bounds,
our worship is unending.

581 Lord God, eternal Father of all people,
you are more constant than the unchanging hills,
as trustworthy as the succession of day and night,
and more reliable than the turning earth.
Your friendship is great beyond any human friendship we know,
and the passing years find you unaltered.
We do not deserve your friendship
but we receive it with outstretched arms and open hands
for our lives and hopes depend on it
and it brings us now to worship you.

582 All things are, eternal God,
because you choose to make them so.
You are all in all, beyond all, and within all,
and your creative power knows no end.
Caught up in your creation's wonder,
    we see flashes of eternity,
    hear echoes of glory,
    sense the power of a great beyond,
and we see, and hear, and know,
only because you have so made us.

583 Faithful and eternal God, we pause in wonder:
    you have sustained the universe from the beginning,
    rhythm of tides and pattern of seasons speak of your constancy,
    hills, mountains, and rocks are tokens of your steadfastness.

You have girded your Church with protective might:
    in times of persecution you have revealed resources of hope,
    you have watched lest success should yield to complacency,
    or our failures utterly destroy your Church.

And you have come to us, each one, in personal experience:
    your Spirit has led us along life's path,
    in our human despair you have cradled us,
    and in times of delight you have deepened our joy.

Great is your faithfulness, eternal God.

Confession

584 As ever, we come in adoration to worship you, God our Father,
and as ever, we come alike in confession.
We have failed you in our appointed tasks.
We have been lazy and ill-prepared for your work.
We have turned willingly towards tasks that attract us
but turned aside from more demanding duties.
Hearts that should have been warm with zeal have grown cold.
We would understand if you turned away from us.
    But no, as we take one faltering step
    you come out to meet and greet us,
    you offer forgiving love
    you revive life in us again,
    you trust the untrustworthy.
We can but marvel at such a God,
and worship you in wondering love,
in the name of the one who has made your love clear to us: Jesus Christ
our Lord.

585 Is this your one and only mistake, eternal God;
an act of divine folly never to be repeated:
    that you put your name on our lips
    and your work into our hands,
    so that we are your Church, your people?
We know ourselves too well:
    touched with glory but stained by sin,
    glimpses of light but shrouded in darkness.
You would have done better without us!

Were you lonely in the vastness of creation?
Did you – even you – crave relationship and trust?

We promise little in response to your call
our need far, far exceeds whatever we can give,
but take our faltering answer as love's token
and our poverty of spirit as a sign of praise.

586 Father, too often our worship is shallow and superficial.
Forgive us.
Reveal the deeper places; refashion our spirits; re-form our understanding;
chide, exhort, probe, and unsettle us,
until what lies on our lips is true to our heart,
and we glimpse the majesty of your glory.

587 Before you, holy God, we make confession:
 our goodness is but half-good,
 we are readily satisfied with slight virtue,
 and left to our own devices we would come to nothing.
But you have given us your Spirit, and with such a gift,
 the best remains our goal,
 the prick of conscience urges us forward,
 the life of Jesus sets our sights,
 and your persuasive love ever encourages us.
We who make confession also continue in hope,
founded not on any goodness within us
but on your eternal mercy revealed in Jesus.

588 Father, your children come before you in penitence.
We are ashamed of so much in our world,
 yet we are a part of it and contribute to its downfall.
We are sad that there is so much darkness in the world,
 yet we are not ourselves constant beacons of light.
We long for a wholesome, united world,
 yet know that we play our part in its brokenness and despair.

Even in the life of the Church our hands are not clean.
We grieve when fewer people worship you,
 but know that sometimes our actions keep people away.
We regret our lack of influence in the nation's life,
 but know we are often seen as those who condemn rather than
 understand.
Father, renew your world, renew your Church, renew your people.

589 In your eternal, lasting peace, God of comfort and strength,
 drown the anger of human hate,
 absorb the hurt we carelessly inflict,
 take wars and bury them,
 receive the cries of damaged children,
 accept the pain of our human sin,
 and bear the long-felt grief of those bowed down by injustice.

And if, in asking this, we bring Jesus to his cross again,
and lay on him, afresh, the world's deep anguish,
then so be it, Lord.
So be it, in his willing mercy.
But this time, give us grace to stand with him.

Thanksgiving

590 God of wisdom and love, giver of all good things,
we thank you for your constant care over all creation,
for the gift of human life,
and for your guiding hand upon us.
We bless you for your sustaining love for all that you have made.

We thank you for Jesus Christ, your Son, our Saviour;
for a life lived in love, and a death accepted in humility.
We bless you for his Spirit, present among us.

We thank you for the Church;
for friendship and duty,
for good hopes and precious memory.
We bless you for the call to worship, the invitation to serve.

In our weakness you are our strength.
In our darkness you are our light.
In uncertainty you are our confidence.
In sorrow you are our hope.

From everlasting to everlasting you are God;
Father, Son and Holy Spirit;
one God, to be glorified now and beyond time.

591 Father, in the quiet joy and longing hope of this service,
we remember with thanksgiving all the past has given
to bring us to this moment of silence and praise.

Thank you for the formative experiences of childhood and youth:
for parents whose pleasure lay in our growth,
for the intimacy and care of family life,
for sins forgiven by human love and God's good grace.

Thank you for those who have travelled the faith journey with us:
for teachers and ministers who raised signposts to learning,
for friends who sustained us in the pilgrimage,
for books that opened our eyes to new truth,
for silence that deepened our understanding.

Above all, thank you for all you are to us as Father and Friend:
for your over-arching providence,
for your unfailing love, and the discipline of your forgiveness.

What we are, and what all these things have made us,
we bring to this moment with thanksgiving, adoration, and praise.

592

Living God, you hold all people within your loving care,
neither colour nor race, gender nor age, curb your graciousness,
and so we come with gratitude and thankfulness
to hold others in our prayers.

We hardly dare to thank you that we are free to worship you,
for even as we pray,
others worship in danger or under the eye of persecutor,
and some must measure their words, cautious of a listening stranger.

We hardly dare to thank you for our health and wellbeing,
for even as we pray,
children are dying for reasons that money could cure,
young men live as though already old,
and young women wonder where their strength has gone.

We hardly dare to thank you for the food we eat this day,
for even as we pray,
babies cry out in hunger,
little children scavenge the gutters,
and parents dream of food they will never taste.

We hardly dare to thank you for secure and loving homes,
for even as we pray,
families are hounded from place to place,
a leaking roof disturbs a fitful sleep,
and youngsters argue, choosing the doorway in which to sleep.

Yet thank you we will and must,
and to our thanks add holy rage,
and to our rage add promised help,
and to our help the hope and trust
that justice may be born anew
and earth become a lovelier place.

593

Father, made in your image,
bought with a price,
recreated by love,
sustained by grace,
and led by the Spirit,
we acknowledge our debt to you.

Father, in your mercy,
you do not seek repayment;
in your goodness,
you make no impossible demands;
in your eternal compassion,
you continue to give.

Father, your mercy begets mercy in us, your goodness calls out our response
your compassion invites our service, and so, acknowledging our debt,
we praise you in the name of Jesus Christ.

594 When placid lives are suddenly disturbed
by fountain springs of joy
    or sorrow's lengthening tears,
then teach us, Lord,
that joy is there to share with others,
and even sorrow's pain
can bring us close
to those with greater need than ours.
    And joy and pain; both,
    can bring us nearer
    to our God.

595 Leading God, you called Abraham from his native land,
and sent him on pilgrimage;
you called Moses to deliver your people from Egypt,
and broke the tyrant's yoke.
We offer thanks. Give us the same spirit of adventure and trust.

God of community, you gave your people a new land,
called David and Solomon to create a nation
and lawmakers and priests to root the nation in your good purpose.
We offer thanks. Show us our Christian task in our own nation.

Prophetic God, you spoke
    to Amos in the market place, calling his generation to justice,
    to Isaiah in the royal court, calling Israel to face up to danger,
    to Hosea in his broken marriage, declaring your forgiving love,
    to your people exiled in a strange land, giving vision for their future
    homeland.
We offer thanks. Help us to listen to your word in our time.

Suffering God,
you stood alongside Jesus in Gethsemane loss,
you comforted Mary by the cross,
you inspired John in exile.
We offer thanks. Stand by us in our times of loss and sadness.

Boundless God, you opened Paul's eyes,
and caused the infant church to break the barriers of race.
Travelling God, you have ever led your people in pilgrimage.
We offer thanks. Continue with us in our own journey.

God of every age and time, constantly revealing yourself,
be our vision and hope, our challenge and guide,
in the time and place where you call us to be your people.

Supplication & Intercession

596

When advertisers present a world led by greed,
and self-content becomes a nation's aim;
>Lord, lead us not into temptation,
>**but deliver us from evil.**

When spiritual values are dismissed,
and loyalty derided as a joke;
>Lord, lead us not into temptation,
>**but deliver us from evil.**

When the second mile is scorned as foolish,
and life is measured by the ease that we can find;
>Lord, lead us not into temptation,
>**but deliver us from evil.**

When little gods are offered for our worship,
and heaven is reduced to earthly span;
>Lord, lead us not into temptation,
>**but deliver us from evil.**

For thine is the kingdom, the power and the glory
for ever and ever.   Amen

597

Dear God, ever-present, ever loving
you are there in the pregnant buds of rising spring,
and in the full-grown wonder of summer;
present in autumn's fading beauty
and in winter's cold and sleeping earth. **Help us to see you.**

You are the silent presence in our loneliness.
You are the warmth of human companionship,
You are the gift within the community of faith. **Help us to sense you.**

Birth proclaims you, as does vibrant life.
Death cannot overshadow you.
You stand within our sorrow and grief
as you do within our joy and delight. **Help us to welcome you.**

Our words hide you yet also reveal you.
Daily we both perceive you and yet miss you. **Help us to recognise you.**

**And in our seeing, sensing, and welcoming, and recognising,
help us to praise you by word and life.**

598
Father God, there are those in this our world
whose lives are dominated by despair and sadness,
who carry burdens beyond their strength,
and in whose darkness there seems little hope of light.
> **Glorious God, we pray that we may become the compassion of Christ
> to those who need support.**

Father God, there are those in this our world
for whom poverty is a daily threat:
mothers who cannot feed their children;
fathers whose willing hands can find no work.
> **Glorious God, we pray that we may become the compassion of Christ
> to those who need support.**

Father God, there are those in this our world
who lack the friendship others so naturally find,
and too rarely enjoy the depths of human companionship.
> **Glorious God, we pray that we may become the compassion of Christ
> to those who need support.**

599
We pray for those who feel that love has slipped them by,
for those who know little of its security,
and for those whose memory of love is tinged with sadness.
> Lord, you encircle the whole world with your love;
> **let all your people know your loving kindness.**

We pray for those who dare not take the risk of love,
for those embittered by jealousy,
and for those who know more of the pain of love than of its joy.
> Lord, you encircle the whole world with your love;
> **let all your people know your loving kindness.**

We pray for those saddened by a sense of love long lost,
for those separated from loved ones by distance,
and for those whose love is stretched to breaking point by stress or
> misunderstanding.
> Lord, you encircle the whole world with your love;
> **let all your people know your loving kindness.**

We pray for ourselves and for each other who, knowing the love of Christ,
long to know it more deeply,
to share it more widely,
and to live within it more confidently.
> Lord, you encircle the whole world with your love;
> **let all your people know your loving kindness.**

600　*The following prayer could be spoken by several voices with a pause between each section.*

Eternal God,
the praise of the church is music to our ears
as we sing of your goodness,
speak of your loving care,
and whisper in gratitude of your forgiveness which never fails.
But now we are silent and listen to the cry of the world.

We hear the cry of the lonely ones:
those bereft of friendship,
those who live alone and wish they didn't,
those bereaved who long for the voice they no longer hear,
parents and children who have lost the ability to communicate,
husbands and wives who have forgotten how to talk in intimacy.
For all these we pray.

We hear the cry of those in pain:
those who go to sleep hungry, wondering if they will eat tomorrow,
the long-unemployed, grown bitter with no work to do,
parents, helpless though they see their children suffer,
children caught in the antagonism of a crumbling marriage,
For all these we pray.

We hear the cry of joy and gladness:
as new marriages are formed,
as eagerly-awaited babies are welcomed into life,
as long-held love is celebrated in anniversaries,
as exams are passed, new jobs begun, and strangers welcomed,
For all these we pray.

We hear the cry of confidence:
from those newborn to faith in Christ,
from those who find their strength in long-held trust in God,
from those who hear Christ's call to service,
from those who hold to truth despite persecution,
For all these we pray.

We hear the inner cry within the human heart:
that guilt be met by your mercy,
that anxiety receive your confidence,
that strength be given in searching.
For these we pray.

And in the end we pray for ourselves

Silence

In the name of Jesus Christ our Lord.

Commitment

601 All is yours, eternal God,
all falls within your power and purpose.
We offer that which excites us, seizing our imagination,
we bring the great events that change our very lives.
> But, not these alone:
> receive the simple patterns of our daily life,
> accept the routine that undergirds our work,
> for all is yours, eternal God,
> all falls within your power and purpose.

602 Father of past and present; hope for our future,
let darting insight pierce the commonplace of every day,
imagination find new soaring wings,
perception probe the surface of well-trodden life,
so that out of fading patterns, weathered by customs held too long,
we find the newer rhythm of your expanding purpose,
and finding it,
begin to share your resurrection life.

603 Lord Jesus Christ,
we have heard your call to walk the Christian way,
and have received your ministry of healing and reconciliation.
Now, send us on our pilgrim way.
Give us strength to keep the faith,
insight to know where you are leading,
and love for all our travelling companions.

604 Lord, we believe,
help us where faith falls short.
We reach out for that which we cannot yet hold,
raise our sights towards that which we cannot yet see,
hold to a faith we find it difficult to express.
It is enough to know
that you are the path we tread
and remain our goal.

Copyright and Permissions

Every possible attempt has been made to trace the copyright sources of the items in this book. In a few instances the search has proved fruitless. The compiler and publishers apologise for any errors or omissions which occur. If their attention is drawn to these they will be corrected in future editions. Items within the book where neither author nor source is given are the work of the compiler who also retains the copyright.

Item

1 Laurence Housman. Permission sought

13 Jane T Clement. © Plough Publishing House; www.bruderhof.co.uk Used with permission

21 Alfred Delp. © Plough Publishing House; www.bruderhof.co.uk Used with permission

23 From *Celebrating the gift of years* (United Reformed Church booklet 2002). Originally from an Advent talk on Radio 4 (2001) by John Bell © 2001 WGRG Iona Community, Glasgow G2 3DH, Scotland. Used with permission

24 © Margaret Connor. Used with permission

43 Lilian Cox. © National Christian Education Council

51 The Hengrave Community. Used with permission

53 © David Jenkins. Used with permission

67 Gerald Priestland. Permission sought

69 Elizabeth Rooney. Source and © unknown

70, 72 © W S Beattie. Used with permission

77 © Beryl Chatfield. Used with permission

78 Rose Macaulay. © unknown

79 © Margaret Connor. Used with permission

80 © W S Beattie. Used with permission

82 © Donald Hilton. First printed in *Sing New Songs* published by the National Christian Education Council 1981

84 © Margaret Connor. Used with permission

86 © Kate Compston. Used with permission

87 Jennifer Dines. Source and © unknown

88 Chris Avis © ARC Music. Used with permission

89 © Philip Wren. Used with permission

96 © Sheffield Urban Theology Unit, 210 Abbeyfield Road, Sheffield S4 7AZ. Used with permission

Authors

This index gives the names of authors throughout the book. Those items which do not indicate an author or another source are the work of the compiler.

Anthology themes

The Index of themes is based on the Anthology material. Bold type indicates major sections.

Theme	Item
A	
Abel	405
Abraham	23
Adam (and Eve)	257, 271, 413
Advent	**20–29**, 452
Afghanistan	542
Africa	504, 542
Agnosticism	368
Albania	81
Ambiguity	460
Angels	307, 359
Anger	552
Anna	23, 28
Argument	315, 376, 455
Arrogance	259
Art	26, 137, 316, 364, 418, 451
Ascension	**358–359**
Asteroid	411
Astor, Nancy	499
Atheism	81, 498
Authority	482
Autumn	423–424, 426–427
Awe	150
B	
Baptism	158, 262
Barabbas	249
Bartimaeus	201
Beatitudes	207, 453
Beauty	364, 417
Beethoven	137
Belfast	543
Bereavement	312, 453
Bethlehem	67, 69, 77–79, 83, 88, 175
Bethsaida	201
Bible	138, 203, 204, 307, 309, 310, 503, 544

Theme	Item
Bible, books of the	
Genesis	307, 369, 409
Judges	307
2 Samuel	152
Matthew	75, 307
Mark	201, 307
Luke	75, 155, 307, 310
John	309, 310
Acts	307
1 Corinthians	370, 495
Ephesians	501
1 Timothy	307
Big Bang	407
Birds	26, 368, 420–423
Birmingham	266
Birth	410
Blindness	201
Books	26
Booth, William	143
Bread	25, 44, 198, 259–263, 268
Bridegroom	22
Buildings	499
Bunyan, John	274
Burning bush	138, 142
C	
Calling	123, **138–150**, 255, 360, 361, 410, 483, 494–497, 552
Calvary	29, 141, 193, 194, 199, 203, 266–268, 271–273, 376
Calvin	413
Candles	67, 79, 89
Canham, Elizabeth	494
Capitalism	544
Carols	67, 81
Cathedral	26, 308, 368